NEW & COLLECTED POEMS

George Szirtes was born in Budapest in 1948, arrived in England as a refugee in 1956 and was brought up in London. He was trained as a painter in Leeds and at Goldsmiths College. He has taught art, history of art and creative writing in various schools and colleges, and now teaches poetry and creative writing at the University of East Anglia. For some years he exhibited and ran a small etching and poetry press together with his wife, artist Clarissa Upchurch. Their children, Tom and Helen, were born and grew up in Hertfordshire. He lives in Wymondham, Norfolk.

His poems began to appear in print in the mid 70s. His first book, *The Slant Door*, was awarded the Geoffrey Faber Prize, and since then he has won the T.S. Eliot Prize and a Cholmondeley Award and been shortlisted for the Whitbread and Forward Poetry Prizes. He was elected a Fellow of the Royal Society of Literature in 1982.

After his first return to Hungary in 1984 he translated poetry, fiction and plays from the Hungarian and for his work in this field he has won the European Poetry Translation Prize, the Dery Prize and been shortlisted for the Weidenfeld and Aristeion Prizes as well as receiving the Golden Star medal of the Hungarian republic. He co-edited Bloodaxe's *The Colonnade of Teeth: Modern Hungarian Poetry* (1996) with George Gömöri, and his Bloodaxe edition of Ágnes Nemes Nagy's poetry, *The Night of Akhenaton: Selected Poems* (2004), was a Poetry Book Society Recommended Translation. His study of the artist Ana Maria Pacheco, *Exercise of Power*, was published by Ashgate in 2001. He co-edited the anthology *An Island of Sound: Hungarian Poetry and Fiction before and beyond the Iron Curtain* (Harvill, 2004). He has also written for children, and for various composers in collaboration.

After four collections with Secker and five with Oxford University Press, he moved to Bloodaxe, publishing his Hungarian selection *The Budapest File* in 2000, *An English Apocalypse* in 2001 and *Reel*, winner of the T.S. Eliot Prize, in 2004. *Budapest: Image, Film, Poem*, a collaboration with Clarissa Upchurch, was published by Corvina in 2006. His *New & Collected Poems* was published by Bloodaxe Books on his 60th birthday in 2008 at the same time as John Sears' critical study, *Reading George Szirtes*. His later Bloodaxe collections are *The Burning of the Books and other poems* (2009), which was shortlisted for the T.S. Eliot Prize, and *Bad Machine*, forthcoming in 2013.

George Szirtes reads a half-hour selection of his work on *The Poetry Quartets 6* (The British Council/Bloodaxe Books, 2000), a double-cassette shared with Moniza Alvi, Michael Donaghy and Anne Stevenson, and an hour's selection on the CD *George Szirtes Reading from his poems* (The Poetry Archive, 2005).

GEORGE SZIRTES

NEW & COLLECTED POEMS

BLOODAXE BOOKS

ISBN: 978 1 85224 813 0

First published 2008 by
Bloodaxe Books Ltd,
Highgreen,
Tarset,
Northumberland NE48 1RP.

Second impression 2011.

www.bloodaxebooks.com
For further information about Bloodaxe titles
please visit our website or write to
the above address for a catalogue.

Supported by
**ARTS COUNCIL
ENGLAND**

Cover design: Neil Astley & Pamela Robertson-Pearce.

Printed in Great Britain by
Bell & Bain Limited, Glasgow, Scotland.

for Martin Bell, for Peter Porter,
for Clarissa, Tom and Helen
and those I love

Look round you as you start, brown moon,
At the book and shoe, the rotted rose
At the door.

WALLACE STEVENS,
'God is Good, It Is a Beautiful Night'

ACKNOWLEDGEMENTS

This edition includes poems selected from George Szirtes's previous collections: *The Slant Door* (1979), *November and May* (1981), *Short Wave* (1984) and *The Photographer in Winter* (1986), published by Secker & Warburg; *Metro* (1988), *Bridge Passages* (1991), *Blind Field* (1994) and *Portrait of My Father in an English Landscape* (1998), published by Oxford University Press; and *The Budapest File* (2000), *An English Apocalypse* (2001) and *Reel* (2004), published by Bloodaxe Books. Poems from *The Slant Door* first collected in George Szirtes's selection in the anthology *Poetry Introduction 4* (Faber & Faber, 1978) are included in that section, along with two poems which have not been collected since then and two poems which were later included in *Selected Poems 1976-1996* (Oxford University Press, 1996). *The Budapest File* and *An English Apocalypse* were thematic selections of new and previously published work, but only the previously uncollected poems from those books are included in their sections here. The whole of *Reel* is included, followed by the section of *New Poems* (2008).

Acknowledgements are due to the editors of the following publications in which some of the previously uncollected poems first appeared: *An Sionnach*, *Guernica* (US), *Hunger Mountain* (US), *International Literary Review*, *The Liberal*, *The Mad Hatter's Review* (US), *Magma*, *The Manhattan Review* (US), *Pequod* (US), *Qarrtsiluni*, *Seam*, *Poetry* (US), *Poetry Ireland Review*, *Poetry Review*, *Poetry Salzburg Review*, *The Rialto* and *Signals*.

'Mirror' was published by Circle Press. 'Dust, Skin, Glove, Bowl' was written for The Barbican Art Gallery, and 'Beckmann's Carnival' for Tate Modern. An earlier version of 'Clear' appeared in *Lebanon, Lebanon* (Saqi Books, 2006).

CONTENTS

An English Apocalypse

PREFACE

When, at seventeen, I set out to write I just wanted to be a poet. First stage. Then, as I went on, I began to feel I had to be specifically an English poet, meaning one who worked from within the language as spoken by those around me. Second stage leading to the first book. But then, in the course of my first three books, from *The Slant Door* (1979), through *November and May* (1982) and *Short Wave* (1984), especially in the title-poem of the last, I found myself moving towards something I seem to have desired ever more urgently without quite knowing it. What was it? The easy answer would be "identity", but it was not so much my personal or cultural identity I wanted to discover – I was then, and remain, sceptical about any notion of identity that has a fixed locatable centre – as, what I'd call now, an amalgam of reality-sense and historical-sense. The desire was blind and unarticulated but acute.

The desire drove me to a first return visit to Hungary in 1984 as a result of which I found myself becoming an English poet with a Hungarian past, or, to be more accurate, a fully baptised but increasingly residual-Christian (to use Peter Porter's term) English poet with a Jewish Hungarian past. This becoming was not a project, more a kind of falling into what now appears inevitable, into that which has been the rest of my life. What was it I fell into? Buildings and streets and bullet holes in walls, the world of the missing and a clutch of dead relatives, not to mention the long-buried, not-quite-forgotten, shadow language that I began to speak again and from which I started to translate.

Once the resultant work appeared, in *The Photographer in Winter* (1986), *Metro* (1988) and *Bridge Passages* (1991) – the poems longer, more architectural, working their way through then-and-now – I found myself re-labelled according to the dictates of cultural politics. I became a "Hungarian" poet. Not having written in Hungarian I found it strange then and it continues to be strange, albeit progressively more understandable. It had nice side-effects in that I got to travel to various places with other poets who fitted under the multicultural umbrella – but certain aspects of it remained comical and disorientating. What I would ideally like, I thought in my most confused periods, is to go back to square one and simply be a poet again, because when I am writing a poem that is all I am doing. I am not flying flags of convenience. But there is never any genuine going back. The books of substantially new poems after *Bridge Passages* – *Blind Field* (1994), *Portrait of My Father in an English Landscape* (1998) *An English Apocalypse* (2001) and *Reel* (2004) – have, it seems to me now, been attempts at moving beyond synthesis into the beginnings of some deeper, less personal understanding of the human condition. And fair enough. That is what poetry is for.

People must live somewhere. All those Budapest buildings with their storeys and stories told me as much. I thought of them as Marianne Moore's imaginary gardens with real toads. Shadow Ithacas with real people in them. Or vice versa.

*

In putting together this volume of *New and Collected Poems*, my editor and I considered the possibility of a thematic arrangement similar to those of my earlier selections, *The Budapest File* (2000) and *An English Apocalypse* (2001), but rejected it. I didn't want a thematic book because the metaphor of the journey through time forms a natural shape and it is what most readers want and expect. Things follow each other in the order they first arise. Themes on the other hand, like opinions, are what you discover about your person. A *New and Collected Poems* – a great privilege – does not feel like that kind of occasion to me.

The journey does reveal abiding themes of course. Apart from poems that could be considered to be *Budapest File* and *English Apocalypse* material, there is a large body of poetry based on visual art of various sorts and an almost equally large number of poems based on personal attachments and what springs out of them: love, desire and apprehension.

Paintings, photographs and films have haunted not only my poems but the poems of most of my contemporaries. There is even a term, ekphrastic writing, referring to work that deals with another art form. It sounds rather too programmatic to me, as if the writing had set out to define the work that sparked it. I suspect most bad writing about visual art is ekphrastic. Good writing is after something else.

Trying to define what that is takes one beyond the realm of the ekphrastic, the "art poem" or indeed any notion of theme. Roland Barthes coined the term, *blind field*, for that part of the world that goes on living and dying outside the photograph. It is brought into play by a point or detail that he calls the *punctum*. That which we do not know is of importance, perhaps of paramount importance. Its hidden presence floods into the frame through the punctum and gives it meaning. The photo still exists in its rectangular frame but its surface has suddenly dissolved and dropped us in the world of meanings and significances under and beyond it.

In the same way the world outside the good poem acts as the pressure against its skin of language and form. Something in the form invites it in. The work, to paraphrase Emily Dickinson, is the house that tries to be haunted. The good text or picture or photograph or film remains itself but the blind field is felt hovering around the rooms of its language. Possibly because I have lived in one house of language but with the shadow existence of another within it; possibly because I have had to rely on the mediation of other, in my case visual, languages to hold the world still enough for me to get any grip on it; possibly because of certain hunches or apprehensions or fears about history, its grand public face, its tyrant sneer, its personal flutters and terrors and the haunted look in its hypnotic eyes – the look, the punctum and the blind field seem to have driven much of my work.

That also goes for the personal poems whose true subject is often fragility: love poems, commemorative poems, poems verging on the edge of verses, tender formalities. Most poets write such poems because most poets sense that they, like all people without fixed stars, inhabit blind fields. The blind field is our realm. We are our own and each others' blind fields. In the best poems the blind field presses in, is everywhere present.

Blind field is not a private space although in my case it sometimes feels like an intimate space. The only crowds there are comprised of ghosts and apprehensions. It is not the public *agora*. It isn't a poetry slam or the cabaret circuit. It can sing and dance and juggle a little, indeed has to juggle if only to keep moving. It rather likes company. It warms to human presence, to the human smell. It could not do without it but it spends its time travelling and, until it gets to its own Ithaca (now where is Ithaca in all that blind field?) it cannot become a citizen of this or that mappable, legally-constituted state of the spirit.

*

Collected Poems are a privilege, but their other name is *Tombstones*. Heavy, flat, hard to hold for a long time, writers are firmly buried beneath them. For that reason, and because I don't think I am in memoir territory yet, the New part of this book consists of the shorter poems that have accumulated in the past few years, not the longer work. The longer work – sequences, experiments, more sustained voyages in that or that leaky craft – is saved for the collection to appear after this one, *The Burning of the Books and other poems* (2009).

It would be good to think that one is not trapped in the coffin-voice of one's historic making. I prefer to think of wilder voyages, crazier, more various craft that may take one to yet stranger places, islands before Ithaca; the peculiarly riotous, dreamlike isles of the restless old. It would be nice to think so before the bits of the self start, in Larkin's words, 'speeding away from each other for ever'. Thinking is easy.

Poems strive to understand where we have been, where we are, and even, at times, were we are going. In the long run there is always Ithaca. Or blind field. If one can distinguish the one from the other.

GEORGE SZIRTES

POETRY INTRODUCTION 4

(1978)

In Memoriam Busby Berkeley

Military straddle the pool.
A gasp of music. Everyone is here.
Thousands cross the street unseeing. Two hearts
Grow breasts. Swirling like a dream with top hat
And cane come eternal softnesses.

Wind them up and let them go. Spin
Little dancer. The rain is gold, and as
The eyes light up it's Keeler! Powell!
The audience, to a man, cry down their trousers.
The lights come on too bright, like chariots.

At Colwick Park

First thing in the morning they went out
To rake over the lawn. The horses
Waited quietly in their stalls, snuffling
At wet latches. Birds were already singing
Behind the roof; dull blades rusted
In drops of condensation. While others were asleep
They worked, sowing their own bodies in Colwick Park.

Their aprons sweep them round. Rakes to earth,
Certain of their footing, they stare
Across the field of their flesh
With no apparent emotion. A sharpness comes
To peel away their noses but they counter it
With work: Swish, swish of hewn wood descending,
Recoil of grass, resilient in clouds
Of green; the regular clicking of arms.

Clouds can only echo their shapes.
The stubble was dragged clear, the lawns
Levelled without anger. Their sullen staring
Is what is left when mythologies disappear.

At the Dressing-table Mirror

She sits at the dressing-table, pushing back her hair,
Lipstick in hand, eyes poised above the quivering stick,

Aware of someone – a boy – moving behind her, watching,
Observing the dark hair falling onto her shoulders

And trying to remove without her noticing
A thing she cannot see from the handbag on the bed:

But she has only to turn to her right to check on his movements
And the reflection that showed her now shows the boy also

And what he does beside her in that mirror, in the room
They both occupy...United for an instant

In that glance, surprised by the net in which they find
Themselves doing what their image shows them doing,

They break on the very edge of laughter, clearer for
A second in that marriage, till she leans forward to

Apply the lipstick, when her breathing mists the glass
And the boy and woman are parted. But still, many years after,

Throwing out old books or turning up a card
In her writing, or noticing a look in his daughter's eye

To arrest him at his work, he sees at once the mirror
And hears again their shared and broken laughter.

Village Politicians
(after Wilkie)

Their heads are too big for a start. Their bodies
shrink to pup-like cowering, all hunched.
Gestures are means of voiding the bowels; air reeks
in the small room where they are bunched

around the table in endless argument.
A frenzy grips them surely! Faces fall
to ape Michelangelo's *Damnation*, a small boy
steals the dog's dinner, woodlice crawl

out of the rotting beams, and a carving knife
lies on the floor among the debaters who
are growing angry. The fireplace is threatened
by encroaching darkness. Time fixes them like glue.

Salon des Independants
(based on the picture by Henri Rousseau)

Flags hang stiffly from the trees, the sky
Is cleared, the obstruction of the clouds put by –
Wind bends the massive emblems and the park
Stretching towards the pavilion is dark
With canvases. A million artists wait
Suspended between fame, death and depression,
Squeezed between the tree trunks and the gate.

Hush! The adjudicators are in session!

Their voices are tiny; the rubbing of antennae
Omnipotent through the early dusk of Paris,
Dealing immortality. Held high
Above the trees the angel's trump
Shakes down gold along the crowded ramp
And sprays its glory down the whitewashed terrace.

The apparently-tame lion underneath
Growls and briefly bares its razor teeth.

The Birdcage 1851

She leans to kiss the cage in the full sunlight
of the conservatory doorway. Walls gleam
down the shade-patched drive, a pair of pigeons, alight
on the apple tree. Everything is stiff as a dream,

and so she strains to the bird's mouth that draws her up,
stretching out her neck – though she could scarcely approve
this sensual exhibition, nor the cup
that tilts to spilling from her hand as she moves –

and draws her hands and breasts up and shuts her eyes...
The sleeping dog crumpled at her feet
stirs a paw to wave away some flies:
wings buzz interminably in the heat.

The glass is vibrant with its rainbows; flowerpots
perched sullenly on the rough sill glow brick-red.
The bird's small feet are sharp and her beak cuts
the pouted fruitage of the lady's head.

At the Circus

No need to ask what the black horse is,
or the dripping tinsel tickling Mamie's hair,
as she perched delicately on her husband's knee,
courses spirals through the blurring air.

Round and round we go the children cry,
next to their respectable papas;
the red-tongued horse invites their crisp applause,
the ringmaster hands round immense cigars.

We fill the sagging tent and pay no heed
to the tin clowns clattering across
the sawdust. The grey air above us bleeds,
the lollipops are cold, voluptuous.

Three Dreams

1

The yellow rusting of the late apples under the trees:
insects to lunch. We are almost dead – ancient localities

stuck in intricate plumbing of decay. Almost dead
almost dead, old masters. Bestuccoed in white lead

we flake off bark or blade, struggling for breath, running
in autumn rain. We watch young girls swing

pendulums into the park's throat – it is we who choke,
go down with flags flying into the still lake.

2

Except you. You don't come down this way – I'm glad.
The marshes croak: I find my place in the *Dunciad*

with Crousaz and Burgersdyck. Everyone else wins
plaudits; I'm overwhelmed by my stripling sons...

3

Words revolt against the weak king. Effeminate, he
is condemned to be locked into a shelf of his library

between the first two volumes of Mickey Mouse. Castrati
lull him to sleep but he's woken at night by the noise of parties

on a lower floor. A heavy fog descends:
the autumn brings pear-falls in the garden.

The Past Order

We reach back into some past order
to reshuffle the pack, coming up
with ancient medallions till now kept
stored away. He who was once King
is reduced to plotting minister,

the greenwood is repopulated
with silver fruits that droop precipitously
from the branches, falling
every so often with a soft sound
that stifles the screaming of mice.

News for Signor Mouse

Who is dead? Who? Who?
Signor Mouse will tell
the kitchen sink of this,
and those bare floors will
stink of disinfectant;
propitiatory; the incense of Paradiso.

One is dead, and two are dead,
now three. Whispers
at the perimeter, closer still
and closer, tickling the thick-skinned grass
from underneath;

faces cut in mid-sentence:
Signor Mouse, hurry –
tell the cat of this.

The Fish

What eye, obsolete and monstrous, blue,
In blue bath of pupil, beautiful,
Occupies this specially prepared room?
No one knows you yet you compel joy.

No one knows you but you compel joy –
Unknown before and hardly discernible,
A joy quite different from happiness,
One that is always present in some form.

How then to address you? A long white spout
Of want is all the rhetoric you need,
The whale of the blue sea is your eye
And winks at all our dear formalities.

I hold you in my arms, could kiss or crush;
I come upon you basking on a rock,
Strange and rhythmic, mermaid, mythical,
I touch, hold, grasp and am vanquished by you.

We smile within our bellies but you laugh
With the sudden wind that rattles at our doors:
O such infinite care propels us here
To hold you, feed you, sing to you, and grow old.

A Windblown Hat

Always time, there is enough of it:
Running down the street after a bus
A man loses his windblown hat.

In the gardens that he passes the lawns sprout
Insistent waves: weeds and nettles press.
Always time, there is enough of it.

Across the road the library has shut
But books are nagging in the crowded house:
A man loses his windblown hat.

A printed form is found behind the pot.
It hints at something vague but hazardous:
Always time, there is enough of it.

So many beginnings, cancel out the lot;
The bin drinks down old papers, dead ideas
And a man loses his windblown hat.

But in the end, you say, well, I can wait;
Something will replace the thing I miss.
A man loses his windblown hat:
Always time, there is enough of it.

Nils

Below me like my mother's scarf
The fields are set in perfect pattern;
Connemara cloth and satin,
Tweed and wool – such mythic stuff.

Up here the air is drunk and cold
Swaying past my neck and arms:
The world is balanced on my palms;
Its dreams and justices are stilled.

I spin away from time and house,
Freezing silver spreads my veins:
Below me disappear the lanes
Of childhood – Faster goose!

The Domino Players

1

Brightness over the wood. In the room
Four peasant women play at dominoes.
One taps CLACK CLACK with her shoes,

Another moves a counter with her thumb,
A blob of spittle on her lip. A third
Wide-mouthed, reveals soft and toothless gums.

The last invites no special comment; smokes,
Leans lewdly forward, headscarfed like the rest,
Listening; like them to a foul stream of jokes.

A boy sits in the corner. His dumb face
Is screwed up. Beside him in the rusted pail
Cold clear water gels to clouds of ice.

2

In the cold, enchanted room
Three witches sat. The boy had come
Having reached the usual age,
And sprawled out, snoring in the cage.
The cat beside him rubbed her back

Against his vast and bloated neck,
But even in his shallow sleep
He heard their scissors snap and snip
And felt their laughter swell, and burst
The banks above, and was immersed.
He swam, a fish: with monstrous glee
He ate the witches, one two three.

3

Are these mothers here with such skinny faces,
Such damson patches at their cheeks and eyes?
Do they realise
How the room has presented them to us?
That dominoes are bodies of dead men,
That the boy in the corner is already enervate
And resigned to the point of boredom?

Soon the clay pipe will be broken,
The cigarette burn away to nothing,
Their hideous husbands come dancing
Over the fields and be annihilated.
But these wait and play at dominoes
Paying attention only to their game,
And whether one calls them witches or weird sisters
They simply sit there without fuss or bother
And they have fine curly moustachios.

4

Caked inseparably to some distant past
The women talk on though their tongues are lost.
Assuming the mantle of the innocent
The boy still listens, quiet and intent,
Sits and listens to how one found
Her old man's doodah under a pile of dust,
Or how this other scrabbled at her love-mound.
But here there's neither love nor light nor lust,
But a rudimentary composition, an ache

In which he'll notice as the night wears on
The fly's dying intermittent drone
That circulates above the grating laughter
Of his close relations, and long after
The company has put away the dominoes
And gone to bed, the wind's commotion
Gnawing at the walls. But under the bedclothes
Comes the final loveliness of being alone;
The downward rushing of dreams into the lake.

The Drowned Girl

(for Peter Porter)

Salt fogs insulate
The harbours, those fishing villages
Wood visited and painted:
Men wrestling after dark;

The white sea, and the tinkers
Arguing over a horse;
Rows of houses like waves,
Drowning in their solitude.

Your lips and tongue explore
These sounds; the spitting 'th',
'w' – the rolling silence of water,
The joyful crowned vowels –

These were the words I learned
Quickest of all – monosyllabic,
Twisted to boys' threats
Like a collar twisted

Over a scrawny neck of land
The sea kisses and bites at.
These were and are the words
That I now teach my children.

*

She turned up in the cabin
Three centuries later; a girl
Some twenty years old, they say,
A mile off Anglesey.

The sleeping girl, broken
By a falling wardrobe,
Drifting among her
Ragged dresses, eyes

In perpetual surprise
That this sudden kiss
Should come with such sucking,
Such uncouth labials,

Stretches out her hand
To push away the swell
Under the door, and finds it
Kissed –

Soft, interminably soft.
Even in the white bone
This heart and hip cushion
My time and my words.

Drowned miles, bleached bones.
Earls of Meath or Ardglass.
Breasts locked in the cupboard:
Lockets boarded under waves.

*

But the low murmuring
Of the cabin expands
At last to music
Of other lives and other voices,

Meaning more dead than she did alive
To instruct my children
In the grammar of countries
Vaster, more important than theirs,

Yet with which they shall in time
Be themselves acquainted;
Thankless and hollow
Like this table or these bones;

Fortunate still in the choice
Of their father's adoptive home,
As was this English girl
In the salt noose, her birthright.

FROM

THE SLANT DOOR

(1979)

Virius and Generalic

My good friend Virius is dead,
cried Generalic the painter
(sixteen years after the event
and his own body withering)

and set to build a tomb of grass
in a field by the church
ringed with space only,
the pronged wire distant,

and placed by the reconstituted
corpse, thirteen candles,
a cock of hope, and a tape
across still starting eyes.

The grass unrolls to support him
and mourners huddle
by the church, led by a pink priest,
Generalic in the rear.

Nearby water thirsts; the dark green
promises a Byzantium of worms
already tickling round the sockets;
images of kings and queens moving into focus;

the rude blond pilots
hidden under sheets of sky
are crying for forgiveness, lacerated
by the cock's beak, tree's spear.

(Generalic and Virius were 20th-century Yugoslav "naive" artists.
Vinus died at Zemin at a concentration camp during the war. Sixteen
years later Generalic painted a homage to Virius.)

The Town Flattened

1

This is Dada architecture; big stars of wood,
amulets of brick and a far church
blown down by the rational wind.
The whole town is like this. My hands
are so cold I can hardly write.
I am fascinated by their patterns though:
white walls and grandpapa dying
along with the cat and the chambermaid
(I only want a little bit of butter for my bread).

These stations are so draughty.
Were I a god I could rebuild all this in seven days.

2

Sun blurs the trees. Along the slats
light rattles like a carriage. The porch
sighs out another century but we maintain
our distance, preferring the panoramic
view afforded by this vacancy
between two paths. Surely if we touched
the trees they would sound like crystal.

3

My window eyes are brighter than a cat's.
I guard these trees with twigs and right-angles
and feel their hands upon my ivied walls,
a creeping caress. No one passes
to disturb our fusion except the servants
who keep the garden trim and wait for someone.

4

There should be a progression in all this.
My hands are so cold that I cannot write.
The whole town is reduced to rubble, like
remnants of a fire. I have walked the streets
and seen nothing but timber and fallen masonry.

You should not have sent the parcel on my dear.
I will let you know as soon as it arrives.

5

In the top room of an old hotel there sat
a spider sheltering from rain. It was
the biggest I had ever seen.
To tell the truth I dared not move
in case it scrambled down the wall.

There are draughts all over the place –
holes big enough to push a finger through.
Were these in walls you ask? Of a kind.
The wall of a head, the secret orchard
with its cobweb of hair. Amazing to think
strands like these can hold together
a wall, a thought, a family even.

6

The apples are burned red this year. In
every groove and ditch broken skins of apples
char the bank and the mist is a fine ash
caught between valleys.
                   But under it the idea of a skull
bearing the load of its leaves and branches,
pure, the dust cleansed off, and the thing
set on a table ready for inspection,
seems to contemplate the striking of a match,
a harvest.

Dwellings

The first was a flat with a courtyard
Several rungs below the piano-room
(Dust stuck in the window there)
Where rust and chalk climbed in a spiral
Of grotesques both round and porcupine.
Children ran together in that courtyard,
Their voices stripping paintwork in low rooms.

The second was a cottage, utterly filthy,
With the saving grace of black morello cherries,
Our dead lights. The hill was stained with them.

They ran or rolled down slopes between the trees
And stopped, lost between house and house,
Loaves a mile long under their stiff arms.

The next was a civilised room. Books hugged
In cabinets, a file for papers, and a wireless
Turning its ear to the loud town. A decent
Darkness spread over the corners. Their heads
Were neat and tapered, hair brushed flat,
Guardian spirits of the wall.
But dust stuck in the window there
Whenever bells rang which was not often.

Now everything is quiet. The bus snorts
Along flat roads between a set of fields;
Chalked walls indicate a choir of trees
In a park perhaps, stacked in neatest rows.
Leaving both behind, small rooms present
Their shrinking surfaces; enamelled baths,
The sliding mirrors of a cabinet,
And a body hanging with showered age,
The skin glistening.

The Slant Door

The red light is on the slant door again
That stands in the garden, up against the shed.
It's time we took the children off to bed;
It's been such a fine day it's sure to rain,
And down the door the rain has worn small grooves;
You don't know what it is that means or moves.

This tiny circle, as fragile as it's flawed,
Becomes a cage where the exotic sheen
Of birds gathers, a blaze of red on green
Whose greater forces instinct will applaud;
A strutting menagerie one tries to hush,
The constant prattle of the sleek and plush.

Let's pack away the tea, I'll wash, you dry
And let the children play for half an hour
With their toys before the forecast shower.
The small rain will creep on purposefully
But we must be quiet if we want to hear
The rain's approach – listen now – is it near?

Quiet, you birds, stop squabbling there below,
I will not make you metaphors just yet
Because the greater power lies in quiet.
The clouds move silently and very slow
To blot out gardens and our slanting door
Which is precisely angled for the downpour.

Group Portrait with Pets

The little group seems perfectly at ease
though drapes and scattered toys confirm the truth,
it was the clever painter's artifice
that fixed the glimmer on each eye and tooth.

I say there will be hopelessness before
the children rise and the chair topples back:
the bright, transparent skins will fold and crack
before the painter leaves by the back door.

That satin, crinoline, so much like blood
splashed across the canvas, find an echo
in the bird's breast, the cat has understood
who simply bides his time while others go,
who has seen terror written on a face
just as the limb is torn and the claw sinks.

The artist too, in spite of what he thinks,
can only measure breath in a small space,
where husbands, wives and children interlink
and find a warmth in the arranged embrace.

Glass

1

This morning I could swear we were made of glass –
tight nervous shards. Our hearts
echo in our mouths – even this desk feels brittle.
Bright clouds scuttle, smeared against the window;
men are being blown to pieces in
the doorways of villages. Women are crying
over the disgusting corpses that were children.

Powdered glass is falling through the doorway.

We are thin and bend in the heat:
slabbed in yellow light our fingers are crystal twigs
shattering over open mouths.

2

Twin asterisks of milk. An
explosion of doors in the quiet house
rouses a sleeping force to pout
under the doors of our bedroom.
Motorcycles are sick outside;
houses and dynamos turn, incendiary.

The sleek bombs wait underground
holding hands for comfort. Under
the stairs spiders are singing songs
with perfect composure.

In the pale sea-egg, all the clocks
of the world break their frail shells
and we come up fresh, smelling
of daisies, feet skyward, heads
under turf, our lips
still joined.

Summer Landscape

Long after you move the trees still bow.
Houses remain far longer than your gaze
Can hold them. Yawning wide, the gardens now

Push hedges out all bristling in a blaze
Of withered sticks. Roads grow steep and white
In driest summer, migrating birds amaze

The dusty roofs... Here descriptions bite
The dust. We end at nothing. You, the trees,
The houses, freeze before oncoming night,

My hands drop down. We hear a flight of bees
Bombard the pane. Bitter ghosts go out
Into the sunlight. Summer dies by degrees.

Recovering

'So you are recovering.' The bed was thin,
Their thoughts unwound and were anatomised,
They missed the touch of one another's skin

And all the love of habit that disguised,
Insurances against one troubling theme;
They feared to find themselves too much surprised.

In spite of this it was a worn out scheme,
As night is simply night however dark
And one survives the grilling of a dream

Whose awkward figures tend to stand out stark
Against a well loved landscape, and the knife
Is drawn quite painlessly and leaves no mark.

Sleeping

You sleep, and I beside you in the bed
Am listening to the noises of the traffic
And the creaking of the blinds. Day's ended

In the usual fashion; the wound clock's tick,
Eyes growing tired, some entangling of arms,
Wrapped and unwrapped, falling. From the attic

Come sighings of wind, the whispering of charms
Against bad dreams. How distant we must seem
Before the light goes out and blankets warm

Us to passivity; when the thin gleam
Of a barricaded moon might let men see
A private love whose skin is pale as cream.

Bones

The doctor came, love's old anatomist
To pick our bones clean, perfect ghostly white.
The frost had hardened on the sill, the mist

Curled round the house in freezing wreaths; our light
Was ancient moon, cold and bright as a rock
Laundered by seawater. He came that night

Administering heat and with a shock
Shook bones to movement, made the dunces spin
A dance beyond themselves whose tick and tock

Measured the pulse of love. Whole skeins of skin
Lay crumpled till the crisis passed, then he
Stalked off, typical of his profession.

Anthropomorphosis

Foreigners, said the lady. Off the bus
Fell two dark men in heavy duty jackets.
The conductor swore; a pair of dogs
Leapt after a ball in gusts of fretful barking.
The men stood at the kerb watching the bus
Disappear over the crest of the hill, then turned
Sharply and walked off in the opposite direction
Pausing only for one to let fly with a gob
Of spit toward the curving wall behind them.

It was as if I'd seen it all before –
That long sail of spit arching over.
By my will I held it there, suspended
Between brick and mouth. Slowly some
Indefinite memory broke, spilling its garbage:
A harbour town smelling of dead fish,
The uncertainty of leaving mingled with
Excitement at arrival. Years of water
Concentrated to a blob of spit
On its trajectory, and the afternoon
Rearranged itself around his act.

And though I could not say what place it was
Or how long ago, I too hung there
Encapsulated in that quick pearled light,
Spewed by his volition, about to crack,
The taste of sea already penetrating my mouth.

Pastoral

The ancient at the gate wickers a chair:
bald-headed, hunched, he is focus
for a metropolis of ants while on the bank
stubble grows aggressive. He is an English Joseph
earning pin-money. Behind him
in the topmost room the god-child slumbers
as the child-wife sings over the oven,
the neighbour's children brawl in the sun
(one's watching him now as he turns away)
and the trees fling their doily patterns high.

No doubt a flock lathers in the valley,
no doubt an owl stirs in the hayloft,
no doubt the spider bridges its rafters:
there are laws and ordinances, local rites,
to say nothing of precedents to be observed.

In the quarry feet start a stampede of stones
and the wind is heard by listeners in the hedge.
The gammer starts a story though the children know the ending.

Fog

Foggy this morning, the fog dripping down
in streaks of grey, and far distances ageing
into dust on glasses of water grown
permanent as poison. There is no gauging
distances at all – blindness grips the town,

and adolescents rising from their baths
feel the load of their quick growing, sudden
and dizzy. In old albums, photographs
bleed down to faint circles and aunts are hidden
in thick fuzz. Feeling faint nobody laughs.

Snow

Look, it has snowed in the night
And the roads are bright as skin
Lit by the moon: the snow *is* moonlight
And there will be no morning ever again,
We shall live in white like brides
Never stirring, nor shall night be over
To discover the bed unmade or the windows thrown wide
Or the street stopped in its course like a river.

Background Noises

The shuffling of folded paper, creaking chairs;
Where does it go, our surrogate music?
Hold off the intelligence and listen
To the survivors; an ear, a hand, a bum
On a chair: solid, untearful matter.

Quietly now. Quiet. Quieter still, until
What listens is part of the same world
And the friction between noise and sense
Falls in irregular cadences.

This is the quietest music where you and I
Fade in accompaniment, pronouncing names
That once had power: I to you
And vice versa, dancing on thin air.

In Suspense

If you were to go out of that room now
You might miss him. Who? You may as well
Ask the sick man what he sees in his mirror
Or the man sitting by his window, waiting
For the postman on his clockwork rounds
What happiness he anticipates. Wherever
We move there are too many alternatives.

And it is no spectral visitor, nor the sun
Illuminating a carpet or a chair, but more
A white walled ornate garden, fresh as rain
Between twinned columns of white, where
An intruding hand clutches its white lilies,
A knee bent under, a head bowed, hair yellow,
And something singing: riotous conception!

Picnic

Two dogs are in love. The children seek
spiders in the scrub and place their hands
gingerly upon stalks, their mouths agape.

Their sisters and aunts pick flowers which they will
press between the leaves of poetry books
marking time if nothing else. Trees wash away
and the dogs' tails curl tighter. Rakish uncle
looks smug with his fair companions.

This is how order is made: the clipping down
of untidy edges, the finding of the spider.

Two Men in a Boat
(i.m. L.S. Lowry)

Are rowing in opposite directions.
Their names are Sid and someone
and they are stuck somewhere in the middle
of a boating lake where ice-cold gulls
lever themselves off a pack of houses.

The boat is rain and tastes of
old tobacco. Reflected in
the water, two swans
do not like each other
and attempt to pull away.

In the dark leaves of the umbrella plant
a man with a lute, a nun with a dirty habit,
and the sea-scum laughing with its bones askew,
and these two seem to be singing to each other
about the weather and the lake,

or Lear's oddikins, those dear men,
rushing round in a sieve,
whirlpool against whirlpool.
At least they are enjoying themselves
though the songs are sad,

because it's kisses they bestow
on one another in the yellow light,
like Siamese twins growing out
of each other's skulls,
away from each other. And the boat will break

with a loud guffaw, brother Lawrence,
and the oars slam at nothing
but winter and winter's comforts,
hollow trees shouting at one another
across the waves.

Silver Age

They don't look significantly different –
Gold silver, iron – touch them and disappear.
Whether they are wielding cudgels or walking
On the grass in postures inherited from
Rococo shepherds, or giving suck to putti
Their dying is a crooking of fingers and makes us feel
How sad it is an age, whatever age, should pass.

But no use, no cure. The weathered glass
Falls with the mercury falling. Earth turns steel
And bone powders like Napoleon's buttons.
It's the cold turns them numb
And prevents them from talking,
Mud in mouths for every lengthening year.
The snow is silver. There's the way they went.

The Swimming Pool in the House

There's a swimming pool in the house – yes, I can smell it,
And it isn't a Roman bath or British one –
It is the water coming up to meet you,
The chlorine lapping in the August sun:
And look, an arm is waving! There's the roof
Returning all the light it does not need
To make the shadows greener, and the splash
Of bodies falling into waves that bleed
A green and hesitant curl.
                    I was young
With the men that swam here once, and the stone
On which they stretched rose hot and angled square,
A surface we could run on though alone,
Each separate in his own patch of brown –
The skin of age unpeeling where they drown.

An Illustrated Alphabet

A. The conventional opening, the most
generous of vowels. King of non-specifics
yet a cunning master of definition.
I am A. You sir, are nothing but A.
I myself have always been A
with aspirations towards THE,
unique and posthumous.

B! Sheer bombast: no Drum
nor Trumpet are ye like to have
but words with fantastical action:
a suicide, a revenge, all fantastical.
Here in the quiet grove
among the faeries lies one asleep
who shall take the knife, and being bold
shall batter and blow to the end
for which our rhetoric was designed.
Banish not him, poor fool. I shall be his bond.

C is catch as Catch Can, ambiguous
in the middle of the piano. Throw one
to St Cecilia. Soft. Throw one to
St Catherine. Sharp. There is no telling.
Berlioz thought C dull and vague
unless in the minor key. Let us put aside
our differences then and concentrate on the melodic
and the minor, the not-too-cavalier.
Can we do it? You must wait and C.

D, says my little boy, is Daddy. I accept his
designation and try as far as possible
to live up to it. (There are three Ds
in Daddy, which is a lot
for any man to cope with.) However one
learns to wear one's Ds with a certain dignity.
But Droll. One becomes grand D, great-grand D. Finally just d.

E is, as everyone knows, the most common
letter of the alphabet. You brush past
Es in the street never noticing their faces,
often dumb as in Brute or
Horrible, sometimes merely implied
as in Alone. From Eggs to Elephants,
from Eden to Dies Irae. The time
will come when Es shall sit in judgment.
Meanwhile there is always the Brute, the Horrible, the Etcetera.

F is for Fellow Sufferers. Friends, the world
is full of us. We are the voice of reason.
Our puffed-up face witnesses to
humiliations and indignities. We have our offices
and our true fury. Friend, why will
you not be friend? Why will you
persist in finding us faintly funny?
O foolish man, examine thine own self.

G. Ugly and glottal, just a pain
to pronounce, you always lie
beneath our vocal gewgaws.
When the others have long climbed out
onto the shore, you still squat there, winking
at upright creatures and gulping air.
I see you toad, red-eyed and lascivious –
no wonder you are ninety per cent submerged
who do not know to praise a lady's hand.

H. Wipe away the condensation. Whose face
is that in the garden? Hoar frost
cools our grass – my face and yours
transposed over each other, staring
out over a thin brightness. The
images kiss but the frost remains.
Our breath obscures precisely that part
of the garden we were looking at.
The frost remains, hidden and durable.

I was hoping to remain hidden below
this table (half naked and too white,
the cold draught tickling my skin)
but I saw the door open as you entered
and called my name. Come out, you said,
come out, the game is up. I lay
as still as I could, unaware
of my protruding feet.
Should I come out? And if I did
who would be left to cower under the table?

J! The sound jars. Why that
suggestion of a hush? Is it above board?
Would you jeopardise everything
to claim a title beyond proof?
Justice will be ours. Already
the jury is assembled and whispers peel
like strips of skin to a clear Jubilate
and the joke dies on your lips.

K is kiss; the joyning of lips
for a token, or sheer exploratory
pleasure as in a hand stretched
out to rain. Billiard balls kiss
and part on perfect cushions –
professionals observe the lie.
But let us make ours one of trust,
fleshly and unskeletal, as it flies –
such is the ideal: comedy and decay.

L, my natural singer, all liquid
and melody, who will not learn
the words but comes forth tumbling
like a juggler at a fair. It is all
so easy for him, such fa-la-las,
so slick and mellifluous.

Beware fool, your idiotic waggling
breaks against the bars. Tomorrow
you must be tied and whipped.

M? When you are stuck for words
or feeling foolish, these ass's ears
come made to measure. Nor is it
merely fluency at stake but pride.
(How easily these ears could become a crown
with the addition of a single peak!)
And is it possible then? Well... says a squeaky voice,
Ah Mickey Mouse, *mon semblable*; Muffin, *mon frère!*

N is for Nose, noble and necessary.
No one compliments us on our nose:
What rich lips or what deep eyes, they say;
you don't have to be a Cyrano or a Gaganov
to realise a point of honour is at stake.
But nose, you are the only character;
we follow you instinctively
and all your indefinite delights,
to smells of bread or coffee from a shop,
to Denmark or to distant Hottentots.
Here's adventure then. Forward nose,
into the cold, northerly and northerly.

O altitudo, somewhere up there,
walking on clouds in the crisp sun
without flame or brightness.
Tragedy becomes white in the mouth:
You promise us Heaven. And it's O O O O
that Shakespeherian rag,
not one but a thousand, as many as you like.

p – softly now piano, uncontemptuous
if you please. Flutter along
the high trebles without offence.
True there are Persons, Poverty of Spirit,
Impertinence, but glide over these
unruffling the morning stillness.
Hush, don't wake the children,
practise quietly; small explosions, small grievances.

Q, queue – a tail. How it sharpens you
this appendage. A dog wags it, a cat
works it into an angry forest, a pig
curls it tight as steel. It's certainly

a powerful weapon. A crocodile
demolishes all Nineveh with one sweep,
and as for the devil – who can forget
that swingeing horror? It whistles in
the dark from the lung and over the teeth.
Tu quoque. Quick. Querulous.

R, gentle reader, stands for you;
always short of time but philanthropic,
ready to fork out for this or that,
placing and displacing volumes on
your shelf, our hoard of words
crushed to a fine juice. Really reader,
you are indispensable, your approbation
rewarding, your anger distant as a lion's growl,
Half myself: I purr and praise reflecting
on all the things you are.

Sss. The kettle puts out his tongue
and disappears. Whistle away
you hot clouds. Everything
that is secret or wet snakes on our glass
and presses the room close.
Outside leaves toss air, here we steam up
and bite at little provocation.
Hiss! Keep your distance. Hiss! Know
your place. Hiss! Wait till you are
spoken to: vituperation
endless as the garden in her clouded stole.

T! Who stole the pig? Who drowned the cat?
Who pulled him out again? My son Tom
has done these things and with him I am well pleased,
who knows the terrors of the tongue
and the tipping of the table and who with his nonsense
tittle-tattle frights devils and protects his mother;
Tom, tall as a tale, whose coughing
breaks the evening's counterpoise.

U! The first language – gruff and crude –
a heap of Un Uns being the vocabulary
of want and claim. (Is it a woman
or a beast or a mound of earth
that is desired?) It is still monkey talk
and sends bricks tumbling with brute force,
trampling on our conversation
which might have been so interesting.

V. A sharp valley bids us welcome. Here the water
rushes among weed and rock.
We must swim upstream into the vapoured falls.
Salmon pass us, fragments of wrecked craft
come hurtling about our ears,
and each time the blood freezes we must leap.
We are the vanguard, guarding nothing
but an expanding vacuum. Our gestures
are vast, Churchillian.
We shall never withdraw.

W. Why do we never meet? Our distance
engenders softness, demanding an explosion.
We wait. It cannot be maintained. We merely
squeeze air till it hurts. Our poles repel.
What is the cure, what weed, what weal-healer?
Only to engender such softness, never knowing why,
for what purpose and when to end?
We wax and wane. Be resolute, say we will. We will.

X cancels out everything: fortune,
kisses, a sheaf of faces, converting
present to past and planting instead
an unknown kingdom, all a mystery.
Once we measured our affections by these
simple methods; walked thirty paces after
the dead tree and meeting on a tall hill
marked out the map of our turning fortune.
Certainly the past is excessive but love
lives on hope. Where is it all buried?
In the head, in the heart, in the belly. Make
your incision then, as soft, as warm as skin.

Y is Yes, the Life Force, not just
the particular and partial but
a grand universal, the happy islands.
Shall we go there? Yes. Shall
we leave now, without waiting,
without putting our coats on? Yes.
Are you ready? Yes. Then here's the boat
and here's your compass. Quickly, go now
for you must reach it before nightfall. We
shall be waiting for your reports.

The lovers file down the hill.

Are you still going? Yes.

Z is laziness itself, under the humming roses,
nodding. We know no wind but breezes
troubling the grass. And shall we
collapse, completely and easily
into sleep? The sun snores
under his coverlet, blood gathers
under the leaves. O fall, fall without pain.
Avoid, and let the phrases close gently as in music.

NOVEMBER AND MAY

(1981)

A Girl Visits Rembrandt's House

Her hand moves on his hand and his face —
Gnarled in grimaces, glamorous as a Turk
Or Sultan with the moon and nightingale,
A sodden mynheer all of cloth and patchwork.

He comes on disguised, wearing skin like cloth,
Armoured, gowned, spurred, inordinately dressed
For imperial adventures, maps of experience:
Skin becomes an ardent imperialist.

She wanders in folds of skin along the street,
The old town slimy with red lights and tourists,
Trams, canals, the dark church in the centre,
With dim eyes, stub hands, smooth outrageous breasts.

The Icy Neighbour

Through you I enter the permanent chamber
thick with frost, the walls' sheer reflection
where you once smiled forgetfully at me,
your very dust frozen on the tables and sills;
the little jar from which you ate, your dog,
your fingerprints, the quick apparatus;

while in the corner of the room
there nibble the two mice, love and death,
and you are too absorbed to hear them
being dead and lovable yourself,
still smiling in your icy way across
the lush carpet, your hands clasped,
the dog remaining faithful,
bearing witness beside a discarded shoe.

It is as if you had never died, and the mirror
with all its distortions goes on recording
the image of your permanent chamber
with your fingerprints, the quick apparatus.

Of Grass

It was the shade of grass – no, something greener
We touched on shortly before sleep, so soft, so bright,
No metaphor could touch or scumble it,
I cannot speak it though my mouth is green.

In a dream following a cobra nestled
Against my chest – we wrestled as in play
Then I lay poisoned in the open air,
I was nothing and the grass was nothing,

Only my fingers were aware and moved
In search of feeling, but they found
Nothing except a tongue and it was yours

Speaking of something in a foreign language
And I being your tongue's interpreter
Understood the word you spoke as grass.

The Phylactery

> *Thou shalt teach them diligently unto thy children, and*
> *shall talk of them when thou sittest in thine house, and*
> *when thou walkest by the way, and when thou liest down,*
> *and when thou risest up.*
> DEUTERONOMY 6

The photographer is an ageing Jewess
with blonde rinsed hair, whose eyes we may not see
because of the phylactery she carries
between them, without which she feels naked.

It is a text to stand between her and Sheol,
the inhabitants of Lidice and London,
the trucks with yellow stars, the word Juden,
an ancient man polishing a pavement.

The firstlings are still set apart for God
who will enlarge or detail or expose:
she too calls many but will only choose
a few. A man on a park bench with a parcel

on his lap which on closer inspection
turns out to be a supine white cat
hangs old hands out against a row of slats,
his face worn and impassive, almost blind.

No character without geometry
she says. The children grimacing at her
out of dog-tooth check look no better
now than they did twenty-five years ago,

their arms and legs make herring-bones, their teeth
are bars behind which their breath identifies
them to mothers working in hot factories
between the first rain and the latter rain.

House in Sunlight

It isn't right, whatever the sun is doing –
It sits on a chair as if it were at home.
The house smoulders behind curtains.

Custom is our guiding light – we make rules
For chairs and tables to obey. We say to cups,
Go there and they go, without question.

A house is full of knowledge; wisdom
Ages-old lodges in it, or we call it wisdom,
At any rate it falls into a pattern.

It is a focus for news which it laps up
With unconcern. We can remember earthquakes
And revolutions, something is always being massacred.

We boast Michelangelo's dome, Bernini's
Colonnade – a house ought to have style
And proclaim the harmony of the spirit.

Through it we thread delicate bones like friendship
And childhood, linger over details of
Kissing, fondling, sucking, licking, such tenderness.

Whoever lives here knows what they are about –
Forms appear suddenly in mirrors and photographs,
We do not think however that they are entirely at home.

At night the doors are locked. We lock them now.

Half Light

She is standing in a darkness that is luminous,
I say, but my cat flicks her green eyes upward
as if to reply, That is a lie, darkness cannot
be luminous unless I choose to make it so,
and she who is standing there inhabits darkness.
That argument is appropriate: I no longer know
who that woman might be. A dark croon of traffic
sings in my ears; plaster and brick
are four-square, both physical and mental space.
Yet someone is standing, waiting quietly
making that darkness luminous. I riffle
through my acquaintance, dead or living. A mother
dead too early burned brightly enough it is true
but would scarcely deign to blow to such thin flame
that darkness itself was the more noticeable –
Whose fingers if not hers then scratch away
behind the lids, causing the sensation of light?

The Car

It was light skedaddling across the bars,
Four supermarket trolleys running on
Over the street with one boy following,
But it might have been Platinum,
Or at least something *expensive*. The ice
Was black, I did not see it and fell,
Meanwhile the mundane apparition passed,
Disappearing inside double doors

That opened automatically. This blinding
Had no religious significance – no –
But it was exceedingly beautiful and sudden.

Later that day the snow began to fall,
Upward, downward, like a dream of war,
And girls were screaming, running on white grass.
I heard one say, 'How wonderful.' So cold
It was yet they ran on bare-headed
As if snow themselves – I almost lost sight
Of them in grey and white now the sun was gone.

Stuck on the drive a car was losing colour,
No one was in it, the snow had risen up
The windscreen and had reached the top,
Freezing it as steady as a crystal.
Concentrating I saw its windows cracked
And splintered into tiny intricacies,
Fantastic Gaudi-like structures hung
Under the mudguard. It was sepulchral.
Wonderful, cried the girls under the snow.

Sheep-shearing at Ayot St Lawrence

The muzzle firmly held between his knees
he gathers the fleeced stomach into pleats
and leans forward across the flaccid belly
to push the razor down towards her teats.

And there she sits, blind-mouthed, flat on her rump,
black-legged on a sheet of polythene
like some old woman at the hairdresser:
she's corpulent and yellow and unclean.

Behind her stands a cottage with a garden
where a real old woman serves out pots of tea,
and further back the church, Palladian,
which acts this Sunday as a gallery.

Someone at the door sells raffle tickets,
the catalogues are handy on his desk:
inside the close-hung paintings testify
to the attractions of the picturesque.

The sun is out, the summer heat is stifling,
pouring across smooth shoulders, washing hands,
a clean, hard light cuts definitive shadows.
The man relaxes, lets her drop, and stands

above her with a needle, plunges in.
The anxious lambs are nudging underneath
their unshorn dams. It is an ideal moment.
The ewe escapes. Sheep stud the hill like teeth.

The Birdsnesters

1

By Dupont's orchard they went, the three of them
One summer evening, having doused the fire
And locked away the sheep, somewhat excited
By the previous night's apparition,
Or what they thought they heard and saw together
But were less than sure of now, afterwards;
Across the hill, round a small farm, Leclerc's,
On their way to an unlikely stable
Exactly as in the Bible story, out
Of time in the year 1874,
Over beyond the city of Cherbourg,
Philippe and Henri Karr and Jean Boulanger.

2

Towards Equeurdreville they heard the sea
Purring in the dusk, and Philippe being tired
(He had injured his leg some weeks ago)
They decided to make a stop. They spread
Their blankets out and uncorked a bottle,
But Jean listening out more carefully
Made them be quiet, as he said he heard
Above the sea a whirring, hustling noise
Which, it seemed to him, must be coming from
The copse of trees hard by; and they agreed
There were distinctly two conflicting sounds,
And Henri said it was wild pigeons roosting.

3

'When I was a boy,' said Jean, 'we'd often go
Down to the woods, a few of us with torches
And stout branches, and surprise the pigeons.
We'd have pigeon-pie the morning after.
It would be a suitable present for
The new-born God, supposing he exists
And we are not all touched with August madness.'
'What was it like?' asked Henri. 'Come and see.'
The three of them approached the throbbing copse:
Between the leaves wings lifted, breasts squittered
In shades of grey and white. They dared not go
Too close at first for fear of frightening them.

4

Henri whispered that he'd seen some branches
Lying further back, which had been sawn off
And were quite short and thick and heavy-looking;
Philippe meanwhile could go and make three torches.
'We must be quiet yet,' said Jean, 'but when
We're in among them we must whoop and bark
To panic them the more. They flap about,
You cannot help but hit a goodish number,
But watch to hold your arm before your face
For being blinded they fly anywhere
And you are likely to be scratched and slapped.
We'll wear our hats and wrap ourselves in blankets.'

5

And so they got their torches and their branches
And made their way across to the loud trees,
Philippe hobbling and shuffling in the dark,
The grass was wet, the nightingale was singing.
By the outermost trees they hesitated,
Stood like marble, dumb with concentration.
'Now!' cried Jean, and the three of them leapt to
Rushing into the midst of the wild pigeons,
Whooping, barking, waving flaming torches,
Failing to put their arms before their faces,
The leaves like wet whips on the naked skin
And the clear moon frozen among the stars.

6

This was the worst – the heavy bodies falling,
Others rising and falling like white rain,
With shrieks and thumps, blue and silver collared,
Green tinsel orange in the sudden flame
Above their mouths. It was the gravest speech
Of a wild tongue, clubs uncontrollably
Wagging, wagging. They felt the rush of wings
In the highest branches and tripped over
The inanimate moaning in the grass.
Philippe himself lost balance and lay flat
Seeing Jean and Henri – but which was which? –
Whirling dervishes in a cloud of flame.

7

There should have been a pattern to this movement,
The dumb parabolas, mute helices,
Horizontal darts from the charmed circle,
Bright villages eternally collapsing,
Broken walls with glimmers of broken glass.
The birds rose higher, seemed to swirl away,
But Jean and Henri had been cut and bled,
And everything was being madly shaken
Except one bird that seemed perfectly still,
Hovering, glacial, directly above
The blurring figures of Jean and Henri
Like some strange and dangerous benediction.

8

How to number all the different pigeons
Since that single one bearing the olive-branch
Returned from the dry peak of Ararat?
Fruit Pigeons of tropical rain forests,
Columba Livia of rock and shore,
The common breed round civic statuary,
The journalist's and soldier's messengers,
Jacobins nestling in the fancier's attic,
Nearest surviving kin of Solitaire
And Dodo, as distant now as Seraphim,
A softness padding out the knobbly branches,
Softer even than white apple blossom.

9

They hardly knew when it was truly finished
But continued swinging about blindly –
It was a miracle they had not clubbed
Each other into insensibility.
The birds lay round them, some twenty or so,
Ring-doves, stock-doves, some with cracked wings or backs,
Some with their heads crushed in. After a while
When they felt steady on their feet again
They gathered up the seven largest birds
And wrapped them in their torn and sodden blankets,
And in a mood of deep tranquillity
Packed up their camp, doused fire and set off home.

MISERICORDS

The Silver Tree

In a hot steamed-up room five girls are spinning
a tree made of silver paper, growing
from a trunk so clumsy only a child
could be taken in by it. Its girth outstrips
the attenuated branches that tumble
from its crown and drop down to the floor where
they coil and lengthen, lovelier than hair,
a genuine silver tree they seem to spin
out of themselves. Their fingers diminish,
twine with foil, are sucked out of their sleeves.
It is the triumph of Aluminium.

And just as they become the tree, the tree
becomes them. They thrive on ambiguity.
As the tree grows they grow, although
infinitely more slowly, and enter into
the frieze where mothers and smart daughters dance
in a cold pastoral. Ice is eating them.

It is desire for perpetuity,
the film rerunning as they petrify
and the forest throws its lank arms about them.
They hang like fruit, sucked out, perfect, until
imaginary gods pass by and cut them down.

Dancing Bears

At first to a tin whistle or an accordion
with buckets and string and broom-handles,
grim hobbledehoys go flinging out a leg.

So dancing bears perform their capers,
tame bears, nursery ghosts,
moving in a circle on a tight leash.

Bravely they swoon it until quite pegged out;
deep in a wood the golden girl takes fright
and leaps from an upper window to her death.

Each knows his own legend. Goldilocks, the bear,
are both charmed by music. It is circles themselves
that are limiting, but grace is optional.

The Fitting

Consider the formation of the toes:
Some spatulate, some tapering; the shape
Can alter in a year or less, but shoes
Properly made will help preserve what's there.
Feet age first, remember; the body grows
Under a watchful eye. The wrinkled hand,
The paunch belly, bow leg and drooping nose
Demand constant attention, but the feet
Lead a private life.

Sit down, I will attend to you at once.
Your tired soles may find refreshment
The pair of comfortable slip-me-ons
I have just completed, hanging above
My shoulder among that row of unsold ones.
Look round the shop. Take time, inspect our stock.

That lace-up job is neat: mark the ribbons,
Made to last for years. One doesn't want to
Keep replacing those.
I would prefer to work on a commission,
A tracing round the foot, the perfect fit;
Shoes you'll never notice. With your permission
I'll remove your pair and draw this clear line.
A flattened instep, dropped arch. It is precision
That counts in the end. There. How does that feel?
As light as dreams, as soft as any cushion
You have fallen asleep on. You won't know
You are wearing them.

The Shared Bath

They crane heads forward and try hard to see,
With shoulders flexed along the batten rail,
The shapes made by their own intimacy
(There's extra water slopping in the pail).

The water laps at sores that do not hurt
And steam obscures the features of their faces;
The nuptial vows of bodies in their dirt
Are growing numb in all the hidden places.

Behind that veil is what they cannot see;
Their children's children dancing in a grove
Of smooth lawn trembling under startled trees,
The intimacy of skulls, the months of love.

Concert

My sister sow pays homage to St Cecilia.
I merely pump away at the bellows
While keeping an ear cocked to her delicacies of feeling.

She has taken the veil but I am mother
To a thriving farrow. She tickles heaven
With her music while the family are tugging at my dugs.

I know my place well, strictly behind the organ,
But keep myself clean in the knowledge that
Whosoever administers to art goes not unnoticed:

But my sister, she keeps herself quite spotless,
The perfect nursery pig. Music charms
The ticks off a scarred hide. It is of immense value to pigs.

Girl Dressing Herself

She is putting on her underwear, squatting on
a low stool. Knees raised, the skirt uncovers her thigh,
slackening about her rump. She lets out a sigh –
moving shadows provide a moment's distraction –
and stops, gripping the item tightly in her hand,
concentrating on a patch of sunlight beyond,

then looks away, resumes her task, stands up, and
the skirt falls crisply enough to its measured length.
Now she has things to do and has the fresh day's strength
in front of her. She hears the sparrows chirruping
and returns the stool to its usual habitat
beside the mirror, goes out. The front door clicks shut.

The stool does not retain the imprint of her sitting;
the high gloss cools, regains its brilliant colour
in swelling light; walls proceed to lose the pallor
and ambiguity of dawn; the room is heating
to a mid-morning equilibrium, a bright
clarity of statement, positively forthright,

and holds there, perfect and poised as the minutes pass.
A spider crawls over the mirror, a fly blunders
into the pane, draughts rise in the door and creep under,
stirring the thin Indian bed-cover. Through the glass
rustling of leaves, hazardry of traffic, voices,
stiffening of light on shadow-blackened faces.

Then afternoon, quieter than before; the dresser
begins to lose definition, its dust becomes
invisible as light withdraws; a few stale crumbs
are swallowed in the carpet; you'd have to guess the
pattern of the cushion on the little chair
by the far wall. Patches are scattered here and there.

Room and girl, fellow conspirators, wait for each other
at both ends of day, their patience is unlimited.
I try to carve them from imagination; the bed,
the stool, the skirt, the light; trusting to the weather
of their eternal and impenetrable country
of which I too am a citizen, or will grow to be.

Song of the Shirt

My head must be too big – can't see a thing,
Just red patches before my eyes. This shirt
Is much too tight of course, it's no use struggling,
Whichever way I turn it's sure to hurt.

> Now that everything has gone,
> Home, life, and belongings,
> Walking down a foreign street
> Without currency, without
> A clue to where I'm heading,
> I could almost believe that
> I am happier without
> Perspectives, almost believe
> That this pounding in my head
> Is a willed pulse that leads
> To the country of the blind,
> And that my shirt is a tent
> Of blood, peaked like a skull.

Perhaps I ought to wait a while before
I pull at it again. I'm hot and numb
And my nose feels so terribly sore.
It is a pity there is no one at home.

> It is quite possible
> That after emerging
> I will find myself
> Elsewhere, at some familiar
> Spot I can take bearings from,
> But for now I am firmly
> Wedged in this position,
> Children playing in Brain Park,
> And the smell of food in pantries,
> Little privies stocked with
> Flies and messages.

I can't get to the button. If I could
There would be no problem – I'd not feel sick
As if my head were being turned to wood.
I am becoming stupid, daft and thick.

> One place is like another –
> Trees grow names, sprout grammar,
> Burst into ideas.

I only am localised.
Somewhere between my ears
Is a palace. I walk
Towards it along glass,
My breath blinding me.
My palace is a shirt.
I grow magnificent –
Grandee of sockets,
Duke of depressions,
Patron of capillaries.

I believe now that I might be Nessus.
Friend shirt, I am lonely for company
But remember no useful addresses.
You'll have to do your best embracing me.

Apples

Apples shake down, their belled aprons udder
To knee length, making progress difficult,
Until reaching the basket, the avalanche
Begins and knees and baskets both shudder
Under the bombardment of a main branch.

Girls keel and tack with aprons or cupped hands
Under the apple shower, are themselves bruised
Where fruits have struck them. It is feverish
Activity fulfilling the demands
Of orchards. They swim in apples, like fish.

The Girls

A mosquito tipsy with blood, the children dozing.
Prams are curdling on the patio.
Here a high buzz of female conversation
Over cups of coffee, intelligent, worn young faces.
The house has a lot to answer for
But no one asks it to account for itself,
Instead they address themselves to the well of experience –
A long long throat before you hit the water,
The penny will be falling for years.

The room is charged with danger. At the bottom
Of the well there lives a toad
Clammy and neglected who forces them to speak.
Words bubble up, the toad is wounded.
They are thick with children.
Look what we have fished out of the water!
Each nurses a genius at her breast
Who sucks her dry. It is beautiful,
Sophisticated, dangerous, dull, charming.

Education

1

This woman is teaching her child the sense of touch.
'Look here. Touch the air now. Is it damp?' He feels
her warm hands on his wrist. 'Concentrate,' she says,
'Feel the air before you, how it gives way.'
He feels the folds of her cloth on his legs.
'Prod it, move it. It's clean, everywhere.' The throne grows
up around them. They must sit down. There must
always be rest after education.

2

See here – life is a voyage –
I must set my star in the ceiling
and be off across the city of fish
where the bells are silent and masts are bones
and all prows echo my own features.
I adjust my loin-cloth and feel the rough slap

of hessian on my chest. The air is rare
and is getting colder. One must
acquit oneself *etcetera*, so cheeribye.
My star draws me like a magnet and
I am rigid as iron. This damn thing is leaky
but in order to get to one's destination
one must get one's feet wet.

3

There is always the question, Why?
Even when the answer is perfectly obvious. Why?
says the glance towards heaven
in spite of its investments there. Why?
the craned necks of examination.
Why? the inviting armchair.

The walls are marble, streaked and veined
in marvellous colours from which
heads project. These accept
and never ask the obvious questions.

And the old man lying there
seems happy enough to see the bothersome syllable
disintegrate into mere cleanliness.

North Wembley

The mongol boy makes friends over the fence,
his cat owns all the local mice.
From hosepipes squirts the Sunday carwash.
Tom and Joan are decorating.

There are trees, grass verges, a parking space,
and alleyways, alleyways by the dozen.
Khan is arguing with his wife.
The train whistles through an empty station.
Blackberries by the railway are quickly stripped.
Jewish boys practise the violin in dark but modern lounges.

Over the main road there is a Sporting Club
with pitches stretching out to distant hedges
from where, one summer night, a lazy rat
emerged and crossed, legally, over the zebra.

Piano

Up and down, *glissando*, vague and searching
without knowing it, turning things over
in a ruminative fashion. Whoever is playing there
might be transmitting fire for all we know,

his thumb beating in a hot arc. He draws
from himself something so abstract
that chance and longing are both cancelled out,
shredded imagery drifting in a pattern,

smoke, black stuff rising, an October sky.
Here the leaves are turning and curling
to an immense, grave loneliness. The piano
stops abruptly, prepares for breakfast.

The Outhouse

That terrifying head thrust in at the window
made blue by light that had crossed continents,
tundra and ice, bleached havens of dugong,
seal and whale, scratched over, an effacement
of all that promised warmth: Spring, her soft hand
clutched in a moment underneath the table
in a sun-soaked outhouse. Such contrast burned
at walls and doors, would let nobody out
beyond the confines of their fear. They thought
that once got clear they might have made
a reasonable attempt at flight, but stuck
in a corner, contemplated by
that particular angel, shrivelled, bowed,
they felt their tears drying as they welled,
and hands dissolving where they once had held.

THE DISSECTING TABLE

The Dissecting Table

Each gash emits a spurt of formalin.
You blink and blink like Dr Johnson
Before falling once more to your task.

The flesh is white and close, the nerves rubber.
This is Poor John indeed, no John Dory
But mudpuppy, blackfish, opprobrium.

We eat our meal with a scalpel, a fourchette
For our houssette. Dark and gangrenous
He paddles at the sea-bed among scraps,

Growing thick and blubber-lipped,
Sucks at another, screams
When torn or prised. What say you, Mr Fish?

'The formalin hurts my eyes.
I am all attent, blinded for hours.
My skin is one hard arrow of desire.'

Daddy-Long-Legs

It was an act of daring then to fling one at the girls,
a kind of modest proposal like requesting the pleasure
of a dance, and their cries, we understood, were pleasure.

Purring and rattling in the palms then out upon the world –
flop-flop across benches and the grass, these maddened ghosts
had their legs broken or pulled off, silent in their pain.

Little brown handkerchiefs animated by bluff currents,
blowing against windows where a veil of condensation
held back the damp larders of grass, bark, potato-leaf.

Those days were shorter. Our legs froze although properly speaking
it was hardly autumn. The television lay muzzled in
the front room. Tap and splay. They hung there, vegetal.

God save these daddies and all their young babies –
repulsive fry greasing the cellar, leathery nuisance.
Put salt on them like slugs, their curling slime.

They lilt against the lightbulb, out of control: in hell
they will be gorged with our blood, now they are brittle
girls proferring leaves and hands, ragged, memorial.

The Artichoke

A scooped crown; the great Globe itself;
sovereign for both phlegm and melancholy,
no wonder the worm gnaws at your heart.

You love all things temperate,
particularly fog. Delicious with lemon;
young, you taste like stone.

A romantic vegetable: the Northern kings
have ridden round that white perimeter.
At night the peasant hunts a monstrous caterpillar.

Your namesake, perversely, is unrelated
And spends his time underground,
A warty tubered thing, and quite unlike.

But fine in soup, served cold in summer,
Pale and green in lamplight. He dreams of Tasso,
Nicolo da Tolentino, dark evacuations.

Brimstone Yellow

A pair of them, as Gosse says, bounding over the fence
in early March, with buckthorn close, in an existence
the very encapsulation of urge and dance,

on wires out of sheer hell, with a brief sputter
like fat in a pan, yellow indeed as butter,
in the burning lake with Sodom and Gomorrah;

thus, both butter and brimstone, they leave an itch
on the eye that tries to follow their toss and passage;
Spit-fire! Virago! screams a language that can catch

nothing of their angelic irresponsibility.
Even Linnaeus saw in them a muse. The Pieridae.
We feed them children and kisses. They take our gifts away.

Discovery of a Boy

Sixty hours he was wombed again – a foetus –
On the third day he rose, his thumb to his mouth.
We unstopped his ears and nose – he did not greet us
But curled uncomfortably.

I slept like him, wrapped up in sheets and blankets,
Sucked at an indefinable mother, tugging
At her hair. I was given a few trinkets
To amuse myself with.

It was brick-dust, just the smell of time. He snuffled
Hoarsely as a dog. Sometimes the doors would shake
Violently with a mad wind that whistled
About the chair legs and sighed

Like lungs full of grit. We were in hospital
Drawing cheques on our blood, everything was red.

These hours are owed. The furniture is brittle
And the mothers are sleeping.

Floating

The swimming pool is black at heart but tame.
A white shower falls as children splash
And noises deaden. Water sleeks their hair
Into a duck's-arse, confusing periods.
Heads are tails. They move backwards out of time
Into a comical underworld that is
Fringed with horror. Hands keep pulling them down.
At night the sea eats away mother's face
Till she is thin and polished. They can
Taste the salt for weeks. Or father sees
The child drifting on a tide. The sun whitens
A sunny beach. It takes a little while
To make out the speck on its narrow bed.

Immediately they are transformed. The game
Is for earnest and their bodies crash
The looking glass, tumbling down the stairs
To depths where any who survive may live like gods
Till water pickles them. They burn in lime
And rise raw red to dazzling surfaces
And raucousness while they themselves have grown
Hoarse under boards. The dry land is no place
For resurrection. Down they go again,
This time with pleasure until by degrees
Their legs and arms float off and nothing frightens.
Moving to the top they give denial
To the slim body plummeting like lead.

The Weather Gift

1 *Cumulus*

The shadow hated him, he was quite sure
and one day lying desolate
on the world's edge, a little way from town,
he described the strange phenomenon
of vaporous reflection, as it turned
viciously inward, showing a devil
of his own heart and blood
to send him scurrying with terror
to more tangible misfortune;
the haunting of a mad, substantial brother.

He trusted clouds. His brother's face in shadow
broke upon him vaguely but with force
beyond his concept or experience –
now let me break off a bit for you,
just a little – it is strutted with light
and supports itself through a sequence of moods
to reflect, refract, press, break into rain
and spring like a lock about the ark,
keeping fate and other evils out –
a true gift of love. Here, take it from me.

2 *Nimbus*

A cloud had settled across her life.
It was a sunless weekday and the traffic pouring,
in a house very much like this one:
a swarm of bacteria, a cloud of tears.
She sat at the table and wept,
there was no one upstairs. All day
the wind had piled grey on grey.
Light was elsewhere, steadily dripping,
rich oils on some Venetian canvas.
It was making her ill this weather.

But there was work to be done, the work
of moments, dabs and scumblings,
a barely primed unsympathetic surface
and rain bullying one into speed, like a giant
each minute threatening bone-grinds.
She moved briskly and precisely, cut all corners,
till a hypothesis forming at the tip
burst, and she ran a great vertical
dark dash of rain, without thunder,
perfect and abbreviated.

3 *Thunderstorm*

The thunder wells and drops its load of light
blasting a tree dead then roars again
across the bridge. The walls blanch to water,
echoing long-mouthed exclamations,
while all that thought crowds to headache,
knitting, knitting into deeper blues
and heavier blacks. Something must come forth,
if only an inkling, a dribble, a spatter of words
to grace the leaves with whippish strokes
until they are hustled into answering.

If we were to walk through the streets in it
we would hear dogs and cats rushing about
in covered places, excited and afraid,
but clouds envelop us, take us into
their confidence, whispering to us with
their age-old hoarseness something that we share,
a love of surrendering mentally
to tears or rage or simply loneliness
that is not exactly isolation.
The rain begins where landmarks disappear.

The Object of Desire

Sleep suits you, but you look much better waking,
He said to her as they both lay in bed,
That light glow of your cheeks, your eyes uncaking...

And stopped there. He was ruining it, was wrong
In saying anything. There was an aching
In his head. The sunlight was too strong.

Years of such fresh mornings had quite wasted
His vocabulary, the sentence lay too long,
Too tedious. How could she have outlasted

Her bad praise? Her eyes were open. She stirred.
It was terrible, her moving. He tasted
Her bitterness and power. Could she have heard?

Nightsong

It was the nightingale and not the lark

Night covers up what day has left undone,
A bed, a journey, love's interstices
To peek through at a fast declining sun,
And pink clouds' grace and the wind's courtesies,
Finger-ends that rub sore in the dark.

Turn in your sleep or roll along the shore
Or in the little foam of the cold sea,
In weeds that star the water-darkened floor
Where sheets run riot. Here think yourself free
To kick up shells like fire till they spark.

Sleep soundly, time is always on your side.
Before you dream there's nothing. Feel the weight
Of someone pressing to you, as a bride
Hugs tight the back of her unfortunate
Bridegroom drifting downward in the holed ark.

May Wind

In this May wind over the gardens,
Forgiving everything – the roughness of bark,
The cat's silk, the lilac's unreadiness,
Even the high-pitched screaming from the park –
The bed moves under us and its main sheet
Is lodged in sunlight from the street.

Made green and trimmed with trees which are like waves
Our red estates are blown about the world.
The Book of Days says: 'a mad happiness...
Remember us poor Mayers all.' The girls are curled
Within the flower-niche. The street is wide
And you lie naked by my side.

The Dead Mouse

This is what polish is for: the death of a mouse
In a mansion made to fit the living,
Where antecedents wrinkle up their noses
At the mice and the music is Aeolian.
Polish is for the floor and for sharp nails,
And the trap too perhaps with its absolute poetry.

Not for the regiment of exploded views,
Not the detail of crafted steel, not halberds
Or escutcheons, the streaming merciless dead
Beyond our control (victims of halberds,
Escutcheons, crafted steel and exploded views).

Poetry has its uses. It can lament the living,
Raise up the dead, show us bright bones,
Twang a heroic harp at the right moment,
Spotlight the anomaly of a louse,
Show nature her own image, or bury a mouse.

Necromancy

It was the daughter-in-law not the son
Who felt the mother kissing her one night.
She had been dead three years. Curiously
He slept. He never could remember dreams.
His hand moved in a slime of known events
Intangible as dreams. A live thing hovered
In the room with the casual ease of air,
Obeying her, though not his, necromancy:
Blood coloured curtains, blankets rucked like tombs,
The bed was soft, the earth fell outwards gently,
Sheets wound as sheets will, folds pushed with manners
Into folds of body, sinking. They were all waves,
An affection without hope, like desire.

The Museum

The music in the wall is next-door's radio,
Schubert I would guess, but even now it dies
And the wall lengthens with car noise, footsteps,
My own breathing rises like a sheet.
I would want to know more: how far
Have these snatches travelled between
One moment and another? I flick at the paper –
It crumples as though burnt. My nail-clippings
Belong to a lost museum, I could never find it.
And upstairs, upstairs the breathing
Of the children lost in their cold museum.

Midsummer spreads the day out. It blossoms
White and pale, folds its petals now
At half-past eight. Someone is beating
Up those stairs in the museum, blindly
Tapping towards some store or office.
Surely the day for him too is bright and long.
No, he says, it ceases at midnight for everyone,
With dead skin and hair, genuine tears.

A Donnée

I woke to find a donnée in the form
of four white pigeons ranged about two black
of the façade of a demolished house.
Their symmetry was disturbing, held me back
from putting pen to paper, rightly so;
rightly so, except that hills of brick
lay curiously scattered on one side
and window-frames and jambs, and lintels thick
as thighs were spread-eagled behind them.
The smashed roof-beams and door panels, the boards
that used to hold the darkness in before,
now offered glimpses, if no more, of sash-cords,
plaster, wallpaper, some broken glass
from kitchen cupboards; little human stuff
that had for years been hidden in the hulks
those houses had become. It was enough
to call to mind the old men irritably
smoking behind net curtains, concentrating
on the television, falling asleep
or studying a newpaper while waiting
for some relative. The pigeons would sit
on next-door's chimneystack and in the gutter,
occasionally dropping their white shit
down the dark walls and projecting lintels.

The bricks must have rained down throughout the night,
the dust was everywhere. Its mottle grey
covered the window-ledge of the last house.
My children ran down a tight alleyway.
The donnée was a dream, no more, but real
bulldozers were being carefully driven
up to the standing wall. The birds were gone,
the ground was flat. This much at least was given:
old men and women, a long chimney-breast,
the noise of traffic, moonlight, a child's cough.
Six pigeons, a façade. The wood was burned
in one huge fire, the slates and bricks sold off.

Mare Street

Has been closed a long time. A black square nets
The door-frame and the lettering hooks light
As it hangs from severe guttering-frets
And a bench straddles the frontage in a flight
Of planks. An abandoned place, or almost,
Unless one takes into account the ghost
Of two frisking horses above the legend
HORSES, in black frame and gilt edging, faded
To a time-honoured vagueness and a blend
Of trees and grass, background suitably shaded
For amorous horseplay in the foreground.
One black horse, one white, moving softly to
Bird and car song, merging with their sound
To thunder, faint and welcome, galloping through.

FROM
SHORT WAVE
(1984)

THE SLEEPWALKER

The Sleepwalker

Into this room, which is a pickled darkness
(Pressure sealed, the blinds drawn down)
I blunder, vaguely, stubbing my toes on wood.

This furniture was handed down to us
By my side of the family, and I feel
My way round a low-slung Swedish armchair

That is reassuringly familiar.
The stage is mine now. As I pull
The blinds and open windows the room brightens

And hours fly in. The sofa has come unstuffed,
Light and air play havoc with the props.
My mother leaned on that when she was young

And a young man like a strong wind hung
About her shoulders and her undone lips.
Where that pillow is they sat and laughed.

It all expands, a soap bubble with colours
Delicate and blinding. The street is white,
The sky a cool acidic blue. I float

Within it dizzily, watching the motes
Of dust settle and swirl in a delight
Of movement after the dead hours.

Lilac, Laylock

1 *Lilac*

Early morning the lilac
quivered, threw out a track
of fragrance to the street,
pervasive, watery-sweet.

The choreography of water,
the drift of scent caught at,
swirling away, blown back,
was the cunning of the lilac.

She bristled sweetness, arched
like a girl. A bullfinch perched
on her crown, immaculate
in his feathers. His weight

bothered the lilac, she bent
a little, her small tent
of pleasure collapsing
inward with the swaying.

2 *Laylock*

The last place before sleep
in the changing cave;
the children rush to play
rolling on wild grass.

Black cherries fatten us
as we run down the hill.
The flies sleep in the bowl
among the newspapers.

The children dream. They run
towards us bearing faces
that are pinned out like rags
against the lilac branches.

No smell, though garden flowers
are in full bloom
and the queen wasp hovers
about the door.

Abundance

You come to me with that young god
whose hand is slipped in yours, but tired somehow
as if all good were bound to take its toll
and past and future drained what happens now.

In the plenitude of etcetera comes a fullness
satisfying both. Those perfect leaves
can have no weight and are not crushed, your dress,
your open mouth, your eyes made to deceive...

The boy who carries grapes and waits to sip
at my half-empty glass already looks
more than half-seas-over. See his lip
unsteady, not, may I say, with reading books.

Hand Dance

They cup or mould or make a shadow
in the full glare of a bedside lamp,
fingers that travel through hair
as on a long journey, or close an eye
preparing for a tiny death or great.
These moved instinctively together
and fell instinctive to such million uses
it seems a shame ever to part them.
How much like each other they've become.
What fine old dances they can twist and turn to,
And think of all the kisses trapped and freed
to catch again, again in the long night
which is longer than their reach or grasp,
which can't be caught by hands and casts no shadow.

Against Dullness

Clouds harbour no cuckoo-land,
preferring fur that wraps up night
like an expected gift.
The chair spins round: a dark unplanned
by schizophrenics comes adrift
and wags a finger out of sight.

I thought you were sitting there,
your hair still dripping from the rain
that lately caught you out.
Tired, you slumped into the chair
and shade and water burned a stain
across the collar of your coat.

Water whispers, makes a dull
provincial sense, and such things may
depress us, being true.
The darkness of the chair was all
that kept the provinces at bay,
half hiding, half displaying you.

Titillations we survive,
and rain too with its gifts of fur
and darkness with its face.
There's little we ourselves can give
but that which loves both rain and fear
and lives in any place.

A Girl Sewing

I do not like you to be quite so still,
only your fingers moving constantly.
I have imagined girls at windows reading,
others sitting staring at a table
lost in the mass of mean forgotten things
that fray or tear almost as soon as finished.
Sometimes the light makes littleness too subtle
so it seems nothing: light so weak that shadows
become indiscernible on a flat surface.

Whole days like this can eat away a life,
leave tiny bones, half powder and half shadow,
freeze the creases of a finished garment
or find perfection in imagined girls.

Attachments

The radio crackled and crackled and the thin man moved
About his room, spiderwise among the chairs.
His skin was cold, his brow inordinately creased,
A cloth wrung out and left to dry itself.

His name I can't remember – but his room, his brow
Seem of one texture with the noise. He settles down,
Offers me a boiled sweet which I cannot taste.
His living is an absence and a draught.

A Scottish uncle writes to England: Since her death
I do the housework but the furniture retains
Each mark. I'm polishing away her fingerprints
And my whole life is measured in that hand.

An Old Woman Walks Home

If we were machines we would learn movement.
There is a kind of grace appropriate
to function. One could roll along delicately
despite particular conjunctions of fat.

An old slow woman pushing herself home
has tailored her dejection to a style
that is becoming. She understands the force
of gravity more clearly than a child.

That she should move at all is marvellous
but not astonishing. Children burn things
on the wasteground and the ash flies up,
and she would too were she equipped with wings.

It is a question of machinery
and built-in obsolescence. How one fears
for her survival, her immensity,
the enormous effort of becoming tears.

Dialogue for Christmas

This white year arrives and leaves
her gift of boxes crammed with time.
Tomorrow and tomorrow, chime
the little bells to warn off thieves,
but thieves ubiquitous as frost
have entered here and time is lost.

Here they come, the Eastern Kings
laden down with Other Things
fit to please both man and God.
Their boxes open in a flood
of colours bright and cold as snow
that cheer the heart before they go.

What arrives in frost and snow?

The broken branch, the late white night,
a word or echo of delight.

What word is that?
                    I do not know.

SEEING IS BELIEVING

Seeing Is Believing

For we walk by faith not sight

Opening the windows on a receding skyline
   Of regular trees, it seems
That streets, however familiar, are a divine
   Form of architecture,
An autocratic mad professor's lecture
   On the logic of dreams.

A child runs off into the distance
   Diminishing like Alice
With just that stern Victorian insistence
   On etiquette. She disappears
Possibly to drown in her own tears
   Or dine at the Palace.

Horns are mute in forests where a battle
   Hardly rages but dances
To imagined music, and the fallen settle
   On grass and sleep for hours.
The horse of reason champs the brilliant flowers
   And neatly prances.

Goya's Chamber of Horrors

Ya ya Goya ('I am Goya')
ANDREI VOZNESENSKY

1 *The Allegory of the Cloth*

His waistcoat runs away down his elegant chest.
The colour pools somewhere just below his heart.
It shakes him with its colds and satins.

The tie that breaks from cavities around his neck
Is a waterfall. His eyes are very wet.
He is indisputably unwell.
Somehow appalled and sentimental all at once
He falls into his own puddle which turns out
Deeper, colder, silkier than paint.

2 *The Allegory of the Dummy*

He is tossed in a blanket
By cheerful bosomy girls.
He accepts this as his own
Allegory of desire.
When they shoot him he blazes
Like an indulgent omen.

3 *The Allegory of Singing*

He listens to a woman dying
Who as she dies insists on singing
Though her voice is badly cracking
And nobody else is listening.
She is appalled and sentimental.
He himself finds this appalling.

4 *Yo lo vi – I saw it*

The enemy about my waist
Tears my children in his haste
Lord preserve me live and chaste
      Fear has a sweet and bitter taste.

They hung my arm up on a tree,
My testicles were fed to me
Before I perished. They were men.
          I would do the same to them.

5 *The Allegory of the Breakfast*

He breaks an egg with a sharp tap of the spoon
(Saturn Devouring His Own Children)
Submits a slice of bread to the Inquisition
Of the Fire, wrings the neck of the salt cellar.
Two old macabres make pigs of themselves
On the walls which are horrendous and black.
He rises from the carnage like Colossus.
He cannot hear the agonising creak
Of the chair leg. He cannot hear the shriek
Of the draught that keeps the fire burning.
He stumps about in one of his black moods.
Ya ya Goya, he says, perfectly serious.

John Aubrey's Antique Shop

Certain objects find their way down here –
Grogged in glamour, porcelain faces peer
through flecks of emulsion and faint dust on collars;
shoes go manky, mortuary, scuffed;
the clocks with marbled gingerbead and barley
tell no time but one, the hour of breaking.
And one could find yet bigger, better, richer:
a bellows-organ say with some keys missing
that some doughty Nonconformist household
bright as a button, collars starched resplendent,
trained to Wesley, Lanier and Newton.

As I've forgotten who once said of Andrewes,
his sermons were too playful. I believe it.
'Here's a pretty thing, and here's a pretty thing'
argues a serious lack of seriousness.
In Hell everybody goes dirty all the time.
I once knew a girl as clean as linen.
What would happen to all these did not
such idle fellows as I note them down?

Redcurrants

Acrobatic, the tiny redcurrants
are sprinkled head-first, swollen into scarlet,
and made to dance on crisply gathered points
Then birds guzzle them or someone picks them
to serve up in a delicate white bowl.
On folding tables in conventional gardens
they glow within an avalanche of cream,
drunk on Lalique, set in a pattern of light.

Sharp, dangerous, the bead memorials
are told without religion, without pain.
Not martyrdom nor a pretence of it
but the fate of jewelry, to go
forth into the world as concentration
without a thing to wear except one colour,
no blood upon the hedge and little taste
and all too small or piqued or plentiful.

Sea Horse

What has the sea done to them? Her distortions
come sailing at us out of a mirror.
She runs a murky administration
of dead bells and skull-music, dull tirra-lirra.

An urchin turns hedgehog, blows bubbles
to pass the time and keep the living company.
Drowning we eructate through our mouths, sly trebles,
timbreless. There's roaring at the tympanum.

Clouds, horizontals with lump-fish and gurnards,
in turns out, our bones become stars, our eyes
imitate the glasswort, hang like grapes, inward.
Hares are lipped molluscs intent on their disguise.

But among our exoskeletal remains
one creature, but one, may yet come, nosing
shyly between veils of seaweed, gazing down,
its muzzle opening and closing,

not some ten-yard fable raising Proteus
on awesome breakers, but three or four inches, less,
his curlicue of a tail catching at us,
nerves and tendons like old rope; a horse

swimming at us out of the mirror, all wrong.
He will tend to delight whatever stars
are out that night and perhaps bring
with him the drowned and rotten but true cross.

Skeleton Crew

Penelope's suitors chirruped like bats.
Hercules' trained band made bird-like noises.
No one knows what song the sirens sung
or when the air turned music in the lung.

You know what time does to antiquities?
We have museums where there is rejoicing
at a prodigal's return.
The boy who falls to earth but doesn't burn

is an immortal like the piece of wood
miraculously rescued from the Turk.
The flying boys are only made of bone
secreted in some hollow, overgrown.

For forty years these bones have sat and waited.
It's their Hawaii, they her skeleton crew,
coherent bodies whose firm discipline
outlives the aircraft that they travel in.

And now they're found, without names, bleached as Athens.
They waited and their patience is rewarded,
the widows and curators will awake,
the clerks will rectify one small mistake.

But not a shot was fired on Ithaca
though bats were black with panic on the walls,
heads bobbing like a shooting gallery
above another war and frozen sea.

Assassins

My people, by whom I mean those curious sets
Of non-relations in provincial towns,
Sit ripening brightly in the *Weltanschauung*
Of other poets. Here is one who follows
A second-hand pair of shoes into the Courts
Of Social History. Another ransacks
His late unlettered father's bedside drawer
And finds dead ukuleles littered there.
What heraldic yet surreal landscapes!
To lie in the bed of your ancestors
And feel the fit. To hear the neighbourhood
Stirring in its ancient sleep and rhyme
The dead into their regiments of pain.
The poverty of old shoes runs away
With its own eloquence. And yet they write good books.

But I think of an England where the ghosts
Are restless solitaries or assassins.
They cannot speak but run about in sunlight
Demanding restoration of the birch
And death as public as the crime is private.
They have lost time. The Russians on Burns night
Celebrate their history of combustions.
Their people lie in complete unity
In graves as large as Europe and as lonely.

Foresters

Cameron, and his morbid fascination
With gremlins, water-spirits and outlanders
Had them pinned and mounted, a sour nation
Of fearful superstitious peasants
Who drifted into town out of the forests
In search of fresh sea-air and giant crow's-nests,
Talked of vampires and the lycanthrope
And used these comic horrors to scare the pants
Off naughty children and give hope
To balding office wolves for whom
A white neck spelt invariable doom.

But Cameron forgot to give this nation
Credit for their gift of adaptation.
Who faced the baleful gods now faced the sea
And made a certain noise even in the city
And gained success as gatherers of samphire
By infusing native charm with touches of the vampire.

Short Wave

1

Somewhere in there, in a gap between a taxi
and some indecipherable station
there is a frequency that's unfrequented
like an island, an administration
of ethereal incompetence, the voice of Caliban
deserted but with remnants of quaint speech,
an accent or two that could be out of Shakespeare.

You tune in but the voice is out of reach
and seems merely to flirt with meaning; dry trees
rattling on an unprotected hillside,
hollow tubes wind whistles through. It speaks
at length through a protracted landslide.

Whoever lives here, the transmitting tower
is out of date, there is no programme schedule
to list what may be listened to, what hour
the one clear and intelligible accent
will burst like a soprano voice along
the curving sea between the taxi, France
and Germany, all Europe in her song.

2

This landscape is eternal night – not hell
or purgatory, just a weave of streets
settling like a cobweb late at night
in greys and greens, advances and retreats.

Only drunkards reel home, slam the door
and wander over to the wireless
to turn the dial in hope of finding music,
celestial and perfect, more or less.

3

These reasonable voices going on
and on, unconscionably long
at all hours of the day and night
mean nothing in most places, not to me.
I speak no Dutch or Spanish, tell the truth
I only know my native tongue and French
and that barely sufficient to get by with.

My lips are sour with lager and my head
has no room for a second studio.
Anyway, what do they mean, these voices?
What are they saying? Well, it can be guessed.
Which is why I sit here listening
and turning dials, eavesdropping
on that Balkan baritone
who tells me what the world believes of me.

4

The planets click like doors or whistle wide.
Their secret messages are understood
by fascinated children in their beds
who're used to lack of sleep and solitude.
Downstairs the broken speech of moving objects
where unrestricted chaos rules the air
and mother is no different from a chair.

We leave the children sleeping and ourselves
lie reading and half listening until
the close-down, when we kiss and frontiers blur
in line with international good will.
There are so many stations on the line,
and other music wells up in the drought
in waves that cancel one another out.

In the Cabbage Grove

The women are walking the cabbage grove
towards a loss they cannot comprehend.
    Quick simple tongues
will click and lips grow wet and spend
their moisture in a ritual of songs
    that pass for love.

They pass beside me, already lost
in shadow and the comprehensive night
    which like a hem
has swept them up, away. What light
perpetuates and mollycoddles them,
    and at what cost?

Admiring their strong legs, their skin
of crusted leather and their death in groves
    of cabbages,
I cannot speak but know their voices prove
the gruffness mine. They are the savages
    I gather in.

THE KISSING PLACE

The Dog Carla

This is what perishes: the soft glut of a chair
in which a white dog perks to her name:
'Come here, Carla. Good dog.' 'What a coquette
you are, Carla, let us be married at once.'
An inverted flower of lace, a crisp head
at the bud, young Philip, heir presumptive
to these darkened rooms addresses Carla.
'What selfish love is this Philip, to imprison
a defenceless dog? You'll pull her tail next!
This is no way for a king to behave.'

Philip is the smallest of the dolls.
So lifelike is he that his hope of love
should not go unrealised. He calls to Carla:
'Here dog, here I am, let me stroke you gently.'
And Carla skips, Carla fawns! Philip whoops
with laughter to his sister Margareta.
The bells on his petticoat go tonguing
eleisons for conjured Philip,
seriously relaxed now, and exhausted Carla.

Brief Sunlight

What's best of all is sunlight that we feel
only for some ten minutes, even less,
a sudden warmth as if sleeping you had placed
your hand against my cheek in tenderness.

But tenderness is no part of the sun.
Our hands bleach in white heat that carries all
before it like a wave. It's what we feel
that's mortal, tender, paradoxical.

And we are shaken by light in the street,
its angles, jaggedness, its blowsy head
appearing from behind a roof or wall
to lie across our path, invade our bed.

Early Rising

At six o'clock in early March the light
came winding like a sheet about our bed,
binding us into our sleep so tight
we moved in stone between alive and dead.

Our feet were much too far away, our folds
were unremitting, and my hands had lost
all shape and disposition in the cold.
The window frozen with its motes of dust

admitted the high treble of a blackbird
sugaring her benedictions on
a stone garden. Who else could have heard
her sculptured fioratura, neat and clean

as a whistle? Love may last as long
as life perhaps. 'Where would we be without
the thought of death to prick us on,' she sang,
whose brood of three would not see summer out.

Flemish Rain

In a spindly rain my daughter sits
astride the toilet and makes her own
spindly rain, the tin and copper sound
of water arching out of her,
her belly round, slotted and tight,
swelling out beneath the ribs
of the almost transparent chest
which cradles her neck and the large skull
within its shimmer of flesh. Life there
forms to an aperture, and her mouth
is pinched into a smile of self-consciousness,
hearing both the rains, her own the sweeter.

How am I to give shape to this music
that pours tinkling out of her
but crumbles and powders as it is heard?
A breath of air and it is gone.
I think of Rimbaud's miserable monk
at his grotesque squattings, his bunched
and withered thighs reddening, the stench
a kind of comfort to him, loathsome
in its preternatural sympathy;
and then of one particular boorish Fleming
wetting the thatch beside a house
(I pick her up and shake her)
while a woman flaps her carpet from the window
and the dust shakes out like sunlight.

The Claude Glass

A tiny house. The tiny couple move
with the huff and delicacy of birds.
He has the best room and finest view
while she keeps company beside the fire,
brother, sister and all the children
shrunk to a Dutch peepshow, a Claude glass.
The weather holds, a lean boy drives the cows
down to the lake from where the view is striking,
hills and crags bareback on one another
and the house still tinier, still shrinking.

Through the window of a rented farmhouse
I see my wife and children moving dumbly
through a history made picturesque.
In their peepshow all is a pearl stillness,
a singing place for eyes and teeth,
a box to keep absorptions locked away.
The sharp cat is fixed against the floor.
Through the glass you may contemplate the sun's face.

Morning in the Square

The square is empty in the early sunlight.
What is it waiting for? It seems to lack
animation – a delivery van
turns the corner like the shadow of a bird in flight.

It is a kind of delicate mourning –
remaining quiet as if out of respect
for a ritual that has been going on
since the sunset of the previous evening.

Best not to take too much from such retreats
though everything that's peaceful seems to gather
in a broad piazza and the day's arriving
with a shiver down the narrow side streets.

Walls

Wall has its topography
of loose cement and dropping moss,
hillside picturesques and water
seeping through the layers of dirt.

Finding here a dwelling place
you let the world slide under you,
turn Umbrian or Florentine
in a maternal Italy.

Run your hand along the brick
as along a furrowed brow,
a mothering detested damp
like childish mud but colder now.

Porch

Here stood George Herbert not daring
to approach the altar, waiting as do
the young innamorati in the last
shelter before their passing through.

Lion, sphinx, pediment
are appropriate. Inside
the cool glissade of hallway
and the noble storeys.

All possibility, an interregnum
between rain and some commitment;
this is the kissing place the god
prepares for us before his passion.

The End of Captain Haddock

Their heads propped on their elbows at the table
are lost in adventures of Tintin and Captain Haddock.
The kitchen grows a beard of fragrance
curling with pomade and vinegar.

Is it Captain Haddock in the pan
cursing softly in his coat of batter?
Whose face is running on the steamed-up glass
weeping itself into malformations?

As I Was Going Up the Stair

As I was going up the stair
I met a woman made of air
who seemed a creature half asleep
struggling dreamlike up the steep
demanding incline which would lead
eventually to her bed.
    It seemed to her a dreadful cliff
which she must climb however stiff
and breathless she became, as if
it only mattered to attain
the landing and be free of pain.
    But she was proud to be alone
and pleased to be dependent on
nothing but a wooden rail
between two floors, and this was all
that seemed to her desirable.
It was indeed a kind of game
terminal and dangerous.

Though rooms vary from house to house
most staircases are much the same;
I passed her almost at a run
and when I turned round she was gone.

The Moving Floor

The floor grows away. What distances
it seems to travel! How it rolls in sleep
like water turning in a quiet bay,
calming and disturbing all at once.

From one year old, tottering and grasping
making bull-like rushes at the chair
to five or six when turning dizzily
it spins about us till it crashes upward.

How strange to think of being under it,
supporting a great ship of frozen marble,
all the water traffic of these islands
moving by on cushions of live air.

Attic

The spider huddles in its angle like a coat
made small and crushed
and all the dust goes flying down the nearest throat
as if perpetually brushed
by some hopeless, houseproud creature, a disturber
of dreams straight out of Thurber.

I used to think that nightmares entered through the ceiling –
and were strangely brought
to my attention like an improper feeling.
They were an alien thought
floating about the town quite randomly
till they took hold of me.

I don't believe that now – I know I can lay claim
to both the nightmares
and the hoarded luggage, and that this uneasy game
is something played upstairs
between the female house, myself and the one ghost
comprised of all that dust.

The Design of Windows

You close it like the good virgin you are
who demands a constancy
appropriate to her stillness. Others would
perhaps lean out (perhaps lean out too far).

By lamplight things appear to strike a posture
that is ludicrous and sad
and vacuous, a bright hole in the fabric,
in every sense an indecent exposure.

Better are the black and unadorned
rectangles of glass, new windows
like negatives, that flaunt their recklessness
in blocks whose shadows leap across the ground.

The Impotence of Chimneys

Silent spouters, barrels, tall comical brothers,
you have reached the age of puberty
and impotence at one and the same time.
The fire in the groin is merely smoke,
the cloud will never rain. How quickly
it disperses and your stumps go gathering
their wits for one pale archaism which
will offend no one. See, even the dead,
how apologetically they fade and blow
above the crematorium, their smoke
invisible, floating about the town
like dandelion seeds. The fat pink Popeye
forearms, the ornate iron hats, are raised
to acknowledge the old Viennese truth
that in between the one fire and the other
we can afford the gentleness of smoke,
secreting pain beneath its decent whiskers
with Lear's menagerie, his nagging cricket.

Turn Again

The pavements lie down narrowing their aisles
against the sunlight which is vanishing.
Their lives are a disappointment to them,
a daily exercise of punishing
self-discipline measured in long miles.

You grab your coat and hat and go outside,
leave doorsteps filthy with anxieties
while treading a fine undulation, cracks
for hopscotch and the promised gold of trees
in autumn, the dull streets of human pride.

Postscript: A Reply to the Angel at Blythburgh

Indeed the Cost of Seriousness
May be death or something less,
A column in the *TLS*
Will do as well.
This long disease my life? Ah yes,
It can be hell.

Hurt 'fades to classic pain' you wrote
Yet pain remains, no antidote
Exists however we promote
The Muse of Graves.
The Church's message, and I quote,
Is *Jesus Saves*.

Not death so much then, but the pain.
Religion's task is to explain
What suffering means in the reign
Of good King Good,
Why Blythburgh angels don't complain
Of martyrhood.

Complain? It is a miracle
That angels should survive at all.
True, the woodworm have a ball
Inside her brain.
Her look is faintly comical,
Zonked-out, insane.

Discredited and dull and tame
The churches fear to praise or blame.
They've got themselves a safer game:
The liturgy.
No one goes there all the same
Incredibly.

Residual Christianity
Is ineffective, you'll agree,
The *ut absurdum* to a T.
The Cross demands,
And gets perhaps surprisingly,
Pierced feet and hands.

The Catholics get God and Art
(To Puritans they're worlds apart)
The Sistine Chapel for a start,
Georges de la Tour,
While Calvinists, though pure in heart,
Tend to be dour.

But Art comprises *grazie*,
That neat Italianate way
Of making ugly things obey
The rules of dance.
A *contrapposto* sense of sway
Rules out mere chance.

Christ sways on his slender Cross,
St Sebastian, scandalous
In loincloth, sways like Diana Ross,
Supreme, appalled.
Thank God, he cries, I'm not a Grosz
Or Grünewald.

To fabricate or to omit,
To make the hazy definite,
All is fair that Art may fit
Into her scheme.
She'll round a shape to flatter it
Or hear it scream.

She'll hear the scream but make it learn
A civilised and formal turn
Of speech, so that the scream may earn
A living wage.
She makes the devils bake and burn
Inside her cage.

Orcagna, Signorelli – Hell
Is on the whole remarkable
For overcrowding and the smell
Of something rude:
No poise, no sway, no swing, no swell,
No attitude.

Its easiest room is occupied
By those who loved us but have died.
Here Orpheus came to fetch his bride,
A wanderer,
But failed. Is it his face enskied
At Blythburgh?

The expression on that face!
Sometimes in the street I trace
The same ironic commonplace
Look of defeat,
A vagrant, idiotic grace,
Pathetic, sweet.

The common cormorant or shag
Lays eggs inside a paper bag
But does not, like some women, drag
A vast array
Of household junk and filthy rags
Around that way.

That Blythburgh look which reconciles
Apparently contrasting styles,
The daft and Gioconda smiles;
The eyes that stare
Down into the empty aisles
Shield from despair.

Peter, if one verse we write
Shields anyone, however slight
The shelter or how foul the night,
Let's think of her,
And bless the angel's loss of sight
At Blythburgh.

FROM

THE PHOTOGRAPHER IN WINTER

(1986)

The Photographer in Winter

(i.m. M.S. 1924-1975)

   for M.V. and O.O.

> *He was hurrying along with frozen hands and watering eyes*
> *when he saw her not ten metres away from him. It struck him*
> *at once that she had changed in some ill-defined way.*
> ORWELL

You touch your skin. Still young. The wind blows waves
Of silence down the street. The traffic grows
A hood of piled snow. The city glows.
The bridges march across a frozen river
Which seems to have been stuck like that for ever.
The elderly keep slipping into graves.

Your camera is waiting in its case.
What seems and is has never been less certain –
The room is fine, but there beyond the curtain
The world can alter shape. You watch and listen.
The mirror in the corner seems to glisten
With the image of a crystalline white face.

Too many marvels. Pagodas, ziggurats;
The follies of the snow. Geometries
In miniature, the larger symmetries
Of cars, the onion domes of bollards, spires
On humble kiosks, stalactites on wires,
A vast variety of dazzling hats.

The white face in the mirror mists and moves
Obscure as ever. Waves of silence roll
Across the window. You are in control
Of one illusion as you close your eyes.
The room, at least, won't take you by surprise
And even in the dark you find your gloves.

*

Where are you going? To work? I'm watching you.
You cannot get away. I have been trained
To notice things. But all will be explained
And you will know why it is necessary
To follow you like this. In the meantime, carry
On as usual, do what you would normally do.

You catch the tram? I'll sit behind you where
You will not find me. I see your every move.
Believe me when I say you would approve
Such thoroughness and objectivity.
So this is the route you take across the city.
The tram goes rattling on. You touch your hair

Before you stand and walk off down the street.
Your hair is swinging loosely. The snow breaks
My picture up. It needs a few more takes
To get this right. Your costume is correct
Historically speaking? They will expect
Immaculate appearances, discreet

Camera angles, convincing details. Please
Co-operate with me and turn your head,
Smile vacantly as if you were not dead
But walked through parallel worlds. Now look at me
As though you really meant it. I think we could be
Good for each other. Hold it right there. Freeze.

*

You can't remember and you can't redeem
The faces altered with a loaded brush,
Faces who drift before you as you wash
The prints in faint red light, pure images
Of births and funerals and marriages.
The snow has lost them. Even when you dream

They merge confusingly. The children throw
White bombs at one another which explode
Splattering their clothes; and, across the road,
A white-haired man reveals his youthful skin.
You see the building he's been living in
And you yourself have aged. He turns to go

But leaves his face behind, a different face
With no expression but the features set.
You cannot quite remember where you met
But go on meeting. Doorways, offices.
The dream creates an odd paralysis.
He seems to move, you're frozen in your place.

Wake up, wake up. The faces disappear.
Your own must be put on. You look a mess
And draw a veil over your tiredness.
The curtains lift. Your hair must be swept back
Before the wind which gives you a loud smack
And forces out an unexploded tear.

*

Some elegance is what you crave, a touch
Of silver in the grey light of the street,
A hint of Strauss to fill the room, the beat
Of the Radetzky March, or other such
Imperial themes. Ironic music, gay,
But not unfitting in its own small way.

Exaggerations, nothing more. You climb
Eight flights of stairs, immerse yourself
In private smells. The novels on the shelf
Begin to yellow. You can measure time
In their coarse pages, in the damp, the space
Between the deadpan mirror and your face.

The mirror throws her silvered answer back.
A breath takes you away beyond the glass
Into a land of fog and rain. Hours pass
Like dim processions, tiny boats, a track
Of dirty water, and the music plays
While breath evaporates. The image stays.

The gods of gracious living pass us by.
They hear you vaguely as the marches fade
Above the humming of their motorcade.
Dear woman, train your photographic eye
On me and the dead wall where I must wait
For you to reappear, however late.

*

Hand colouring. It was a form of art,
And when you bent over your work I saw
How art could not obey a natural law,
That faces flowered and that teeth shone pale
As distant neon: memory would fail
To keep the living and the dead apart.

To be quite honest, it was creepy watching
This process of embalmment (as it seemed),
To see the smoothed-out features, the redeemed
Perfection of the unbelievable, showing
No signs of ever having lived, but glowing
Pink and white. I found it strangely touching.

And that was art, you said. The difficult.
But you were lying or just didn't know,
And even then, so many years ago,
The images had started to assume
The frozen aspect of an empty room,
Imperfect, white and granular as salt.

And now it's winter, and this dreadful weather
Is always at the very edge of spring
But cannot make or fake it. I can't bring
Another year to light. You sit alone
With all the pictures that the wind has blown
Away and art must somehow fit together.

*

This winter is not metaphorical.
The sun has broken into tiny pieces
And goes on fracturing as it releases
More and more light, which decorates the walls
With stud-medallions and hangs up crystals
On high wires, where they shudder, trip and fall

And break again. Sometimes it is water
Creeping down a window, a sharpened pen
Above the lintel, a white screen which men
Must penetrate like knives, a curious shriek
Which cuts the eye. A square of film must seek
To capture intact this wild and wholesale slaughter.

I go on taking pictures all the same.
I shoot whole rolls of film as they shoot me.
We go on clicking at the world we see
Disintegrating at our fingers' ends,
As if, by stopping time, we made amends
For all that time destroyed outside the frame.

I watch her working. Now and then I've tried
To catch her eye but found the snow had grown
A brilliance which sunlight made its own
And broke on impulse, as it breaks a train
Of thought, or breaks (it seems) a windowpane
That seems to show her on the other side.

*

What awful cold we seem to have had this year.
A winter of betrayals. Even words
Drop dead in flight, and, afterwards,
We try to sweep them up, quite uselessly.
I can hardly see a hand in front of me.
Everything is speckled. Nothing is clear.

Imagine trying to focus through this swirl
And cascade of snow. It's dark already.
Impossible to keep the picture steady
In the wind. An early evening filters in
Behind the white – my gloves are much too thin
To keep it out. I think I am a girl.

'To be alone in winter is like dying,'
She sings. Here everyone is alone. We die
Of the cold. It can be dangerous to cry
When tears freeze on your cheeks. We must have courage
And think of winter as a happy marriage,
The kiss of snow, the wind's contented sighing.

We must have courage till the spring regains
Her confidence. Courage is everything.
I load the camera and slowly bring
The landscape into focus. My heart stutters
But my hand is firm, and as I click the shutter
I feel the cold blood thawing in my veins.

*

I see you standing there, not quite full length.
Successive sheets of ice preserve and bear
You up, first as a girl with wavy hair,
And then a prisoner, a skeleton
Just gathering new flesh. The layers go on
So fast that I am troubled by your strength.

But fainter now, you're sitting in a chair
And wasting away under a fall of snow.
Once more under the skin the faint bones show
Their X-rays. The fragility of ice
Is starting to break up and once or twice
The water spreads across you like fine hair,

Fine hair confusing everything, now dark,
Now light, whichever way the double vision
Catches it. I'm angling for position,
Betraying you with your own camera.
The winter offers vague ephemera
And leaves behind no trace or watermark.

There's nothing to betray. I am exposed
And doubled. I have grown two-faced, split skins,
Become a multiple. Something begins
To bother me – I think it's my own voice.
The situation offers me no choice –
The shutter's open. Now the shutter's closed.

The Button Maker's Tale

Once I had a shop where I made buttons,
but buttons sank like lead, without a trace.
I lost my money and I lost my buttons,
but I was young and didn't give a fig.

The next time I put money into figs,
but figs were almost unobtainable.
I lost my money and I lost my figs.
The whole affair was most embarrassing.

After that I couldn't do much better
than put my money into foreign postcards.
(Saucy postcards! Who'll buy saucy postcards?)
The moral climate changed within a year.

I can't help it. I have this sort of hunger
for risk and failure. So I took up hunger,
which wasn't then a scarce commodity –
people bought it and paid me with their curses.

So last I put my money into damns.
The time was ripe and all the tills were ringing,
my little chicks were coming home to roost.
But my lot was with damns and not with chickens.

I was waiting for the Revolution,
but when it came it caught us unprepared.
We lost our money (some of us lost lives)
and ceased to trade at all, except in jokes,

of which this story is a specimen.
You'll not deny it has a certain length
generous for the times, and, much like buttons,
serves to hold these tattered clothes together.

The Swimmers

Inside the church the floor is like black ice:
The past moves underneath it as it glimmers
In the light of the long windows, and you read
In brass the images of the dead swimmers.

Shoal on shoal, the fluidity of bodies
Supports the weight of the whole edifice.
The names, resemblances and epithets
Run by beneath your feet, under the ice.

Nowhere more than in churches are you aware
Of treading water. Surely you must sink
Under the weight of your own body: the building
Itself becomes nebulous and starts to shrink,

But the swimming goes on undisturbed. The dead
Press water and each other down the centuries
Of darkness: dear small girls, their sisters, mothers,
Husbands, families, their towns, whole countries

Float in the river which runs steadily
Dissolving everything. No wonder
The churches smell of damp and sadness.
The present drips from walls, the rest go under.

*

Like Venables Hinde, infant of the parish,
Along with John, Martha and Bess, of whom
None lived beyond thirty, though each lived longer
Than seven infant Hindes in the same tomb.

History is prodigal with numbers
And Venables Hinde was simply singular:
I think of him now drifting in his coffin,
Properly snuffed, tucked and rectangular,

With solemn messages about him; warnings,
Talismans, to *Remember Eternity*,
Or else to *Redeem Time*, or a plain *Here Lieth*.
For truisms we have immense capacity

And Venables had not yet grown out of them,
A small round passive cliché, hardly elliptical,
His utterances flat and loud, mere noise
Between one or other mortal receptacle.

Poor swimmers, hardly strength enough to move
And yet constrained to buttress a whole chapel.
Tread lightly here, respect the concentration
Of these verbose and delicate people.

*

Who's lost, who's found? I've looked here for you sometimes
And tried to feel such correspondences
As time redeems, remembering... I've strained
To hear you speak coherent sentences,

Cloud-cuckoo tongues, High Dutch or a pure Greek,
A tongue as washed out and as disinfected
As the water; full of hesitations
And precise declensions, but quite unaffected.

How foreign they all sound. How far downstream
From the familiar parish. Their formal prose
Has stiffened into marble but the tongues
Wag on, like plants, in a tide that comes and goes...

Drowned hands and skin; the water drifting off
Becoming water. Their bodies are unknown
As are the names you lived by. Who'll lay claim
To this faint draft of skin, this line of bone?

Whose element is water? A vacuous bright room
Waits upstairs. You approach it quietly –
Like rising through the sea and hearing nothing –
No names, no objects, no singing, nothing but sea.

*

Some forty years ago a girl was drowning
In the icy Danube, one of a great number
Shot that day in the last week of the Terror.
Time and again she seemed to have gone under,

But rose once more, raising a stiff arm.
Between the floes she drifted perilously.
It has been said that some die hard like cats,
And a cat was what she was most obviously.

But cats as swimmers? Yes, a miracle,
Her jaw shot half away, how she pressed forward.
The Danube was as dullish red as she:
That single arm conveyed the creature shoreward.

Those who remained below grew slippery
And featureless. Unfortunate the disparity
Between high-fliers and the deeply drowned.
She had something of an angel's clarity.

I hear that splashing as they throw her in,
The ripples spreading grey and red and white
From the small body, echoing in the stone.
The hymns begin. The cats sing in the night.

Notes of a Submariner

There's not a single window on the craft.
Each bunk is curtained off in tiers of black.
All day you pass along the narrow shaft:
all night you try to jump the passage back.

A form of claustrophobia; the dream
is much repeated and becomes a bore.
You're buried alive but no one hears the scream.
The lid comes down as someone shuts the door.

Then dreams again. You dream in chorus now,
some hundred bodies, separately interred,
gesticulating, one unholy row.
Then order once more, the official word.

No terminus in sight, the night sways on
and burrows deeply. The propellers turn
on unseen wonders that have come and gone,
Edwardian splendours of the age of Verne.

Such harmony of words informs the sea
and regulates the opening hours of clams.
Our lives are disciplined elaborately
into procedures, charts and pentagrams.

Returning to Jules Verne, I thought I saw
the ghost of old Professor Arronax,
his mouth stretched wide in one great gasp of awe,
drifting by beyond the curtain tracks.

We shoulder aside the waves and scoop the deeper
infrastructures of the vegetation,
its outlandish architecture, while the sleeper
nuzzles forward towards the nightmare station.

The voyage is phantasmal, no mistake,
adhering to a magical routine.
A paper girl bends so far back she breaks
across the pages of a magazine.

Old Arronax, Ned Land, the inky squid,
observe the progress of our nautilus
with sinkings of the heart. Our dreams will bid
to settle our accounts and weep for us.

TRAINS

The Courtyards

1

As if a mind subsumed its intellect,
an ear tuned in to noise within the skull,
a mouth spoke words of greeting to a dull
audience of teeth, or an eye observed
the rigging of its fibres and the curved
elastic walls where images collect;

as if a street had turned its stately back
on public matters, and had found a way
of contemplating its own poverty,
had rattled up its years of emptiness
and counted them out on an abacus
of winding stairs, or on a curtain track;

the small lift shuts and forces itself up
a narrow throated shaft with groans of chains
and pulleys, and the whole building complains;
but as you rise through slices of pale light
the brown intensifies to cream, and white,
a trancelike ring of silence at the top.

2

Think of a glove turned neatly inside out;
think of your hand running along a rail
as children run down galleries grown stale
with refuse; think of hands reversed; of keys
and locks; think of these blocks as hollow trees
still echoing to something inchoate;

think of fear, precise as a clean hand
searching in dark corners, with the skill
that years of practice manage to instil;
think of locks where keys will never turn;
of rooms where it takes experts to discern
a movement that the eye can't understand:

The inchoate is what gets lost. You hear
a crazy woman singing, ...*Tannenbaum,
O tannenbaum*... but then her words become
confused with curses, shouts of God and Fate,
and this is not exactly inchoate
but in such imprecision there is fear.

3

Outside, a rusticated, vermiform
ebullience; outside, a cluttering
of pediments, pilasters, pargeting,
embroidery; outside, the balconies
expand in their baroque epiphanies,
their splendid Biedermeyer uniforms;

outside, the casement windows under rolls
of stonework, rough or smooth or both; façades
with manners courtly as old playing cards;
outside, the straining figures stiffly bent
to hold up yet another pediment
disfigured by a web of bulletholes;

outside, the falling masonry, the hard
emphatic counter-patterns of collapse,
the shattered panes and almost hingeless flaps
that bang like toy guns to disturb the dust.
Inside, the ironwork, the lines of rust;
inside, the piles of rubble in the yard.

4

Inside, the caretaker; his wife; his cat;
a cage for small bikes; rows of potted plants
reaching for light; stuff that no one wants
left in the stairwell; little dingy signs
for manicurists, tailors; heavy lines
of washing stretched out tight from flat to flat;

inside, a sort of life. At one o'clock
the ringing feet of children up the stair,
the scrape of chalk where someone scrawls a bare
diagrammatic girl with breasts like bells
and leaves a message in rough capitals;
inside, the noisy opening of locks.

Inside, I think of someone else, a blind
and aged woman treading the fourth floor
as if it were a jetty from a shore
suspended in a band of warming light.
She feels her way to the door opposite.
The hollow building trembles in her hand.

5

Think of an empty room with broken chairs,
a woman praying, someone looking out
and listening for someone else's shout
of vigilance; then think of a white face
covered with fine powder, bright as glass,
intently looking up the blinding stairs.

There's someone moving on a balcony;
there's someone running down a corridor;
there's someone falling, falling through a door,
and someone firmly tugging at the blinds.
Now think of a small child whom no one minds
intent on his own piece of anarchy:

Think of a bottle lobbing through the air
describing a tight arc – one curious puff –
then someone running, but not fast enough.
There's always someone to consider, one
you have not thought of, one who lies alone,
or hangs, debagged, in one more public square.

6

As if the light had quietly withdrawn
into a state of grace; as if the sun
had moved out to the country, or had gone
abroad; as if the shadows had grown old
and grey, or found their recesses too cold
and spread themselves across a civic lawn.

Then what is left? I see the woman grip
the handrail as she feels her way along.
She clutches fervently a ball of string,
an old steel key. She turns the corner, calls
to someone downstairs; and the steel key falls,
suspended like an odd metallic drip.

As if the past could ever lose its teeth:
As if the eye could swallow everything
and leave the world in darkness, blundering
about the courtyards! As if all the words
not spoken here could congregate like birds
and block out the faint noises from beneath!

7

Uncertainly she calls out from the top
of the thin stairs. The key won't fit the lock.
The key won't turn. The key is firmly stuck
inside the door. Then how to get up there
but run up every storey by the stair,
and hope she'll still be there when the stairs stop,

and hope she'll still be there when the stairs stop.

Level Crossing

Hearing the transmission of the rain,
    the ticking of static and the insect lectures,
and seeing those corroded pictures
    flaking across the screen beyond the pane,
merely the sound of water on the sill,
    you reassemble time and hold it still.

It makes a pattern that is audible:
    you hear the history of voices, continuous
as traffic, concealing some ingenious
    device for transmuting the bored, trivial
natter of your days. How could you guess
    those intricacies lodged in pettiness?

Re-entering that noise is much like waiting
    for a train. You're at a level crossing,
hearing at first the usual nothings
    of the wind and birds, then a faint curious shaking,
a tickling in the spine, a purr and spring
    before the final awesome clattering.

A lit train, carriages of light. Its going
   is so cheerful. There's no turning back,
only the vague murmuring of the track
   whose love will leave us perfect in our knowing,
to stand in showers, breed memories like rain.
   The stations sing and then it's quiet again.

North China

A man is walking, or appears to walk,
Rapidly backwards into the lit town
Beyond the darkening platform, where a crust
Of light encases him in the dust
Of his own translucence, his head a stalk
Beside our furious clatter.
   These things will cease to matter.

A stutter of pale boards, the names of sleep:
How soon the semiology of shape
And dying fall takes over. Neither past
Nor future, we discover here a lost
Continent of moments, whose elegy
Begins with a drowsy numbness.
   Such continents are nameless.

A city in the extreme north of China
Freezes each year to fifty below zero.
It has an enormous Culture Park where snow
Becomes a polished lawn and festivals
Of sculpture feature houses with ice walls
Embedding bits of china
   Crowned with ice antennae.

Such baroque, such opulence, such darkness.
We're on the edge of all that's frozen, formal,
Furious and unattainable.
The great fantastic trains, like twists of barley,
Go nosing forward rather eerily,
Even a good marriage
   Is more than half a mirage.

Ghost Train

Is it an illusion? It must be. Cesare
Pavese, sitting on a train, in a third-class
Carriage, alone with a woman who smokes.
He is too embarrassed to smile or make a pass
Among those empty seats that other women
Have at times vacated. It is history,
And the long train croaks
And shudders, smelling of upholstery,
Remaining empty, no place for encounters.

Public transport has been stitching together
The unfinished business of old Europe.
Believing in ghost buses that fail to stop
When requested, that appear only in foul weather,
Inhabitants of inner cities glamorise
Familiar places where the traffic chunters
Like some vigilant but dull
Official, an Argus with myopic eyes
Who cannot watch over his human cattle.
The ghost buses are empty, driverless.
They come upon one suddenly, with a noise
Of thunder and faint bells, their progress
Unsteady, vast overgrown toys
That have run away, and found this special route,
These special streets. Now someone tells a story
Of those who have managed the trick of boarding
By somehow leaping on, getting a foot
On the platform and grasping the ghost bar. According
To him their fate is terrible, a gory
Compound of brown wire, a cross between
A prison and a farmyard, shitty, poisonous.

Such buses and such trains keep rolling on.
Infected landscapes watch them, half asleep
And, perversely amorous,
They listen for flirtations in the spin
Of the wheel or the hiss of the smoke.
Now Cesare Pavese will not keep
Appointments, nor at this time of night
Is it possible to stay awake
And see the stations sweeping out of sight.

*   *   *

Windows, Shadows

A single carriage whose quartet of ghosts
dies in faint echoes to both left and right;
     mirrors and windows
where one man's letter moves in darker light
he may not read by, and a third man boasts
     a clutch of shadows.

We rush across the landscape like a fake
legation. Can we speak with the same voice
     despite the windows?
Exclusive as they are they leave a choice
between perfections, though it's a mistake
     to count on shadows.

It's freezing here. Beyond is a whole range,
a gallery of portraits that belong
     only to windows.
Yet something on this side will faintly long
to shadow letters, faces, and exchange
     a life for shadows.

No companion could be more attached.
No brother show a greater sympathy
     than these black windows
making fiction out of fiction, and a body
out of nothing. Some windows may be touched
     only by shadows.

The Green Mare's Advice to the Cows
(i.m. Marc Chagall, d. 1985)

> *It seemed that the cow was conducting world politics at that time.*
> MARC CHAGALL

1

What matters is the price of the mare.
What matters is the colour of the street.
What matters is that streets have no colour to speak of
Until we give them colours. The same with names.
What matters is the sound of arguments
And not their content. Arguments are blue,
Which, incidentally, is the colour of the street
(And hence, you see, I show them arguing).
What matters is the Love of God
And never mind if God does not exist.
You make him yellow, just as Christ is white,
But that damn cockerel keeps getting in,
And cows with their seductive eyes and udders,
And violinists who can only scrape.
It is another music altogether
That we dance to – and it isn't much
But it will do, believe me, it will do.

2

Surrender to mere *brio*? Stiff
Heads float off in disbelief
And fingers multiply in grief.

A clock strikes midnight in the air
In homage to Apollinaire.
Let Malevich adore the square.

Those who are less innocent
Castrate, carve up, dissect, invent
With a much sharper instrument.

A brush is fine. In mute arrest
A country bumpkin cups the breast
Of tender Vacha. Cows are best.

Cows will run the government.
Cows have a delightful scent.
Cows produce their Testament.

You watch the carnival proceed
Down muddy streets. The cows will lead
The moujiks home while altars bleed

With gentle bovine sacrifice,
Both melancholy and precise.
You cannot kill the same cow twice.

You see the calf, you see the child
Within the womb: Vitebsk, a wild
Impatience, dirty, undefiled.

The commissars may rave and row,
The housepainters obey you now
And hang the banner of the Cow.

The frozen cow hangs like a star,
And you yourself a commissar –
You start to moo. Yes, you'll go far.

Remember Grandfather, who stood
Before you with his feet in blood:
'Now look here, cow, we must have food.'

First grub, then dreams. But Lenin stands
All topsy-turvy on his hands.
What sacrifice the state demands.

The cows will take you at your word,
Advancing on you in a herd.
One cow takes wing, soars like a bird.

But look up there. The dream clouds fly
Above nightmare artillery
And cows are raining from the sky,

Dead cows, contented cows. It pays
To trust their unaffected ways
And leave their ghosts a land to graze.

3

The Man who is a Cello and the Fish who plays
The Violin are suddenly struck dumb.
The Goat in the Sky grows horns of logic. He weighs
Too much and every puzzle and conundrum
Begins to feel the lack of a solution.
The puritans claim back their revolution.

The poet, no longer cut in pieces, does not lie
Flat on the grass in the formal posture of death.
The egotistic lovers neither kiss nor fly.
The riddled milkmaid sinks down out of breath.
The dead man's candles cannot light the street
And broken bodies rest on tired feet.

The village processions reverse their steps. They realise
The city they inhabit has always been there, waiting.
The samovar slips off the crooked table. The eyes
Of the dead calf are finally shut. The dating
Couples are dated. The pendulum is still
And time runs down like water from the hill.

4

Returning to the green mare. She is grinning
At the wild commotion. All those words and colours
Merely confirm her own view of aesthetics:
No artist ever paints quite what he sees.
No artist ever tries to paint his dreams.
An artist only paints what he believes in.
And she is winking, full of self-belief
And green intestines, though she knows the town
Is changing irredeemably behind her.
She tells the cows: your freedom is exciting.
She tells the cows: prepare for government.

BUDAPEST POSTCARDS

Rebuilding the Cathedrals

Everything has turned to foam.
Look, the tower rises and disintegrates
into thrusts and counterthrusts of lace,
a jostling of fine bones.

The hill has fallen into the river.
What remains rears up and stiffens.
The roofs are a shower of epaulettes,
ridiculous uniforms.

Nothing is as it seems – everything changes.
Foam tumbles and snaps like bone;
the lace inclines to rain;
the rain breaks up the fountain; time stands still

Balloon Adrift, City Park

The children drift like feathers
    about the closing park.
The birds themselves are returning to the ark
    of the trees. A night
of softness is promised, an undisguised delight
    of late spring weather.

One balloon drifts upwards
    and slowly diminishes,
swaying slightly with tiny flourishes
    of its rabbit ears.
It takes some time before it disappears
    and quietly explodes.

Attendants of the Metro Museum

How carefully the old custodians
of national treasures polish their black shoes
    and play up to their audience
of children, tourists, television crews.

It's something – even this – at such an age,
to trim your nails, refrain from picking your nose,
    to swot up an official page
of gangling facts in unremarkable prose.

They have a faint religious glow, like mystics
of some ancient orthodoxy playing host
    to a congregation of statistics,
attendant angels on a holy ghost

who is longing to embrace them finally.
They are proud to be the servants of the state,
    part of that great family
of dead who sit round patiently and wait.

In the Puppet Theatre

I never liked the way the usherettes
drew the curtain. We sat in a cigar box
    watching wooden faces
performing before coloured blocks
that made up into complicated sets
    of houses, palaces,

their legends hammered to a public shape
and rigged out with a song or two. We sat
    and watched and applauded,
singing and laughing at all of that,
but feeling still uneasy about the drape
    as if something sordid

were being acted out by woodentops,
so stiff and masklike – a whole mode of being –
    that we could not summon
arguments against it. And the puppets, seeing
    in this nothing uncommon,
rattled through their lines and moved the props.

Tenement

The face has its own architecture. See
    the tenants shift behind
half open curtains. It is like those maps
phrenologists would draw last century,
as if each mind contained a hundred minds,
so many minds the building should collapse
    under the weight
but somehow holds together, stands up straight.

How can one keep an eye on all these people,
    these obsessive couples
in their fury of daily living? I can hear
but cannot make out every syllable.
They speak in tiny streams of coloured bubbles
which issue from their mouths and disappear
    in the blue sky
which swallows them. And soon the mouths are dry,

*   *   *

The Child I Never Was

The child I never was could show you bones
that are pure England. All his metaphors
are drawn from water. His ears admit the sea
even to locked rooms with massive doors.

Look, let me make him for you: comb his hair
with Venus comb, a wicked drupe for mouth,
twin abalone ears, sharp auger teeth,
an open scalloped lung, a nautilus
for codpiece, cowrie knuckles, nacreous.
Let him shiver for you in the air.

The English schoolboy cannot understand
a country that is set in seas of land.

The child I never was makes poetry
of memories of landscape haunted by sea.
He stands in an attic and shows you his collection
of huge shells, and with an air of introspection
cracks his knuckle bones.

A Small Girl Swinging

When first they pushed me
    I was very scared.
My tummy jiggled. I was
    Unprepared.

The second time was higher
    And my ears
Were cold with whisperings
    Of tiny fears.

The third time up was HIGH,
    My teeth on edge.
My heart leapt off the bedroom
    Window-ledge.

The fourth time, Oh, the fourth time
   It was mad.
My skirt flew off the world
   And I was glad.

No one's pushing now,
   My ears are ringing.
Who'll see across the park
   A small girl swinging?

Who'll hear across the park
   Her mother calling,
And everywhere her shadows
   Rising, falling?

Meeting, 1944
(L.S. and M.S.)

I opened the front door and stood
lost in admiration of
a girl holding a paper box,
and that is how I fell in love.

I've come, she said, *to bring you this,*
some work from the photographer –
or rather it's for a Miss D...
Would you pass it on to her?

She's my sister, but she's out.
You must wait for her inside.
I'm expecting her right now.
Come in. I held the front door wide.

We talked a little of the war,
of what I did and what she earned;
a few minutes it was, no more,
before my sister had returned.

You're going? Well, I'm off out too.
And so we rose from our two chairs.
I'll be back shortly, Lily dear.
Shall I see you down the stairs?

That's all there is. We met again
until they took the Jews away.
I won't be long. I'll see you soon.
Write often. What else could we say?

I think they were such simple times
we died among simplicities,
and all that chaos seemed to prove
was what a simple world it is

that lets in someone at the door
and sees a pair of lives go down
high hollow stairs into the rain
that's falling gently on the town.

Boys Watching an Aeroplane Drop Leaflets
(an incident from 1948)

Where does it come from, this blown paper
littering the city squares,
these feathers left by birds on grass,
those clouds drifting unawares
and breaking softly against glass?

Appearing suddenly, the aeroplane
rocks the bay. All those waves.
She sets trees shaking and boats
bobbing, narrowly shaves
the hill, avoiding its throat,

But not its children, playing at war,
who do not hear the oracle
but see the falling of white leaves
as something of a miracle –
the liberation of handkerchiefs.

Cultural Directives

As Michelangelo, the great Italian composer,
once remarked: Artists have responsibilities.
Hearing music is like contracting a disease,
a beautiful infection. It brings closer
the point of no return. One must be strong.
There's no such creature as a harmless song.

Painting too, as the English artist Shakespeare
pointed out, can be debilitating
unless you aspire beyond paint to real things.
A painting freezes movement. The eye, like the ear,
is a channel of impotence. Mere airs and graces
often induce an unproductive stasis.

And as for words, I only need quote Mozart,
the Swiss poet: They're tainted by unreason.
Language is discourse, words slippery. To seize one
we must lay traps, as for mice. The throat's part
of the respiratory tract, and you may clip
a speech, like air, by tightening your grip.

Too many of you are wasting your time and ours
with gewgaws, bric-à-brac and frolicking.
It's time to give you all a rollocking.
We're not impressed, I fear, by your endeavours.
The role of the past is to prepare the future
and your task is to welcome it with Culture.

After Attila

(a version after Attila József)

The storm arrives, a froth of black,
A dark and sullen lumbering;
Lightning snickers, cuts a track
Of light across the slumbering
Landscape, like a shot of pain
Under the scalp, and then again,
A velvet shimmering and rumbling
Sets the jasmine quietly trembling.

See, apple-blossom – the twig is snapped –
Her petals, those poor butterfly-wings,
Attempt to fly, the foolish things.

Down the gentle slope the trapped
Mobs of wild grass bend and sway
Fearing the dark has come to stay.

Their shuddering, however frail,
Is good to teach their little ones
To bear the terror of the gale;
Learn then, my dear, when trouble comes
To sing your terror soft and low
So that the very grass may know
Your voice, and think that, as you pass,
You yourself are only grass.

The Birds Complain

Tiny birds hatch tiny strategies
to lead men from their nests
hidden in low shrubs or wayside hedges;
they scream or tut, expose a barrel chest
or flash a wing.
We cannot guess their scale of suffering.

A brave performance, playing on the nerve
instinctive as despair,
will get all the applause that it deserves.
Though much of it's mere sawing of the air
yet we are gripped
by truth, the very crudeness of the script.

Cruse

Holding this cruse of bone, the human head,
    how brittle
the world appears. The strange occipital
    tenderness
of couples curled together in a bed
    is all they possess,

something to be packed away in cases
    of stoneware,
Meissen crockery, addressed to nowhere.
    They retain
their proper outward form, their public faces
    like old porcelain.

Such frailty (when the head's a passive thing,
    defenceless
without aid of arms) is almost senseless
    and unfair.
How lovely is the bone beneath the swing
    and softness of hair.

Glass

He kept on dropping things. While I was there
He dropped two glasses, one bottle, tripped over my bag.
Each time a nervous smile, a slight sag
Of the shoulders, a vague look into the wild air,
Then out would come the broom. Behind the bar
    The glasses trembled,
    The glasses shimmered,
The place resembled
A jeweller's window, the muscular
And nervous delicacy of the timid.

To be so clumsy was embarrassing.
He looked down frequently for crumbs of glass
And went on serving in that curious
Unsteady way of his, a wretched thing,
Enormous eared and fisted. Behind the bar
    The glasses trembled
    And dissembled
In the honey-
Coloured light, displaying the muscular
And nervous delicacy of money.

Meetings

Drowned men return, the travellers come home,
All is forgiven in that breathless cry.
The statue weeps secure beneath her dome,
Delightedly she wipes her stony eye.

It is the end of literature to meet
With what was offered once and then withdrawn
To make up stories and to give the sweet
Illusion that we're only as alone

As we would wish. I wish now we had kissed
Before you left me, but it is too late.
I cannot find your ear or lip or breast.
I'm going back to books. The rest can wait.

FROM
METRO
(1988)

The Lukács Baths

1

It's circa 1900 and five women
have gathered here in semi-darkness
prepared to prophesy their own extinction.
The water shimmies down a pebbled wall,
a fountain hesitates. Their swimming costumes
are wasps' nests soaked through, softened by the gush,
their bathing caps are a green efflorescence.
They are the light at the bottom of deep pools
wobbling in uncomfortable sunshine
with rheumatic feet, imagining a Greece
ravaged by wars, prepared, they say, to sink.

2

Inside every grandmother there sits
an attractive young girl mouthing pieties,
complaining of sore lips or God knows what.
They prophesy the past with unerring accuracy;
history for them is painful gossip
half way between myth and memory.
They are on nodding terms with skeletons
who take the shape of husbands in dull rooms,
and they can tell the future as it shrinks
into its faint determined pattern.
It's hard to like them, harder to dislike them.
Their faces are light wrinkles in the water.

3

An enormous beech is jutting from the yard.
The walls, just as in crematoriums
are stuck with plaques in a handful of languages.
My shoulder's better. I can move my leg
God bless these healing waters. I can walk.
Inside and on the roof the swimsuits bulge.
I'm watching two old women as they swim
and push away the past like tired waves.

The House Dream

I dreamt of a house in which a man was killed.
He loved the yellow bones of houses and tall windows.
Their shining bodies stood about him. He was tiny,
a child at under five foot two. His hands were minnows.

An empty niche dimpled the wall outside,
a portrait of his buxom wife hung vastly
in the biggest room. His desk had twisted legs.
There was about him something smelly and ghastly –

in retrospect at least, knowing him dead
and horribly so. His old housekeeper wept
among the statues. Where he wrote his slight poems
the wife of a drunken architect now slept.

And yet the house was beautifully at rest,
the mansard like a tight cap on his head,
a vague greenness moved and grew outside
and flowers sung gently in the flowerbed.

My dream or his? I thought I'd like to leave
some tiny vestige of self, collateral,
a History of Since Then, perhaps a poem
to celebrate the peaceful and unnatural.

I knew the name beyond my face and saw it
enter the hall and wipe its foot on the scraper.
The wind was in the gutter and the light
was flaking off the walls like painted paper.

A Card Skull in Atlantis

The *Atlantis Paper Co.* to be precise –
purveyors of artists' materials from their warehouse
in Garnet Street, a stone's throw from the river,
vendors of paint, small bottles, aerosols,
but paper chiefly – cream, pale oatmeal, speckled,
translucent, edges stiffly cut or deckled.

A pirouette of spectacular bones blew softly
in the draught of the door. You could construct
the skeleton by cutting and glueing together
the pages of a book with delicate labels:
the thing required patience to collate,
life-sized at last, if rather underweight.

There is a crystal skull, I do believe,
in the British Museum, more articulate,
more valuable perhaps, but card will do;
it grins among the sketchbooks with its patent,
its ethmoid, larmical and zygomatic,
it could even whisper something politic

of skulls like paper, piled high in ditches,
two sets of grandparents, an uncle or two,
of cousins boarding trains, securely labelled,
and people watching one another from windows.
Under the eyes their bones flare for a minute,
collapse to powder on a distant planet,

subside and sink, and form a kind of silt,
washed down by rivers, drifting among boots
and waste from sewers, sticking to dead branches,
caught by the ebb tide sun along the bank,
sucked finally to sea in salt-sour smells,
and settling dumbly among rocks and bells.

Grandfather in Green

My grandfather, the Budapest shoemaker,
    wrote plays in his spare time, and then he died.
His body became a pebble on a beach
    of softness across which swept the pale green tide.

Pale green, I think, would suit him as a tint –
    under his eye, or thinly flexed across
the hooked bridge of his nose. His sour complexion
    was cooking apples, a summary of loss,

each a pucker in the flesh. His waistcoat
    was grey as clouds, a pale green handkerchief
blossoming from the pocket. Even his tongue
    would sit in his mouth, soft and green as a leaf.

And so he returned to nature after all,
    the pale green gall within him in the shut
cavern of his stomach, and the green
    smell of gas still lingering in the hut.

On a Winding Staircase

I climb these stairs which might be by Vermeer.
Light drools like spittle from the rails. They wind
towards a window, and even from down here
I make out the faint iron bands that bind
the house together in one act of will.

The writing on the wall says *Carpe Dym*
attached to the name of a national hero, or
it could well be the local football team.
Upstairs are voices I have heard before
that hook and draw you up as on a line,

to something cramped, imprisoned and defined
by yards and corridors. I run my hand
along the wall and feel it sweat and grind
its teeth. A brilliant light is in command,
a fist of light within an iron frame.

One purpose, one cohesion. People spill
from monumental gateways, accidents
of sun and shadow, leaving at their peril
the fortress of controllable events,
venturing out and over the world's rim.

I wait to see a family descend
down thirty years, each of them framed alone
before the window as they comprehend
the force that welds them with the light in one
unbreakable and static composition.

They owe a debt to history, that calm
and droning music which slows to a dead march.
Look at these maps, as wrinkled as a palm,
repoussoir instruments, an antique arch,
a girl with a trumpet, bent on playing *Fame*.

METRO

What should they do there but desire?
DEREK MAHON

1 *At my aunt's*

My aunt was sitting in the dark, alone,
Half sleeping, when I crept into her lap.
The smell of old women now creeps over me,
An insect friction against bone
And spittle, and an ironed dress
Smoother than shells gathered by the sea,
A tongue between her teeth like a scrap
Of cloth, and an eye of misted glass,
Her spectacles with the image of a lit room
Beyond the double doors, beyond the swing
Between the doors, and my head in her bosom
At rest on soft flesh and hard corsetry,
And in that darkness a tired and perfumed smiling.

*

Across the city darkened rooms are breeding
Ghosts of elderly women, nodding off
Over the books their grandchildren are reading,
Or magazines or bibles or buttons to be sewn,
With letters, patterns, recipes, advice.
Some of them might have the radio on,
Like her, my aunt, who will remain alone
Within that room in which I visit her,
Ascending to her skin, which is rough
About the mouth, with hard nodules, like rice,
(Her face glows like a lantern) and she says,
There is a God, the God of the Jews, of Moses and Elias,
But this is not the time to speak of him.

*

And here my aunt is happy, and her sister,
Both happy in their roles. And the child
Is happy in the reading of a tale
That ends in triumph over the wild
Succubi of his imagination:
The dwarfish furies of the forest, the lank
Raincoated ghosts who pester
The living daylights out of night,
The stepmothers who live beyond the pale.
The city waits like an armchair. A slight
Woman sits there, watching, as the evenings shrink
About her, and the city opens its arms
And welcomes her to its administration.

*

152

There are certain places healthy to have lived in:
Certain streets, hard cores of pleasure:
Their doorways are ripe fruit, stay soft and open,
Exhaling a fragrance of drains or tobacco,
Others are more proper, starched and sun-eaten,
Doorways where things happen
In a particularly fortunate way, which echo
To words of parting, or thrill to an exact measure
Recollected in the pleat of an arch;
Doorways which see military bands march
Across a square on a blazing hot afternoon,
Or catch a particular angle of the moon.
There are places to be happy in if only you can find them.

*

The Metro provides a cheap unending ride
If you switch trains below the city.
There is a whole war to be fought out under
The pavements; I can hear the faint thunder
Of artillery in Vörösmarty Square:
The cobbles shake, move gently from side to side
With microscopic accuracy, and ice creams
Wobble in their goblets. The cavity
Beneath the streets is filled with the blare
Of surface traffic. The city is all dreams
And talk, and rumours of talk. The place below
Is treacherous. You don't know
Who your friends are, who you are yourself.

*

It is everything that is past, the hidden half,
A subcutaneous universe in which
Our fate is to be the dramatis personae
Of geographers who place us more precisely
Than we can ourselves. I place a woman
On a train and pack her off to Ravensbruck:
I send out a troop of soldiers to summon
The Jews of this fair city.
                              Off she goes,
Repeating her unknown journey, and I must look
To gauge the distances between us nicely.
I see a voice, the greyest of grey shadows.
Lead me, psychopompos, through my found
City, down into the Underground.

*

2 *Undersongs*

I love the city, the way it eats you up
And melts you into walls along with stone
And stucco till your voice assumes a tone
As crinkled, crenellated, creviced as itself,
And you can recognise it in a shop
Like something heard through windows. Human forms,
Detail and allegory: the twelve
Months of the year, the forces of nature, or
A frieze of leaves and angels where the worms
Have eaten away the substance of a voussoir
Above a flaking open door,
A spray of lace or foam, a mouchoir
In plaster flung at the late empire.

        *

The empire underground: the tunnelling
Begins. The earth gives up her worms and shards,
Old coins, components, ordnance, bone and glass,
Nails, muscle, hair, flesh, shrivelled bits of string,
Shoe leather, buttons, jewels, instruments.
And out of these come voices, words,
Stenches and scents,
And finally desire, pulled like a tooth.
It's that or constancy that leads us down
To find a history which feels like truth.
The windows cannot speak because we pass
Before them all too often but the bricks know
What they stand on. There is no town below,

        *

It's only bits and pieces, as above.
You have to watch your language though: the words
Are muddy, full of unintended puns
And nervy humour. Waking afterwards
You feel soiled and dirty, the one you chased
Has vanished, shown a clean pair of heels.
The Metro thunders through like heavy guns
To shake the waking streets. They are effaced,
And reconstructed, effaced again.
Now where are you, psychopompos?
Who'll pick up your thread or catch your train,
Who'll follow you and bear your mouldered cross
Through tunnels tight as fingers in a glove?

        *

Desire again, the undersong. The lost
Children feel it in their sleep,
And turn uneasily to the wall through which
Symbols pass and cool their blood like ghosts.
My mother's family has passed through it,
Not one remains, and she is half way through.
Her brother disappears, the glove has closed
About him somewhere and dropped him in the ditch
Among the rest. The ditch becomes a pit,
The pit a symbol, the symbol a desire,
And this desire's the thread. The tunnels creep
Under the skin, the trains with their crew
Of passengers can glide through unopposed.

*

Their voices are not heard but seen, are moving
Lips and tongues. They're well behaved and quiet.
To give voice is to lip read, to construe
The contortions of a mouth, to place the living
Where the dead are, your money where their mouth is.
The body longs for touch: no words are spoken,
But sentences break up, are made new
Into fictions which will occupy the city
Like a foreign army. Their all too tangible bodies
Litter up the place, these men and women
Travelling. Her voice is underground.
Her poetry (unseen and without sound)
Lies not in pity but in clarity.

*

The Metro runs along to City Park,
That is a fact, and all along the line
The shivering persists beneath your feet.
The same with facts. It is a chance remark
That lingers in the tunnels, is embedded
In pavements, under skin or in the grain
Of your bench. She steps in, finds a seat
And is whisked off to meet my father in
A flat in Rózsa Street. His heavy-lidded
Eye remembers, re-encounters. The street
Of the rose. The rest is not my business,
But a picture in a frame. Under the skin
She wears another skin, another dress.

*

155

3 Portraits

At fourteen she went skating on the river
And caught a cold. *The boys would come from far*
To sing outside my window, there were many –
Because I was attractive and vivacious.
The cold developed into rheumatic fever,
Thrombosis followed. Then would follow a litany
Of lost relations, lost names, and the brother
Who failed to love her, who was beautiful.
The town was Cluj, then known as Kolozsvár,
The district Transylvania. From this
Follows the following, expand the cool
Shadows of biography and synopsis.
Even now I know little about my mother.

*

From this and something more, the skeleton
Of something – body, city, staircase, wall –
Which feels impressive, is part visible;
From this follow internment and arrest,
The family hatreds and the fierce ungracious
Vendettas of my childhood, and the fiction
Of history which makes up Budapest
And what one thinks of as oneself, that one
Who thinks he sees, who wears both belt and braces
In photographs, an infant contradiction,
A narrator, himself of morbid interest,
Whose scented aunt and God have settled down,
Whose eyes shut windows in the city's face,

*

A peculiar little old man of a boy,
A kind of dwarf, benevolently wise
And puzzled, deep voiced, comical almost.
He kneels under a table, his bare bottom
Sticking in the air, a bendy toy.
He swings between the doorway, opens his eyes
And thinks he sees the faint trace of a ghost
Among the coats left hanging on the hook,
Touches the piano, examines the vast stove
Which dominates the corner of the room,
Deploys his troops on battlefields of blankets,
And colonises every possible alcove
Of his world with a vague unfocused look.

*

The early fifties: Uncle Joe's broad grin
Extends benevolently across the wall.
The boy wears a Young Drummers uniform
(A blue tie with a toggle), shakes the hand
Of dignitaries at some parade. He is thin
And pinlike, almost cavernous. The school
Is pleased. He's learning to perform.
She works and he works. She checks his work for him
And terrifies him into excellence.
He has a line of stars in his book. They're hers.
He watches her pupils contract and expand.
Uncle Joe's moustache will shelter them.
This is the era of benevolence.

*

Her likenesses are caught on film. Her hair
Has flared into a dark corona, black beams
Of sunlight, thick, now piled high, now falling.
It hides her face. She stands on the ramparts
Of the Bastion, her teeth gleam.
Her finger can bend backwards in a curve
That is quite frightening. She deploys her arts
Of fascination as he does his troops.
She sits down on a chair,
Invites him to her lap. He will deserve
Her attentions. He listens to her calling.
His father enters and pulls him through the snow.
She smokes a cigarette and parts her lips.

*

He's easily frightened; when she lashes round
In a monumental fury he keeps her sting
In the bottom drawer. It is his occupation
To bring it out at night and scare himself.
For a long time he can sit and watch her working,
And feel her warmth, and listen to the sound
Of her breathing. It gives him an odd sensation
Of belonging/not belonging, half and half.
This half and half will always seem like truth
(I too can see him only with one eye).
He'll keep her face and others in the drawer,
With her own photographs, her frozen youth,
Her unsent letters, his unwritten reply.

*

157

4 *Flying backwards*

The accident of being who one is.
The accident of being in a place
At one time not another. It is not grace
Of form, but grace of accident that gives
A building power, and lends the body strength,
The necessary structure to survive.
The tattered dress of fortune parodies
Our specious dignity. It makes us eat
Our words, as I eat hers, takes breadth and length
And swallows them whole. It is the street
Of Roses. It is the beautiful brother.
The things that might smell sweet by any other
Name we give, or recall by accident.

*

I have her brother's face – a studio piece
Of *circa* '29, and then again
Some two years later, hair cropped tight about
His delicate skull. She stands beside him, pouts
And stares, waiting for him to release
Her trapped hand. Photography, her trade,
Is this security, this collateral:
My fiction turns to sepia in its presence,
All subterfuge is instantly displayed
For what it is, a brief ingenious pattern.
And he cared so little for me if at all.
I tried to find him later but in vain.
My words for what she meant, in a general sense.

*

The uncle with the chocolate factory,
The uncle who was magistrate,
The father who travelled to the States
And worked as a labourer. The middle-class
Jews of Kolozsvár are the lost history
Of which she hardly spoke. Mother's bob
Is a fashionable frame for her neat face,
Which the edges of the photograph reframe.
They bind the sepia, prevent it spilling
Across the desk, hold names
At an aesthetic distance, where, by willing,
We can work them into fictions and animate
The past, which remains forever another place.

*

But it does spill over. It is what we are
And what we see and time and again forget.
It's there in walls, in Uncle Joe's moustache
Which is the wall. The other place is here
And grows moustaches, breasts, Edwardian collars,
Wears miniskirts and co-respondent shoes.
Whatever preserves the late imperial texture
Of before, that keeps the pattern true
And cynical, expresses its regret
In the rhetoric of faded architecture,
The blatant half truth / half light of a picture,
A vulgar hybrid of fleeting, local colour
Where only light is faithfully reproduced.
The rest is reconstruction and conjecture.

*

The rest is data such as: *At the hour*
When the Germans entered Budapest we were
Sitting in the Astoria, or *The man*
Who called for us wore glasses. Or *She used*
A certain colour lipstick…Such power
As we retain resides in these. I build her
In Meccano. Here's the skeleton.
The bare bones of the story are reduced
To ashes and a name in Golders Green,
Behind the Hippodrome, behind the station.
Recovered from thrombosis, at eighteen
She left for Budapest, an invitation
In her handbag (possibly her pocket).

*

She worked as a photographer. The war had started
But you'd hardly know it. She met my father late,
When he returned from camp in Proskyrov.
It was February, 1944.
Next month the Germans entered Budapest
And he was recalled to unit. The date,
Nineteenth of March. Facts, bare bones, the rest
Are silences. A 'safe house' in August
With father's family two floors above.
September, October, the Arrow Cross, the raid.
Her feet are clattering in the gallery,
His family are hiding or departed
And only she remains to be betrayed.

*

5 Betrayals

Betrayed? She felt and thought she was. But who
Betrayed her (if it was betrayal) and how?
Betrayal by omission was the way,
Betrayal by those she trusted. Down below,
The soldiers in the yard, the quasi-military.
They called her down. It was a minute's work.
But why was she out on the gallery
When it was far more sensible to hide?
And why did no one tell her? Who were they
Who should have done so? Why did they shirk
Their human duty? The wound was always fresh:
Even at fifty-one, the year she died,
It bored and tunnelled deep into her flesh,

*

Katona József Street. The Swedish house.
My father's family came from the North,
Moravia and Bohemia, tailors, painters,
Vendors of musical instruments, a broker,
And father's father was a shoemaker.
How much is all this information worth?
The list is endless and monotonous,
Their season's over, summers, autumns, winters:
Few made the final spring of '45.
My father had been brought up by the aunts
Who coddled me in my turn. To survive
Was an achievement, but my grandparents
Were under-achievers all of them, bar one.

*

My father's mother. Large-eyed, beaky-nosed.
We must have met but I've no recollection,
Except of something owl-like, something scented.
Her absence gave her little enough protection
From mother's fury. The matter was closed,
No letters exchanged. In '56 she went
To Argentina, wrote, sent messages,
But his replies were censored or forbidden.
Her case was settled. Sometimes she sent me presents,
Pale useless things, the kind my mother resented
And fanned her hatred for her. It was the hidden
Secret of my childhood, what she'd done.
Even now I don't know what the truth is.

*

160

My aunts (or great-aunts to be precise)
Brought father up. His home was there. The owl
Had farmed him out. When evidence
Was weighed at home this counted much against her
And nobody replied in her defence.
Numerus clausus, numerus nullus: twice
Father was hit by laws against the Jews,
His education stopped, he worked in knit-wear,
Was twice promoted then forced out. A friend
Advised him, trained him, offered him a place
He couldn't decently refuse:
Apprentice plumber, master of the bowl.
For both of them it was an hour of grace.

*

Inevitably, labour camps. How many
Perished here: the artists, writers,
Musicians, plumbers, brothers? Escapades,
Adventures, tragedies, the company
Reduced, disbanded then recalled.
The dark-eyed girl in February, back home.
Road building, retreat, escape. The waters
Close about my grandfather and fold
Over him in Auschwitz. Brief episodes
Of dire intensity, each trivial sum
A fortune lost. The dark-eyed girl moves in
With father's mother, sister, baby niece.
It's lists and rosters, jigsaws piece by piece.

*

They fall together, stand and fall together.
The day the soldiers came she was alone
And heard them shouting. On another floor
The female threesome. She looks for them. The door
Is open. She calls their names, the mother,
Sister, niece. They do not answer. Where have they gone?
Where are they hiding? Nothing. Not a sound.
She wanders out, is spotted. It is fear:
Fear of discovery, fear of strangers. It's done.
They have not answered. Someone shouts, Come down!
And who is it pretended not to hear?
The rough voice rises. I speak for another
And buy my ticket for the underground.

*

6 *In Her Voice*

Like a girl listening behind
A membrane for a footfall or the knock
On a door, the rattling of the blinds
In a secret room of her head, I unlock
My eyelids pressed
Against a darkened window in a house
Whose eyes are asleep,
And quietly get undressed.
I have a thousand eyes to guard my neatness
Against the gods of lust, who quaintly creep
To music as they blind me and I wake
To hear the scuttling of a mouse
Here on the fourth floor at one o'clock.

*

I was on the fourth floor when the yard
Filled with uniforms and we were called
To order, and I ran into the flat we shared,
The old woman, her daughter and the child,
And all was empty. I whispered their names
But they did not answer to their lasting shame.
They should have answered me out of the pit,
Like any prompter from his own hell-hole,
But they closed their mouths to my pitiful dole
So I went down and here's the end of it.
Those men have strolled at ease about our yard
But God will grant them their reward
And punish them according to their lot.

*

They took me in their wagon, up the street
I used to walk, with all its empty faces
Staring from the coigns and pediments.
Great figures started from the roof in tents
Of stone and tiling, forgetting the discreet
Darkness of their long discolouration,
And tiny figures flitted by the bases
Of the portico of the academy.
My mind showed little sign of occupation:
All life was going on outside, upheld
By the conventions of the weather,
My tenants were expelled
To railway stations where we lost each other.

*

They put me on a train, east, west or south
And we rode off in our different directions,
Myself, my body and my heart. My eyes
Were saying something to my open mouth
Which had remained open in surprise
And every passenger had his own questions:
My nose asked, what's the smell?
My fingers wondered at the touch of cold,
My hair was busy interrogating the wind.
We were all agog to know the world at last
As it knew itself but never before had told
Anyone. Nor did I mind
Whether this was heaven, earth or hell,

*

As long as we were moving in the air,
As long as the city barked its orders out
Through doorways I imagined everywhere
And heard the porters shout
Behind closed eyes and behind the narrow wall
Of my most valued multi-storeyed skull.
But they told me no great truth or if they did
I have forgotten it. It was long ago
And I have doubts whether such a truth
Exists at all, as something we might know
Or understand. I have my hatred
Which is proof that something happened in my youth,
And the house itself has not yet been blown down,

*

My body is still standing. The wind blows through it
Like a language of which not a word
Is what it seems, and yet it survives.
The train is rushing past the fields and woods
Of all that was. The words renew it,
Rephrase its truths and falsehoods.
Behind the thinnest of walls a city thrives,
The empty buildings, the unfurnished,
Whose history remains unfinished.
     I rush out to the gallery, alone
And watch the soldiers massing underneath,
My brothers all, their justice bone for bone,
Their eyes are my eyes, their teeth are my teeth.

*

7 *What should they do there but desire*

Disorientation, loss: the doors that close
Just when you think that you have gained your entrance.
A glimpse of hallway, hat-rack, mirror, more doors.
Beyond the doors and on the left perhaps
A window giving on to a neat yard
With trees and flowers. Straight ahead of you
A lift-cage dressed in iron broderie,
A smell of coffee brewing, an envelope
Slit like a wound, the darker recesses
Of sitting rooms, momentarily opened.
What troubles me is the uncertainty:
Is this really a valuable darkness,
Or am I part of the darkness that's locked out?

*

The wind is scrabbling at the glass – perhaps
The trees are wanting to be let in.
The branches say nothing
Expressing only an incoherent thirst
For music, a music so violent and awful
That it can only leave them waving their arms.
Imagine the cellos sprouting dark green tongues
And moaning softly of their lot; their past
Of growing, cutting, hewing, shaping
To this one point of supreme helplessness.
What's eating them? And yet it's good to be eaten,
To become the food of passion and to feel
The stomach rise in suicidal independence.

*

*The wind stands in high places and looks down
And comes out at your arsehole and your mouth.
I do not speak now as a lady should,
Not even as a woman, but of parts,
The one dissociated from the other.
When I think of you I only see your head,
Sometimes a hand. The wind runs through your fingers
And cools the blood to a blue stream of air,
And when I hear it scrabbling at the glass
I'm filled with pride and understand the light
That leaps inside me and across the table
To reach out for some part, a head or hand
Or thigh or foot or armpit, something of you...*

*

Some years ago I met a man by chance
In a foreign street. I had not seen him since
The time when I last saw my brother
Of whom I carry about this sepia
(I seem to be my brother's only keeper)
Which is paler than he was. I blame the weather
For his fading and our having grown estranged.
He was handsomer than any man I knew,
As handsome as a woman could desire.
　　There was a policeman once who doffed his cap
And showed how in the lining he arranged
His family in tiers of small brown snaps.

Photography, I need you. Freeze me too.

　　　　　　　　*

Even here there are shadows of places: serene,
Impassive, idiotic, undemanding,
Without bitterness or rancour.
We are travelling in darkness, standing
On each other's feet but at one remove.
The door of the wagon rattles a pale music.
An elderly man is sick in the straw.
A child clings to my thigh. Two grown men kick
Each other in a fury, or try to gnaw
A third man's head. What do these things prove?

It is the peculiar happiness of buildings
To be witnesses. Here are the stones and mouldings,
The molten forms of clinker.

　　　　　　　　*

Dear brother, I have talked to everyone
But no one knows you. I am sitting in
A wooden hut, rather like a kennel.
You're well away from here. A woman kicks us
As she passes. I do not trust the women.
The men we're used to, they are what they are,
The usual sheep, but I'm a woman and
I know that pitch of the heart,
Am living in it. Who are they paying back?
Their elder brothers? Wherever you are
This non-existent paper will locate you,
In the angle of the wood, the nursery,
Or up the cherry tree with its sticky black cherries.

　　　　　　　　*

8 *Stopping train*

Here's Ravensbruck. I stop dead at the gate,
Aware I cannot reach you through the wire.
I cannot send you poems or messages,
No wreath of words arranged across blank pages,
No art that thrives on distance and desire,
But can't cope with fulfilment, that writes white
When happiness breaks out, that lights a taper
On a frozen lawn and bounces off the stones
Of hard luck. The dead have no use for art.
You might as well bring on the tongs and bones
As chamber music (Schubert's great quintet).
Not all the white ink in the world can set
Their coming through, their verses on black paper.

*

And if I bring you here and push you in
It's only because I know you once came out.
You cross the black bridge thus. *Ich bin allein,
Ich stell die Aschenblume ins Glass voll
Reifer Schwärze*, deep into your mouth.
And if I attribute to you desire
It is to replace what was voluptuous
In bodies full of warmth, *das aschenes Haar*
Which is also mine. I wait outside your school
Of hard correction, mouthing words too soft
To bear a lasting mark, a feminine tongue
In my head. I float on my own craft,
And try to write the half dead a live song.

*

Dead grandfathers, dead grandmother, dead uncles.
Item: to my children, All the aunts
Their grandparents can muster, this bequest
To be taken by them for granted. Tender plants
Turn vast familial trees in paradise,
Which is nothing else but superfluity,
Where every woman has an extra breast,
And every generation's spoiled for choice.
*A balloon floated past our window and almost
Touched the bricks. Small green leaves covered
The trees.* So wrote one Nelly Toll in Lwow.
Superfluous in base things, we are lost
In distant towns whose names sound much like Love.

*

See, in this drawing a girl is making Lwow.
Her mother and she are playing dominoes,
The sunflowers are growing in the shadows.
Small green leaves cover the trees. Above,
A balloon floats past the window. *I visited*
The children on paper. Paper of deep black
Is lightened by her painting. Even the dead
March cheerly in their prison, and look back
On paradise, and know that God is Lwow.
Ich stell die Aschenblume ins Glass voll
Reifer Schwärze. The camp choir sings a mass,
The camp dogs chew their bones. And in the glass
A brilliant ash-grey flower for Nelly Toll.

*

She tolls me back to the bleak scene before
The entrance. The women march to the factory.
Their wooden shoes are tottering on the ice;
It sounds like someone knocking at the door.
Thirty years on the knocking hasn't stopped,
But now your heart wears out its battery,
Is running down, its tick-tock less precise,
Is more like memory, which soon is lost
And drifts above the garden in fine dust.
Like Lili Marlene I wait outside the gate,
A lamplit watchdog expecting no returns.
Imagine my surprise when you walk out.
The crematorium waits, the oven burns.

*

This is our lucky day, like every day.
The white ink settles on the page like snow.
The sunflowers are growing in the shadow.
The crows are circling looking for dead meat.
Your hair turns into flowers streaked with grey:
I put them in a glass. The room grows warm
With soft grey flowers, responds with its own heat.
The pillows, blankets, curtains are in bloom
And open into grey. The grey flies swarm
About the lamp. This is our mortal room.
A train is arriving at an empty station.
A voice is speaking, but it isn't mine.
The passengers are spilled across the line.

*

9 *Fraternal Greetings*

Beauty and terror, just enough to bear:
The Rilkean brother, a little lower than
The lowest angel whose indifference
Is murderous to those who marvel at him
And expect him to return love like a man.
Disdain is an improvement on despair,
And hatred perhaps a kind of confidence
Which can be shared like intimacy,
Unexplained antipathy or dim
Persistent loathing. No analysis
Avoids abstraction. For some there is no physic
Or improvement. When instructed to kiss
His baby sister my uncle was violently sick.

*

And so there's guilt, guilt and indifference:
He in his turn became idealised
As all disdainful gods are. That is why
They are gods. And this was no pretence:
He could be human, true, but not to her.
She called him 'freedom fighter', 'partisan'
Once she had lost him. For a god to die
Is only to gain in potency, to rise
A few clouds higher – and it might have been all true
Although I heard he was a prisoner
And laboured, like my father, like a man,
And then might have been shot, aged twenty-two
Somewhere in Slovakia perhaps.

*

Perhaps. And yet he simply disappeared.
Tall forehead, dark hair, full and sensuous mouth,
Intense, intelligent. But to be sick
At touching her? Are gods sick at our touch?
It's possible of course. The bright one's beard
Is sensitive. It bristles at our youth
And emptiness. To him, we stink of pitch,
Are lymph and chyle and hatred. When we raise
Our holocausts to him he looks away.
He's not pleased by the smoke of sacrifice,
Or tawdry festivals or holy days,
Is tired of them. The gods have seen so much
Of fire they begin to turn to ice.

*

It's not that they mind the flattery: the smell
Is what offends them and they cannot help it.
So he's a god too, and whatever pit
His murderers interred him in he rose
And faded, entered other realms like hell
Or heaven. And she in her hell yearned
For his beauty and affection all the more.
Desire and pain. Around her bodies burned
In their own fevers or behind the door
That was always round the corner. I propose
A yard, a hut, a fence, a row of beds
And shins and shanks and ribs and collarbones,
And one familiar among shaven heads.

*

Those burning babes, visions of Christmas day,
The small photographers, provincial towns,
Perversities, distortions. They move down
The escalator, spread along the platform.
The train arrives and takes them. More keep coming.
Each face desires another. They pray
With a look, communicate by grimacing.
Each one of them is in some uniform
Of obsolescent dullness. Each bears a name
On the collar or the sleeve. Their names are numbers.
Above their mouths a single flickering flame
Sustains their spirit, and like spirit, it burns
And dances and reduces them to cinders.

*

*Dear brother, I have talked...*the voice is distant
As the past it conjures, as the little boy
Under the table...*but no one knows you.* To know
Is not to see or understand. The grey
Fly hovers at the curtain without knowing
That any particular thing is so
Or otherwise, but his drone remains insistent.
The walls keep mouthing at us with their doorways,
The trains keep coming and going.
The ghosts must pass through the walls alone,
Take on the character of stone,
Seek out the angle of the wood, the nursery,
Climb up the cherry tree with its sticky black cherries...

*

Burnt offerings: a little bonfire shivers
At the far end of the street, all rags and card
And insignificance. A wheelbarrow
Is propped like an old man kissing the pavement,
A stiff frock coat, the mud on the wheel his beard.
The flames leap and fall in rapid rivers
Of light, a confusion of elements.
I see small fires along the narrow
Passages between main thoroughfares.
The heart, the eyes and passions maintain
Their vigilance. The holocaust goes up
In smoke. Somewhere a soldier prepares
To set fire to fine details on a street map.

*

The map is always burning. Its consumption
Is conspicuous enough, imagined cities
Of fugitive colour, changing light on tiles,
Faces at windows, hands at doorways, feet
On trams and buses, clothes in smelly piles
In empty hallways, the sonorities
Of gossip and greeting. My friends and I meet
At restaurants, complaining of hard times
In the benevolence of an August night
That smiles on our children. We are an exception
To the rules of sleep. Our children will sleep light.
After the fireworks we tell old jokes
And pay our debt to history with rhymes.

*

The city dreams an island. It has always
Been here, stacked on its mound of days,
Lapped by cold sea, pickled and saline,
Wearing, breaking off. Hard water furs
The kettles, houses fall, rejig the shoreline,
Everything is continually in friction
With the wind off the sea. The women with scarves,
The men pottering in sheds, seek protection
In distance, the insularity of it all.
Sad, great, shaggy country. The soldier hears,
Takes aim and fires but misses. Foreign flotsam
Adheres to the feet of piers by decaying wharves.
The ferries shuttle. Waves crack on the wall.

*

The crack of a gate. Time opens backward to
A heap of pebbles suspiciously like bodies.
The wind whistles through trains whose nightmare crew
Of passengers have fallen quiet, stopped
Their grimacing and squealing and have dropped
Where they stood, dropped off to sleep at last
In broken postures, parodies
Of grace, recumbency and carelessness.
It is only by imagining the trains
That I can enter the gate, walk across the field,
And wait for the signals to announce the express
Europa. Its carriages are sealed,
The wheels go rattling over broken chains.

*

Too long rejected, we meet up in the street
Below a lamp post, yellowed as old papers.
What news? we ask each other. Our faces
Are the cut-out shapes of childhood, full of creases
And torn edges, smudged and circled
In soft chalks. We've brought along with us
Giraffes and elephants in a discreet
Procession, with dolls and packs of cards, and pieces
Of furniture arranged in packing cases.
Nothing but dust and detritus.
This is the news, hot off the world's press.
It's late at night, you say. We are light sleepers,
I reply, our sleep is a kind of emptiness.

*

Somebody has escaped at last. Somebody gets married,
Has a child, another. Somebody remembers
Someone else or something, certain numbers,
Certain streets and faces. One is worried
By forgetfulness, another by clarity.
Someone is not sure they should be here.
    Down into the Metro, down the stair:
A drunken woman's weeping on a bench,
Another's sitting in a pool of water,
The horrible familiar stench
Of loss. A fat policeman nudges
At them. The crowd skirts round the edges
Of the frame, spreads out into the city.

*   *   *

EN ROUTE

My Name

A voice in another room calls out a name
you do not recognise but know is yours.
So many ways with so few syllables
    that you must claim
along with clothes as dead man's metaphors.
Your very heart comes to you bearing labels:

a citizen, a Jew, bourgeois, brunette
or invalid, and each speaks differently:
your parents with their formal admonitions,
    the aunts who pet
and tease you, the lovers who will gently
bend your ear with their murmurs and petitions;

a coin, a patina, a doctor's file,
accretions of diseases, school reports,
employer's references, catalogues
    Shakespearian style
where murder lands you in the kangaroo courts
of popular feeling. You are one with dogs

and cats and household familiars like germs.
Your shaven head, your wooden shoes, your bed
with its number; your fleas, your lice, your store
    of serious worms
that wait on both the living and the dead
whose numbers you will swell. I keep the score

and tell the days religiously on which
my name took on new meaning with a hat
or spoken word. I keep up with the fashions
    and have grown rich
on music composed of lists. I have sat
in contemplation of my ruling passions.

I tend the days like tiny photographs,
each clearly labelled with a name not mine
but valuable: features, smells, a profile,
    a mouth that laughs,
a hand in my dead hair, a lip to sign
and seal me, and your vacant missing smile.

The missing items haunt me. Ghosts that fade,
too lightly pencilled in, underexposed,
time is always threatening to efface them.
        My hands have strayed
in filthy water. The river's doors have closed
on teeth and bones, not mine. I cannot place them.

The Love of Windows

I love the height of windows – they are bodies
at attention in their black and blue,
are blinding truths or lies, or silent studies
in deception, something seen through
once and then again, they frame us, me and you.

Your eyes are windows too, a blank display.
I cannot make you out: the life you lead
turns on no sudden light to make night day,
is only words too small and faint to read
like something in a contract or a deed.

Guards

I remember the windows in the evening;
five grey guards above the bed, their thin
pale uniforms were not assuring,
what monsters might they not let in?
Might they not all float in unobserved
and let loose the damnation we deserved?

Wry-faced clouds and empty dinner plates,
cloths hung on the pipes under the sink,
webs in the attic, shattered slates,
the faded ink
on newspapers whose eyes dissolved in dots
and yellow patches,
a scumble of coal dust and dead matches,
the earth round flowerpots.

I screw up my eyes in the dark, and see
your open brown eyes staring back at me
with all the artlessness
and heartlessness
of childhood, until the tears come.
The guards as usual are waiting, playing dumb.

Pigeon Chests and Alarm Clocks

I see the apple blossom puffing out its pigeon chest,
I see the clouds, dressed like doves, in down,
strips of corn and vines, a field of sunflowers
        goggling at the sky.
There are farms beyond the edge of town,
churches buttoning their jerkins neck high,
    and pines like thick brown showers.
I feel a heaviness, a dull weight on my breast.

We're off, we're off! Do you remember the excitement
when our parents visited their friends
in the next town? They bought us chocolates
        and bags of sweets to clutch
and took us to the station. I can hear the sounds
of tickets being punched, kids crying. I watch
    the hedges, banks and gates
all whisked away, a landscape of retracted statements.

The big cities are waiting on the line. Their backs
are turned to us. They plan their moves alone
without our help. Their streets are like cracked glass
        or folds in old dry skin.
In either case they crack. Their walls are bone
and just as brittle. The very air is thin.
    When we wake up we'll find the scenes we pass
wound up and ticking at the windows like alarm clocks.

Father in America

When father went off to America
he wore a white suit. Later he shaved his head.
Our ancient town burned white throughout the summer
and white flowers blossomed in the cemetery –
the flowers of course remain though he is dead.

It was everybody's most idyllic picture –
white suits against pale brick or amber corn,
and gentlemen and ladies in such posture
with parasols and petticoats in pastoral
benevolence before his head was shorn.

I fear shorn heads – I touch my own skull now
and feel skin pimpling in between the roots,
with father's skull beneath. I feel it grow
progressively more bulbous under mine,
his brain is still developing new shoots.

I feel, but know that feeling isn't knowledge.
The glass distorts in the amusement park,
your skirt blows high, you cross a swaying bridge,
you hear a scream, you stand before the mirror
and face your masters in the gathering dark.

I wish this train were going elsewhere but
a wish is powerless. The skulls appear,
one on top of another. The doors are shut,
and I'd be lying if the truth were told
on picture postcards, wishing you were here.

A Soldier
(after Károly Escher)

A young man with two flowers in his cap
Has turned away across the platform
To move towards two women wearing headscarves.
He is the country I am leaving.

175

He is beautiful, a beast decked and garlanded,
He stands gently and placidly, tall, slim,
Melancholy, prepared for sacrifice,
A peasant soldier, simple as they come.

Death has half closed his eyes
Ready to devour him at a blinking.
Behind his head the blur of a wagon pulling out.
He seizes one of the women, embraces her,

Presses himself against her.
As we depart I am tempted to shout
To attract his attention. I can only guess
The occasion of his death, his tenderness.

Border Crossing

You leave one body, enter another, thinner than
The one you wore. Having nothing to declare
The customs do not bother you. You pass
To other gravities, no longer man or woman,
But neuter as the clothes you wear
As thin and transparent as glass.

In the glass you see anatomies,
Bacteria and germs in broken places.
You see the future in slivers and shards,
Faint, farcical lobotomies.
I try to discover my disease in traces
Of tea leaves, life-lines, livers, tarot cards.

Impossible to read the auguries:

The future waits on fiercer surgeries.

*   *   *

A Greek Musée

When I look at my room I see powder. Life as a footnote
to unwritten literature. The chair with its thick varnish
picked up at a junk-shop, heading for a junk-shop,
is preparing, even now, to vanish.

A few thousand books gathering dust and amber
and half the books not read.
Literature is this torn old pair of slippers.
The plaster flakes and weals above my head

continually aspiring to the condition of literature,
the facets of a crystal. I listen to a record
knowing every voice on it is dead but breathes
volumes into my chaotic word-hoard.

I inhabit a communal Musée
des Beaux Arts where all things learn through error,
perfecting their falls from grace. I read the papers
for anthologies of terror.

And look, a shepherd watches a child fall
on to Greek soil, followed by the mother, followed
by a man's leg, followed it seems, by the sky.
Literature is Chicken Licken's fellow.

When I look at my room I see Greece. The bloody Gods
are resting on my two seater settee,
modelled on Habitat and falling to pieces now.
All will be patched up in God's new city,

all will be literature, as perfect as the armour
in the basement of the Fitzwilliam; the plates,
the pots, the pictures and samplers, and the drafts
of Auden, Spender, Tennyson and Yeats.

The Old Newspapers

I discovered Atlantis when I drowned.
It was a pleasant going down. My gutturals
were smoothed out as the sea rose higher
with all the colours of petrol.

Old warehouses of stuff from '51,
left over from the Festival of Britain,
faces from Ealing comedies, dead Sellers,
dead Hancock, a benign pattern

of cheerful decay. I heard the manic laugh
of Secombe and saw the exaggerated curve
of a girl's rump slipping behind the piano
crying, *I am what you deserve!*

(She squeezed her breasts to emphasise the point.)
Boxed gardens bristled with box and swam in a slough
of their own despond. Ducks, geese and chickens
would regularly plough

the soil to lead and silver. Up they drifted
and rose too, the dried kit of winter games,
flakes of dead grass, the smell of newspapers
with urgent crepuscular names:

the *Evening This and That*, the terraces
where headlines lost their vim, sodden
and mushrooming with fringed clouds in a cellar,
in a rhetoric forgotten

by Cassandras, Crossbenchers and Spot the Ball.
My face dissolves in print, a ticket
for the underground gone under.
I feel the weight of the pound in my pocket,

and know it to be the same, a green sea lettuce
wrinkling like a face, its lips pursed for the kiss
of fossilisation, knowing the softest leaf
must shrink and solidify to something like this.

Preludes

1

All evening I kept running over leaves –
their small dry hands were spiders scurrying
until I broke them. They were in a panic,
some cataclysm might have overtaken
the whole leaf population as I started
down a B-road behind the motorway.
East Anglia, Home Counties, darkened twisters
of hills, punk hedges, sleek old villages
in lamplight, shops with lawnmowers and chainsaws,
the distant sky a television glow
between high trees. I thought: this is my prelude,
the beginnings of a gothick fantasy,
half-pulp, half-mysticism, school-of-Palmer,
the understatement of an English landscape
whose skin is tight and heavy, lumps of shine
receiving a faint covering of moonlight.

2

It wasn't like this in the soft green books
of Dickson Carr, Ngaio Marsh and Christie.
The libraries, the dens, the inglenooks
have only ghosts to fear,
though when you look the moon is far from clear
and the moor is slightly misty.

How can you take a murder seriously
when everyone's in costume? Bumbling inspectors
stage their re-enactments with mysteriously
poor results. Old cars
are found abandoned under fields of stars
rusting away with harvesters and tractors.

A lack of motive, boredom, pressure, panic.
A television shivers into light
against an empty wall, with its babbling manic
insistence on being heard.
Whatever was going to happen has occurred
and is repeated hourly through the night.

3

A single man could creep out of the hills
and, moving purposefully, disappear.
A smell of petrol and an unlit car
on which the well-intentioned moonlight falls
with its mandate for restoring law and order.
The latest pastoral involves a murder.

Discarded anoraks, kagouls. The killer leaves
a trail of functional overgarments, camps
and boots, four empty tins from petrol pumps,
and, underneath the hedge, a pair of gloves,
reminders of the hands that broke from wrists,
a flaccid emptiness formed into fists.

Her hands, or someone's. As the leaves shake free
of barrel-loads of rain he sees her hands,
sole presences in stadiums, a stand
of favours, green and purple like the sea.
A pub winks in the distance. Music sweeps
across the fields: the damp grass bucks and dips.

He goes to ground and finds a hidden nickname –
Some rural creature, rat or mole or fox
which show him only their inhuman backs.
The earthworm fits him and invites him home
to supper where they share a piece of turf
and someone strangles him with his own scarf.

4

A lorry bent its head and seemed to graze,
a tall brick house backed on to CRODA GLUES
and the grass was rotting baize.
The fields of rape hummed at a ragged sky,
long strips of surgical tape were laid across
young lettuce. I watched the hulks of sleeping sheep emboss
a pasture, having dragged along the hedge
their trail of dirty candy floss.

A Pakistani read *The Yorkshire Mart*,
a headless windmill guarded British polder,
a shaft of sunlight opened like a guillotine,
and a white horse drank his own reflection
in a muddy field. Everywhere the green
retreated into dampness, growing colder
and colder, to a sub-zero diction
of bulletins that stirred my foreign heart.

FROM

BRIDGE PASSAGES

(1991)

Night Ferry

And our idea of hell is the night ferry.
A deep slow swell, the purser in his booth,
A thumping head no aspirin can soothe
And two or three lads quietly getting merry.

It's normal, that is all, the bottom line
Of nightmare, meaning nothing, emptiness
Which finds us though we leave it no address
And leaves a pain that art cannot refine.

It's almost three o'clock. The vessel rolls:
We draw our coats about us. The idea
Of sea enters our minds and washes clear
The bodies by their sink and toilet bowls.

Recording

A distant night train and a dog. Then crickets.
And fingers turning the leaves of a book.
Insects hover at the window. The hedges lean back.
Their curving arms are paths of rockets.

The final sensations are necessarily fragmentary,
like voices on a tape recorder repeating...
and there's the horror. Somebody goes on quoting
fragments, unattributable, without memory.

BRIDGE PASSAGES 1

Drawing the Curtain

'Observe the convolutions of this frieze.'
The voice comes to me like a tourist guide
explaining the explicable.
To slide your hand behind the stucco, seize
the mortar and move gently round inside
makes sensuous and tangible.

Curved galleries like zips, a moral fall
of stairs and liftshafts, and the flickering
inconsequentiality
of every human movement – material
and light – make an expanding, shapeless ring
of meaning and capacity.

An accident defines what breaks the heart –
the history of architecture, not of form
but aberration, lapse of taste,
the way an elevation tears apart
its brick integument before the storm
that lays the human pattern waste.

It is quite possible to love a face
the moment it appears and then is lost
in the darkness within windows, shut
within the belly of the commonplace,
that achieves the equivocation of a ghost
or a telephone with wires cut.

It turns to radios barely heard, until
the loud convergence of external moments
threatening familiar sound,
when history packs her bags and pays the bill
long owing, and the intimate events,
the lives of chairs and beds, are drowned.

Compulsive patterns of crude ironwork
in the glass panel of a door, the dangerous
geometry of aerials
on roofs the colour of air, and every quirk,
irregularity, each hint of madness,
are her discarded materials.

The miracles of value, allegiance, loss
are hardly different from a moving curtain.
A hand appears and a shape holds
a single space before they're drawn across,
and in that movement everything uncertain
hurts and gathers in the folds.

A Domestic Faust

Now come into the room. Turn on the light.
It's almost evening. Make yourself a drink.
The hiss of gas and the faint lisp
of match on sandpaper, the sudden bright
crown of quotidian fire, and then the sink
with answering crown and cusp;

the thrust of water like a rod of glass
that stuns enamel with its arrogance;
the breaking up and filling out,
the borborygmus of containers; mass,
acceleration, smell and permanence,
the ordinariness without

that turns to ordinariness within
in homely physics, domesticity.
Even of danger. When you strike
your head on a cupboard door or cut your skin
on paper you excite a kind of pity,
person and place being too alike.

You could be anywhere. Indeed you are
and always have been. It is where you go,
a mini-Mephistopheles,
a footling Faustus with familiar.
What ho, apprentice! What is there to know?
You are the master with the keys

to your own secret universe: a drawer,
a hidden box, addresses, numbers, names
and letters. All the magic charms
that gain you entrance to the inner core
of nothing/everything, the language games,
the smell of your underarms.

And far out there, responsibility
to every piece of unforgiving matter.
You run your hands across the bed
and look out from your window on the city,
draw the curtain, face the daily clutter
of the body beneath your head,

which I can't see from where I sit and gaze.
I know you are there, somewhere above
the traffic, neither near nor far
but in the middle distance which displays
a darkened rectangle that I must love
for itself and not for what we are.

The Flies

Forgive this garrulousness. As I write
a fat black fly crawls up the windowpane.
He feels the winter's over. Spring
anticipates itself and sets alight
worn patches of grass. The promise of warm rain
is like veins on a fly's wing.

And now the fly drops past the radiator.
The time is wrong for him. He scrambles up
fizzing furiously, leans
against the glass, revving up his motor,
then into gear and upwards. He can't stop
and think. His legs are small machines

that run until run down. I let him out.
The dot grows quickly smaller, disappears
in detail, in the dappled air.
Two distant birds swoop down and wheel about,
no bigger than flies. If I strain my ears
I hear their automatic whirr.

Look far enough, the human flies emerge...
I can't maintain this game of telescopes,
having never been a god
or sportsman though the hunting urge
lives in me too. I know the black fly gropes
towards his notion of the good,

his personal heap, however much it stinks;
that being here is an aesthetic choice
for those who have it, and for now
we are among this few. What the wall thinks
is my concern. We give the wall a voice.
The cut worm forgives the plough

and to the fly the plough is the cold wind
brewing beyond the Buda hills, the frost
making a belated entrance.
It's not the business of weather to be kind
nor of the market visitor to count the cost
of gypsies and of peasants.

Eternal polished faces a few streets off,
clutching embroidery or dogs for sale,
their arguments and raucous cries
exhorting us to buy the useless stuff
of lives which from here quickly lose their scale,
grow small and disappear like flies.

*   *   *

The Coolest Room in the City

This is the coolest room in the city,
three windows see to that, and leaves
like dark stains
lend a kind opacity
through which the whole room breathes,
and later when it rains

the windows answer anxiously,
knock for knock, and let the damp
cloud up the panes;
a cataract through which we see
reflections of a lamp
lit only when it rains.

Rooms are at their friendliest
when keeping something out. To sleep
is best. Bright chains
of water dangling at the breast
preserve their calm and keep
silence when it rains.

The Comfort of Rooms

The comfort of rooms is that they live within
and yet without the history of those
who walk across their carpets, wear new clothes
and shed their hair, bacteria and skin,
whose human walls are terrifying, thin
and useless as the petals of a rose.

An old man crawls down a short flight of stairs:
he's drying out, each time he smiles the cracks
across his face widen and come unstuck,
the paint flakes off his eyes, a muscle tears,
his marrow rattles in his bones, the layers
of vision shift in alarming parallax.

This is the parallax the windows learn
between their doubled panes. Their wings are tense,
prepared for flight, to carry the immense
hopes of the house beyond the known pattern
of its creatures. Look how the flowers burn
in the hot vase, desiring innocence.

BRIDGE PASSAGES 2

A Woman with a Rug

Three loud cracks. A woman with a rug
is beating it against the rails. A rich green
flares and droops from her hands, then snap!
it's gone. It is as if she'd pulled the plug
on the street: everything is quiet again,
back within its trap.

In the nearby theatre Tuzenbach's on fire
with one of his neurotic rhapsodies.
Irina draws away from him.
He's ugly and half German. They quickly tire
of his lolloping anxiety. They tease
him because he is vague and dim

even in a passion. He seems to miss
the tragic dimension which is rightly theirs,
their words and images,
the poems embedded in their memories.
He drifts and stumbles among chairs
down unlit passages

of dialogue. Meanwhile the woman tucks
the rug under her arm and looks across
in one of those lost moments
that can't be measured by the usual clocks,
so immobile and permanent, its loss
will never be noted in documents.

Neither will this. This moment and the next
have splintered into far too many sharp
small fragments. Unreclaimable
the bright green rug, the Baron's buried text.
Vermeer waits while time begins to warp
around his carpet-covered table

between the curtain and the string of pearls
held to the light but never quite in focus.
Irina, Masha, Olga freeze
against wild grass which has no time for girls.
The world of things remains as various
and indifferent as the leaves

in the garden which itself is lost, and where
the band is gaily signalling the fracture
of a life. A single crack is heard.
The human voice surrenders to the air:
the rug flares in the trap, its architecture
hangs clear and then is quickly blurred.

A Sea Change

Far down below in next door's yard a heap
of part-dismembered cookers. On the sixth floor
shelves of plants like trailing wires
and old toupees. They've entered the big sleep,
said long goodbyes. But that's not all, there's more,
the winter merely stores desires

under the bed, in envelopes or tins.
It is a time of scuttling, wrapping close,
watching the waves of pigeons beat
against cold air. Even now something begins,
if ever so quietly, something so various
it is impossible to repeat,

that happens only once each time, perhaps
once any lifetime, a sea change so immense
we cannot see it happen but
no one can stop thinking about it. The maps
are restless, all the boundaries are tense;
they have this feeling in the gut.

On the playground pingpong table someone scrawls
the words *New Fascists* with terrible irony.
The fearful and the ugly stalk
the spring as always. The fog's white terror calls
at dawn, remains with us. Its tyranny
lends dark edges to our talk,

but that won't stop us talking, listening.
The university bells begin to toll,
the central heating gurgles and ticks,
the starling chatters on and telephones ring
in nearby rooms. The world is audible
at last above its politics

and talks to itself. Behind the frosted glass
someone takes a shower. These things are done
precisely as before but feel
a little different now. The yellow grass
is its own particular shade. The railings run
more purposefully and reveal

precise configurations in the gaps.
It matters that you give things the right name
and measure their extent, their power.
It happens rarely. Now's the time perhaps
for understanding what remains the same.
The water thunders in the shower.

In a Strong Light

Behind the shower-curtain thunder sharpens
into light. The douche destroys
the human figure and does its best
to murder space. Everything that happens
is the echo of something else, which merely deploys
your shoulder and your breast.

The white striations shimmer without contour
exhaled in the relieved sigh
of water. You dissolve in pools.
The sun breaks on bare twigs in a winter
truce between opposing powers of grey.
Even as the body cools

the room still breathes its freshness and the scent
of soap continues to haunt the walls. Alone
the body loses resolution,
and feels at home in its abandonment.
The lost flesh settles down against the bone
with the lightness of a cushion.

To feel complete and disparate at once
is rarely possible. Think how the sun
breaks down a house yet makes it glow
in burning fragments or deconstructs a fence
into mere rhythm. All the harmony is gone,
but something leaps where shadows throw

their careless and flat members. Your body is warm
and slopes so gently. Hands have narrowed it
to wrists and ankles, formed the bolder
curvatures of your temple and your arm,
explored your ears, lovingly parodied
your brittle collarbone and shoulder.

To snap out of the body, find it stiff
or burned or crippled, to become objective
as sun or water are, will not
completely cancel out a world. And if
it did there'd still remain the live
arguments of the planet:

the child in the pushchair; quiet empty places
where the streets are full of dogshit; hats and shoes;
grotesques met in an underpass;
the delicate careful pity of faces
in memory or mirror; the everyday news
of bridges, trees and grass.

*   *   *

The Lost Money

I'm lying down flat on the floor just reading
when the money starts to fall out of my pocket,
not merely money – keys and tickets, shreds
of paper handkerchiefs – but it's the money
that appears most real, and I keep thinking
my pockets are not deep enough because it trickles
through my fingers even through the cloth,
and I remember or redream the time
a pickpocket once in the Tuileries
slipped her hand into my pocket and I
grabbed at it, her scrawny wrist
a fish fresh out of water, the coins like scales
spilling from my pocket till I wake.

If it comes to that I guess I've never known
the value of cash, unlike my parents,
one of whom was paid in lard, the other
perhaps in salt, I can't remember which,
and they were anxious that I might go hungry,
which was annoying then, particularly
since I felt guilty, having made them worry
about having to go and get more money,
and here I am at forty, vaguely aware
of something slipping from my pocket, a dream
or dreams which feel too much like cash,
but go on reading, gathering up loose change
and thinking it's all right and still not worrying.

Unlike I suppose the pair that I keep seeing
drifting about town. Let me describe them to you.
The man has a beard and lurches violently
from one place to another. His beard is short,
his face square. While she stands at the bus stop
in apparent indifference, he gets down on his knees
and peers between her legs, from front, from rear.
She stands unmoving, looks away. He lurches
again, growls at a passing woman, mutters,
then resumes his work. The bus arrives. He sways
on to the platform. She turns round, her cut lip
and bulging eye immobile, follows him.

Next time she stands before the subway entrance
and he appears behind a pillar, beckons,
and she starts to walk in his direction.
Her trousers are striped, her jumper a dull yellow.
In the nearby block a woman takes a dirt tray
down to the chute marked RUBBISH
and discovers a human couple in the primal
position. Darkness. A hasty pardon.
She withdraws. When he does, it is to piss
into the chute and when the pair pack up
they pass into the street, continue their game
of follow-my-leader. Her cheeks are heavy, swollen,
shining, faintly blue, her bruised lips bear
a faint glaze of saliva which disturbs me
as if loose change were spilling from her mouth.

BRIDGE PASSAGES III

Nachtmusik

Miraculous night when all the lights go out
except the bulbs on the high galleries,
and the radio spills its beans
of rattling music and surrounds the heart,
when the blood within the veins begins to freeze
into serene patterns.

The beautiful sad melancholy voices
of a conjectural landscape, Heimat. The lull
of belonging. To act,
to make things happen, to make choices
are all conditions of the beautiful
and the exact.

The air itself dissolves. The wind is pushing
it around so it changes consistency,
allows more rain, more light,
more darkness through. Nature keeps gatecrashing
the city parties, devalues the currency
of our affairs which legislate

for the predictable, the violence
of skin and fist, and the executives
of reason. Even nausea
begins in nature, and the elements
line up numerically like captives
in an alien sphere.

But music, what to do with you
now lights are out? You always simplify,
invoke. The crudest song
still rings a bell which echoes through
the system and proclaims that though we die
we nevertheless belong.

It doesn't tell us where, that is the catch,
the air always dissolves. The wind allows
the notes to congregate
then blows the gaff on them and leaves a snatch
of something without form. The empty noise
of radio waves. It's getting late.

I'm putting the words in order, miles away
from any sea. I read the papers through
and hear the creak of doors.
The foreign airs are moving: *lullay, lullay*.
The tune billows and scrapes. Such singers do
without accompaniment or scores.

Bridge Passage

You could be anywhere. The broken islands,
the excellence of fog from off the sea,
Well, I was there once, by the pier
where a loud amusement arcade lit the sands
and on the beach lay an abandoned body
and discarded tins of beer.

And the sea just went on mumbling as it does,
lightly clicking its tongue against black stone,
and everything was out there: lust
and loneliness, the neon razzmatazz
of passing time, and time too passing on
to things a passage can adjust.

But certainties remained beyond its range.
The rubbing away, the spartan cheerfulness,
the small talk of cold waves,
preserve an ambience from too much change
too suddenly unless, beyond the ness,
it rears the emptiness of graves.

The waves are ridges, roofs at their own pitch,
waiting in long queues. You move inland
with the incoming tide, arrive
at shallow docks and promenades, at rich
hotels and boarding houses, and the grand
perspectives of the downward drive.

Inland again. The trunk roads. Towns beyond
the motorway. The service station. Lights
and more lights. Lamplit necklaces
of roads in conurbations, brilliant blond
commercial signs. Estates and building sites
and po-faced sixties terraces.

196

Recounting these things tells you just what is,
a gazetteer with no particulars
in view but Europe's lingua franca
of luminous directions, boundaries,
and the fixed stare of endless waves of cars
cresting in truck and petrol tanker.

But this too tells you nothing, though behind
the roof-racks something glimmers. A thin line
where islands hang and stare at rings
of water vaguely pressing at some blind
corner where things must quickly find a sign
to live by, to remain mere things.

The Service of Remembrance

I still remember you. The oldest words.
You're sitting in the kitchen like a wraith
who passes easily through the wall.
You're weather now, part of the afterwards,
the having been. Yours is the narrow faith
that leaves me empty, insubstantial,

queasily watching the sea remove
a mouthful of small pebbles and then throw
back the remainder. A figure stands
by an open window. Outside the branches wave
to no one in particular. Their leaves blow
one way then another, hands

to match the one grasping the windowsill.
The slight breeze lifts a few hairs from your temple
in a kind of farewell gesture.
Some cars are crawling up the hill.
People are coming home. There is a simple
characteristic posture

against the moving world. What is memory
but scent wedded to immobility?
A man enters the house, a sparrow
flies on to his shoulders. This territory
is dangerously laced. It's not just pity,
but Eros, the boy with the arrow

who threatens the stillness here in Colindale,
in north-west London, anno imprecise.
He shoots the bird. The time we pass
has made us valuable, fit for sale
to one another at the knockdown price
of desire as common as grass.

So now I see the kitchen clear but can't
remember where the usual things are kept,
I can't find anything at all
though I know too well that something quite important
is hidden in the room, a life so stripped
it's almost frozen beyond recall.

And this is where we are, at least for now,
except today a quiet breathing heats
the window, whose wing opens
to movements of the air, and a light bough
is tossing in the wind and a few sheets
on the line lift their white hems.

*   *   *

APPROPRIATIONS

English Words

My first three English words were AND, BUT, SO:
they were exotic in my wooden ear,
like Froebel blocks. Imagination made
houses of them, just big enough to hang
a life on. Genii from a gazetteer
of deformations or a *sprechgesang*:
somehow it was possible to know
the otherness of people and not be afraid.

Once here, the words arranged their quaint occasions,
Minding their Manners, Waiting in the Queues
at Stops and Hatches. I got to know their walls,
their wallpaper and decorative styles,
their long louche socks, their sensible scuffed shoes.
Peculiar though: their enigmatic smiles
and sideways looks troubled my conversation
swimming in clouds above the steam of kettles.

You say a word until it loses meaning
and taste the foreignness of languages,
your own included. Sheer inanity
of idiom: the lovely words are dead,
their magic gone, evaporated pages.
But this too is a kind of spell: unread,
the vocables coagulate and sting,
glow with their own electricity.

I cannot trust words now. One cultivates
the sensuous objects in a locked museum:
their sounds are dangerous and must be heard
voluptuously, but behind thick glass.
Their emptiness appals one. One is dumb
with surprise at their inertia, their crass
hostility. They are beautiful opiates,
as brilliant as poppies, as absurd.

Salt

It begins in salt, a pinch of white
added to a mound on a tablecloth
in a friendless boarding-house, where she talks
of striptease and he looks vaguely embarrassed,
makes sucking noises with his mouth,
and hates the elaborately curtained and terraced
six-room establishment with its 60-watt light
and its proximity to coastal walks.

It begins here, eating out the centre
of the past, an indifferent turning-away,
leaving an ache for the vanished
that goes on vanishing, eroding under
wind and sea, an ancient fishlike bay,
a resort that ages badly and turns blander
with each year that heads for winter,
and still the story isn't finished.

Sealed tobacco tins and open drawers
of pale devices, magazines that burn
in hands, the smell of adult beds.
A lit room in a window, the reflection
of a boy writhing like a worm,
the black panes each with its clear section
of interior, of walls and doors
that bear the familiar burdens of his head.

This was the parental home the sea
brought in, its end in its beginning
tail-in-mouth eternally. This cold
and even light that levels out the tones
of summer autumn winter and the spring
within a narrow harmony of bones
and fossils will lend domesticity
to secret lives. And now they can be told.

Bodies

A brawny driver with enormous hands
is injured in an accident. At night
he shows his scar. His wife looks frail
as she describes the junction and the dark
where it all happened. Her eyes are bright,
dilate with impact, her shadow stark.
She begins to dance beside him where he stands –
immense, protective, vastly out of scale.

It is hard to know just where to place a thing.
A paper tissue blown against
a branch, the sea's seminal calm
shoving and caving. On the long settee
a couple smooches; a blonde-rinsed
girl, the man moustached and military
like a conjuror. They cling
together swaying palm to palm.

Every night a new performance.
Every night a new forging of links.
There's something in it quite methodical
and rather less than modest.
He wonders what the heavy driver thinks,
and what that frailness looks like when undressed,
what insinuations make palms dance
and how such largeness must be magical.

Like broken glass, the sea-spray
splinters, leaves her bodywork, her slap
of brakes. All couples are accidents,
mothers and fathers, bathers on the beach
among the towels in which they wrap
their changing bodies. They will teach
their children modesty. Their flesh is clay,
and kneadable. It smells of innocence.

Mr Reason

Dear Mr Reason, hook-nosed and Punch-jawed,
is nevertheless handsome and a hero
to the class of ten-year-olds who love to hear
his voice expand like an enormous football.
He is the ultimate inflated zero
of their short experience. Sometimes he'll call
on God in accents mild or cry him abroad
with trumpetry. He is their Chanticleer

and Unicorn. But now, hair powdered
by the blue dusk falling through the glass, he seems
an angel of some sort. The milk they hold
in their soft hands is what is drunk in heaven.
He speaks their names and summons them through dreams
of being good – Nigel, Sarvin, Trevor,
Jimmy, Wendy – tripping light-padded
among their words, gathering in his fold.

St Catherine's Lighthouse, Alum Bay, the Castle
where the king once slept. This miniature
isle of brightness is the heart of something
so indigenous it drags at small hearts
with reminiscences of furniture
in old men's rooms. There he too waits, a part
of sunlight, dusk, the seashore and the puzzle
of archaic words and comfortable singing.

His terror too: once in the pavilion
the groundsman found a mess, a human mess,
quite foul and brown, no bigger than an egg.
His furious inquest made them all ashamed.
But now well-being, warmth and doziness
creep over children pleased with being named
in Mr Reason's grace. Next afternoon
they'll hear a sermon by the Reverend Legge.

Miss Pickering

Miss Pickering, like a pickled walnut,
dithered among palettes, swam in a haze
of thin spittle, shrank behind glass
till she attained a precious quality.
She coaxed and rutted tiny words of praise,
A very nice thing, dear and *Oh how pretty!*
and her pearly eyes opened and shut
on the big room and swallowed up the class.

They would, if they could, have learned from her
some grace or delicacy, but colours ran
in grey pools over scored lines
that represented nothing and were graceless.
Their hands remained stubbornly simian.
They dreamed of running fingers over a dress
or exploring the intricacies of long hair
through endless and romantic lunchtimes.

The girls themselves were consciously superior.
Their bodies moved beyond Miss Pickering
answering questions she would never ask.
They'd take from her as much of delicacy
as they required, then pass on, leave her twittering
about the small bones of a leaf, or the lacy
complications of flowers. They saw much clearer
the powers around them and took larger risks.

I think of Miss Pickering dead, a needle in
the darkest of haystacks, of filigree,
of egg and dart, of finial and crocket
and the worrying precisions of needlepoint
like white foam stitched to the borders of the sea
riding its back astride the slopping paint.
It's something, after all, to sidle in
and keep a little in so small a pocket.

Seaside Postcard

The sea contracted to a water pistol
is pointed at a child's head and explodes
in laughter. It is autumn. Leaves litter
the pavements. Dry, they are as delicate
as dead skin. Even the wet roads
ignite under our feet and store the late
weak sun till evening comes. A dark pastel
obliterates them all. The nights are bitter

as fine chocolate and as sweet. The games
continue in and out of private gardens,
round fat public trees. Manners grow stiff
at neighbours' open gates. The scout huts beckon
their lost hearties: small boys, churchmen, wardens.
Front rooms fill with TV. The American
comics dance across the screen, trail names
of power through grey and white in low relief.

The child appears, wide-eyed as an icon,
learning the words, staring at a space
beyond the inner one of Now. He wears a comic
pullover, hair parted in horns of light.
The wind is striking at his open face,
gets in among the teeth. The sea is white
against the rows of houses, waves break on
walls and grey-green tide marks stain the brick.

The situation has been well prepared,
preserved in frozen worlds of *Beezers*, *Toppers*,
Beanos and *Dandys*. A dog leaps from a gate
with sharp teeth snapping, worrying at his heels.
The words have gathered in his heart like coppers
which can be spent now, freely. He appeals
for help, his hands extended, running scared.
His yell is comic and articulate.

A Picture of My Parents with Their First Television

I see them before the television, the proud owners
of a wooden case in which the four-o-five
presents its milky versions of success
with the last official faces of a time
that was always more dead than alive,
when Hanratty cleaned the windows and a crime
was solved by men with briefcases and bowlers,
when gentlemen made jokes in evening dress.

They fought their way to this, to Lady Barnett
to Bernard Braden and John Freeman, Kathie Kay
and Alan Breeze, to all those names of power
that solved nothing but could somehow fill
the hours before they slipped away
to private lives which grew more private still,
past old reliable faces by which they set
their clocks precisely to the latest hour.

Some blurred depth in their eyes won't come to rest:
perhaps they're trapped in what they bought,
in all their trappings, in the slim white frame
of the square photograph they sent back home
to show the television. Now they're caught
and solemn. Slowly they become
the stillness by which they are both possessed.
They're listening intently for a name

which once had power, on lips that formed the sound
in darkened flats, in beds in which they slept
and touched each other. Some act of violence
has pitched them here before the screen.
The actors know their speeches, are adept
at pulling faces, know when to go. They've been
elsewhere and are there still, on neutral ground,
of which this patch of grey is evidence.

Losing

We lose each other everywhere:
the children in department stores
return as parents, *fils et père*
collide by the revolving doors.

The pavements' litter, burning flakes
of bonfires, tickets and franked stamps,
the fragile image drops and breaks,
the fugitive awakes, decamps.

The carriages uncouple, trucks
return unladen, suits appear
on vacant charitable racks,
the shelves of darkened stockrooms clear,

skin lifts and peels. A cake of soap.
The human lamps, the nails, the hair,
the scrapbooks' chronicles of hope
that lose each other everywhere.

*   *   *

BRIDGE PASSAGES 4

A Game of Statues

The pond seems to be still, but everywhere
small points of tension gather and stretch.
Dead leaves float in cowls.
The slab breaks up. The foil begins to tear.
The grass is smeared with snowdrops, bluebells, vetch.
The air is a parliament of fowls.

Broad avenues and city parks are dressed
to kill. Houses put on airs and graces.
A hidden population of statues
emerges from the shadows to be pressed
between the brickwork till the terraces
are packed with ancient vices and virtues

pouting and posturing. Their breasts and biceps curve
against the sunlight which first called them out,
even the crippled ones assume
survival rights. Forsaking their reserve,
they brandish their stigmata. Blank faces shout
from pediments, burst into bloom.

An air of celebration. Time replies
with memory. She mounts a ruined staircase
through heaps of rubble. She has come
back from the camps and wagons to surprise
the world. Each broken window wears her face,
her footsteps are a muffled drum.

She knows what she has to do. No need for food,
affection is the cure: the street's hot breath
on neck and earlobe, words and sighs.
They let her go. The air in the room is good
but better still to pass through it, through death,
to this demi-paradise

of iron, stone and stucco. Across the city
thousands are marching past, and poking heads
and arms through niches, waiting there
for common symbols of eternity.
Think of them struggling in their vertical beds
against the continual nightmare

of the wall. The whole street seems to pose
and catch the light. Across the ruffled pond
birds are frozen into screams
of joy. A single, vaguely comatose
statue holds real flowers in her hand.
The flowers are dying as she dreams.

Street Entertainment

The March wind turns up suddenly and shreds
loose canvas on the awnings. Inverted flames
of cloth billow and long to escape
the world of definitions. Even people's heads
seem to be on fire, grow lion's manes,
echoing some comical shape

of terror. These are territorial wars.
You half expect them to rise and spit at each other
just as the rain is doing now,
to arch their backs and growl. Well, here are cars
hunched and growling, part of the same weather,
low clouds learning to bellow

with best or worst. You should have expected this.
You should have worn your coat or slipped the brolly
into your pocket. They are so neat,
so easy to carry. The weather has given notice
it intends to change. It thinks of human folly
as a faint tickling under its feet.

The street entertainers are out. One old beggar
blows his harmonica so faintly the sound
is blown back in his face. A boy
with a recorder stands before a figure
of Mercury, with his schoolcap on the ground
like an abandoned toy.

The ones that interest me are a pair
dressed vaguely as musketeers, in puritan hats
and rose pink gowns. They wield
long sticks. They do nothing but stare
at the growing crowd, till someone puts
a coin into the box, when a wild

mechanical movement seizes them and they
are frozen once again in attitudes
of sinister aggression.
Their faces mimic something, yet are empty.
A girl runs between them and poses. The crowd
laughs at her silly expression.

I'm merely a reporter whose truth lies
in diction clear as water. In the pool
which I imagine by my shoes
I try to see my features, read my eyes.
It ripples. My face is indistinguishable,
the water darkens like a bruise.

National Anthem

The spring begins an age of festivals:
the outbreaks and foundations, liberations,
appointed days, appointed modes
of putting on. The flags hang from the walls.
The weather bustles by. The operations
of the state. The empty roads.

The corridors too are empty though the sun
has laid its fingers underneath each door
to beckon us out. It's quiet:
something bothers the sky. Something remains undone.
April now but it could be May: Nature
that great abstraction is set

before us: small green arguments of leaves,
the proclamations of blossom on each branch,
the flowers with their furious dance.
Meaning! Meaning! they jostle, Whoever believes
in us, must give us meaning! An avalanche
of meaning! Let us have significance!

They shimmer and shake in silence before windows,
in tall black rectangles beyond which only
gods and geometricians see.
I too am sitting in one. Windows close
and open, doors swing to. There is nobility
in loneliness and vacancy,

but meaning too is rooted in a place,
is like a statue always looking past
the same old clump of trees
winter and summer, the same look on its face.
How long can faces at the windows last?
They disappear by slow degrees

each disappearance quick in its own terms.
Mother, father, child. They call out names
that no one understands but them.
They wear their universal forms,
their worn-out clothes. The sunlight frames
each figure like a theorem.

We're here, such as we are. We will be missed.
Some children gather opposite, look down
into the courtyard where
music's playing. A lone saxophonist
proffers the national anthem. The notes are blown
random, slow, into the air.

*   *   *

The Chairs

Where did you stay that winter?
(Singapore? Hyderabad?)
No, we waited in the snow,
All dressed up, nowhere to go.

Where did you sit while waiting?
(In a taxi? In a train?)
We took the armchair from the hall
But did not feel we'd moved at all.

What did you think of, waiting?
(Summer sun and fresh sea air?)
All we thought of was the end
Of summer and the north-east wind.

But didn't you sing while waiting?
(Christmas comes but once a year.)
We ourselves, we couldn't sing
But we heard others carolling.

Then sing now. What have you to sing?
We'll sing of leaving. When we've gone
You can do as we have done.
Here's a chair for sitting on.

BRIDGE PASSAGES 5

Rain

Rain all night. Those sitting in the roof
can hear it talking but they cannot tell
the nature of its message.
It broods and blows, gathers, grows smooth
and seamless. In the stairwell
and the basement passage

it spreads as damp, the closing smell of sweat.
A fly is buzzing round and round. You wouldn't think
a creature small as that
could emit so thick a blare. It deals in threat
and sings of filth. You seem to hear the stink
of old outhouses and dried shit.

Those who speak are moving in the houses,
closing doors, wiping their faces. One picks up
a paper, another puts one down.
Familiar looks, good nights. A car cruises
by outside. Lost and out of step,
history leaves the empty town.

The rain is a mad typist clattering out
endless streams of letters without a break,
littered with quaint symbols
You can't pronounce the words, nor can you shout
for lack of vowels. The language starts to ache
and slowly crumbles.

If rain talks it talks nonsense. We lie beside
each other on the bed and think of all
who lie there listening.
Bodies and bodies and the rain outside.
The small intimate whispers of the wall.
The loud fly's translucent wing.

Chinese White

Do you remember that scene in Ashes and Diamonds *where*
the hero rushes forward through the clotheslines and bleeds
to death among the sheets? Or was it
in Canal *(I can't remember now.) A square*
of white turns slowly red. The redness fades
to black and white. The picture is a composite,

a form of poster. The War, the Resistance,
something about betrayal, all mixed up
in a child's mind who didn't see
the war, for whom it is a haunting presence
of sheets and blood. An image hangs and drops
in a grey passageway or alley.

His name was Zbigniew, and he wore dark glasses,
and later he jumped from a train (a true life fact)
because, well, Poles are like that,
they get drunk, morose, et cetera. The girl who kisses
the boy was blonde as always. Was it an act
of bravery him getting shot

or cowardice? We could look it up in books
but that is not the point (we pull our serious face)
but something in the falling, the how
and where of it. And so wherever one looks
the same old images return and find their place,
a square, an alleyway, a row

of ordinary houses suddenly still and hot
and people falling lying as if on a square
of film. You see the victim's head
as someone aims and shoots him, and you cut
to tanks or bodies or a sheet hung out to air,
a white square slowly turning red.

Funeral Oration

The objects are on stage: their shadows link.
The sunlight turns the towel opposite
into the likeness of a man,
but the gallery is empty, on the brink
of someone's entrance. Empty chairs sit,
waiting. Someone draws a curtain.

Perhaps they'll step out and sit down. Perhaps
a child, more likely the blind woman who
has always lived here. The ledge
is hung with assorted greenery that drips
between the iron. Leaves bubble through
the railings. Somewhere there's a bridge

between the actor and his ghosts. A voice.
Some trick of speech. A broken window speaks
like tinkling glass, a bullet spits
into a cherub's puffed and vacant face.
Even the old rusted awnings creak
in chorus. Everything falls to bits,

the plaster and the stairs, the life within
the rooms, but one still steps out for a breath
of fresh air on the gallery.
It is as if he stepped out of his skin
or casually walked out of his death,
past the neat artillery

of railings, past the chairs, until he found
the one reserved for him, that had been waiting
like an open vowel
to close beneath him. And when the light turns round
you begin to see the human form, the sitting
figure hidden in the towel.

*　　*　　*

A Walk Across Fields

(for Winifred Upchurch)

Not to have known the landscape was my loss —
a scoop of cloud held all the land, the sky
was panes of glass, and rain in quiet gutters
shook like leaves.

The streets for walking, rooms for dreams, the grass
in parks for small adventures: one could die
in forests, magic castles, doorways, broken shutters,
in urban graves

where books held all the secrets. Wind blows across
the river. The trees are bending. Thick clouds lie
like wadding on them. Distant predators
move in droves

beyond the bands of rain. The sleeping palace
wakes to potent thunder. The children dry
their clothes. I think of parents, grandmothers,
the natural loves.

BRIDGE PASSAGES 6

Burning Stubble at Szigliget

We stepped out on the balcony. The sky
had grown romantic and the breaking pods
and stalks were rapid volleys of light.
The air was damp, but somewhere it was dry
as fury, spitting heat. The little roads
were silent and the trees clung tight

to the black park, which had for years been theirs.
The statues held their poses even though
no one was there to see them, lost
in dark and dark grey, minding their own affairs.
The alien world lay immediately below,
and waited patient at its post.

Deep alizarin crimson, bleeding down
to ochre, orange, yellow. Spectacular
colours and a crackling rain
which wasn't rain but something overthrown.
The light was falling like the morning star:
the sons of light were dark again.

On lamp-posts, upside down, hung shrunken skins
which once were men. Tractors like tanks appeared
and crushed the street to crisp white flour.
A woman was kicking a corpse. The thin grey curtains
of smoke trembled and behind them cleared
a space for buildings and a shower

of broken stucco. A sentence broke apart,
each word a promise made in any street
and broken here. I couldn't sleep.
Beyond the park I heard the firing start
and the snap snap snap was tiny running feet
of shrews and mice, of lives held cheap.

Well, it was tidy and the cheapness ours,
our cheap hands on the pillars, our cheap eyes
seeking the heart of flames between
the foreground darkness. Now for a few hours
the fields would burn and the tall smoke would rise
as delicate as mesh to screen

the lake beyond the fields, the towns astride
the motorway, high white estates like teeth,
the factories, our balcony,
and all the others who had come outside
to stand by blazing windows ranged beneath
the rolling smoke, the thin grey sea.

Wild Garden

Vadkert. The wild garden. Sunlight. Notations
on a stave, an airless music in the ears
of bridges, masonry and trees
which spread themselves like railway stations,
heading off towards the park to hear
plain footsteps, plain itineraries.

But who are these, these wild ones in the garden,
the calves and chickens, peacocks, ducks and rams
at whom pre-conscious children wave
fistfuls of crumbs, for whom the old unburden
themselves of stale loaves? Why do the rattling trams
carry them both towards this grave

ceremonial greenness? Such incongruity
is simply another game of let's pretend
that nothing happens. It calls you back,
reminds you how you too felt gravity
tugging at your spine like an old friend
who gave you a playful smack

then set you up again. A mother waits
by an empty push-chair. Her child puts a finger through
the chicken wire. Birds peck at it
disappointed. The menagerie congregates
around us, black, white, purple, peacock blue:
brilliant and profligate.

Happiness is very simple really,
it flows out of the horn of plenty, abundant
as rain or grass but wilder, rarer
than the rainbow. Are you here with me?
Will you stand beside me for ever, as constant
as these farmyard birds and fairer

than the peacock, startled and beautiful,
with with his improbable Japanese elegance?
In the city they're counting votes
and learning how to speak. Feel gravity pull
your sleeve to closer acquaintance with all gardens.
From this distance you may make notes

on the society of worms and ants and clods
in their private infinity of lives
lived in terror of the creatures
of the garden. And beyond them lie the woods,
the lakes, the sea and the enormous waves
on which we inscribe our human features.

In Memoriam Sándor Weöres

I met him only once. So light and grey,
his handshake hardly registered. He might
have been a speck of household dust,
his absence the most palpable quality.
He settled in the chair and made a slight
noise, as if he'd caught a crust

of dry bread in his throat. He signed my book
in a childish trembling hand. He was depressed.
His cat had died. He could hardly speak
but smiled, shyly, vaguely. He had the look
of a February morning, waiting, dressed,
for some final naked event to break,

when he, at last, could be that sublimate
his body had aspired to, simply vapour
burning above a mound of ash.
But this would be a pyre to celebrate
his substance – words and pen and ink and paper
all the luminous trash

of magic and art. The conjuror could take
a parasol and out of it create
an ecosystem, or beneath
the parasol, meander in the wake
of *realpolitik* and contemplate
its dreadful colonnade of teeth.

His invented psyche was both male and female.
Two breasts had risen somewhere in his breast
like towers, so that when he took breath
two bodies rose and fell with it. His pale
shadow left the boy, the light caressed
his skin. He couldn't tell life from death.

He never was good company, would disappear
without one noticing and be discovered
wrapped in a blanket on the tramline
in the middle of the night. He never was there
and nowhere else. Everything he suffered
glowed in the language, turned to wine,

but such a wine as city children, bred
in stinking courtyards, would find in the street,
and when they drunk it, they would know
their nonsense validated by the dead.
He was the poet they'd queue up to meet,
in whose lost shadow they could grow.

*   *   *

Two Rondeaux

1 *Unter den Linden*

In Unter den Linden and Wenceslas Square
the candles wink their *laissez-faire,*
people are trampling over borders,
packing their luggage. Cassette recorders
hiss like steam in the cold air,

cameras roll and spokesmen prepare
brief noncommittal statements, tear
pages from notebooks and wait for orders.
Prisons open: prisoners and warders
    mix in Unter den Linden.

In Prague and Budapest they wear
rosettes, wave flags. A furious year
gathers to a close. The wind disorders
ships of state and fleets of boarders.
Men link hands, dance and boldly stare
    across Unter den Linden.

2 *Clumsy Music*

A clumsy music: years lurch on
and fugitive clocks on the run
must settle debts by Hogmanay.
At Christmas guilty parents pay
the devil who pays debts to none.

Important things remain undone,
the boxes open: one by one
their ghosts are spirited away:
the piper stands by set to play
his clumsy music,

artificial yet homespun,
a rondeau much like this, begun
in hope as much as fear, to lay
his fears and keep wild hopes at bay
with dancing, linking hands, best done
to clumsy music.

FROM

BLIND FIELD

(1994)

BLIND FIELD

When we define the Photograph as a motionless image, this does not mean only that the figures it represents do not move; it means they do not emerge, do not leave: they are anaesthetized and fastened down, like butterflies. Yet once there is a punctum [detail], a blind field is created...on account of her necklace, the black woman in her Sunday best has had, for me, a whole life external to her portrait.

ROLAND BARTHES, Camera Lucida

An Accident

You're simply sitting down. It's getting late.
The sky is a thick slab of premature dark,
metallic, of imponderable weight.
And noises start: a scratch, a whoosh, a bark.

Sometimes you read of accidents: a child
killed in a car, a freak wind raising hell
in an obscure American town, wild
storms of atoms raging inside a shell,

and it's like the room is just too full of you,
your senses, your own presence in the chair,
your breathing hands and feet, all pressing through
a visible integument of air.

I watch you sitting down as on a stage.
The accident begins. You turn the page.

Inuit

I have fallen in love with this baby
whose empty eyes and wrinkled mouth
appear to be essence of baby,
his death a perfect pathos
without sentiment, still as a photograph
of stillness, without potential energy,
with how he looks and does not look at me.

Could he be the Christchild under an Eskimo moon,
part moon himself with pitted eyes,
proverbial round cheese, a comforting thing
in uncomforting space, registering surprise
at the thingness of anything and everything?
And why is he more touching than any live baby?
More nocturnal, more animal? And might he wake up soon?

I hit a deer once, doing a steady lick
at dead of night. Its quivering body
was a thousand startled eyes. I didn't see him fall
but felt his dark soft leg, a heavy stick,
hammer briefly at my metal sheath
then disappear as we sped on, unable
to adjust to his appearance, or
the knowledge of his death.

It was on the brow of a hill. We were heading north,
the notional arctic, but would later bend east
toward Norfolk as the sky lightened. I want to speak light
for the baby, that he might understand. Let him at least
hear the noise of our passage over the earth
and watch the live deer crashing out of sight.

Elegy for a Blind Woman

1

The house beautiful was no longer beautiful
yet high pink walls and recessed panels were gentle
and the lift was an old woman who would forget
where she was, and dark incidental

figures on landings hesitate in the sun
before doorways and kitchens with pans and bare
pipes that snaked free of walls before passing on
behind ornamental railing, down into the stair.

If there were children in apartments below
or above hers they were like pigeons that roosted
briefly on balconies. One wouldn't quite know
when they had arrived but would find them clustered

then flown, or hear – not exactly their voices –
but pittering feet and small beaks. They were
really children and elsewhere, with tangible faces
in a world quite real though invisible to her.

2

Unobserved, unadmonished, the china boy
embracing the china girl's ankle was daring,
while she, for her part, pretended not to enjoy
his attention though one could see by what she was wearing

that she was made for it. Her mother's eyes
stared piteously down at all she could not see:
letters on the cupboard, spoons on tables, dead flies
on windowsills, her hand on her own knee,

and two dead husbands, visible in her head,
the last one kindly, with large yellow teeth,
a bald, rubber-lipped darling of a man. Instead
the cassette player with its stories, the death

of time, the tapping about in the kitchen, the loud
coarse voice she discovered in her throat and the panic
at any small loss. She moved through a hostile crowd
of animate objects, in a darkness thick

with temper. Even her friends were impossible,
and her stethoscope fingers trembled with fury
for moments on end. Their obtuseness, the trouble
they caused not realising her injury,

whole seconds wasted looking for words, and the kind
woman smiling piteously down, also infuriating
because unseeable, like furniture in the mind
which mind keeps moving about, disorientating.

3

She was never lovely, but once as a child
she was sent to a lycée and she returned plump,
delicious, mature, speaking fluent French,
and there was something about her skin and clear eyes

which was perhaps lovely. Later her pebble glasses
misted at weddings, froze in brutal February ice
and there never were children. The greyness set in
as everywhere in the country, with fevers, opiates,

thin chalets on the hill, a uniform dereliction.
Behind the screen children did not touch
her dangling hand, let alone kiss it. Grey
turned to black or whatever colour she called it,

red sunlight, lilac cold, sepia tablecloth.
Her brother came, glistened, fidgeted, died
like the ancien régime which seemed now almost
benevolent, rubber-faced, like an ugly child

in a house without fabulous statues or butlers,
where the sun would hesitate on the landing,
clear its throat and pass on, out of the yard,
across the green park, heading for the river.

Window

Out of this single moment a window opens
and out of the lens or the gun a sadness spurts,
and all the broken glass and the spent cases,
the taps and sinks, loose shutters and other patterns
assume a statuesque pose, turn stone faces
to the present whose silence hurts
because it's sweet with the smell of distance.

The dead swim through their pictures. Their grey water
soaks our hair as we dream of where we were
while others are still fighting, smoking, posing
before buildings in an unexplored quarter
of the city and a shutter keeps opening and closing
to trap them in mere words, but our lips blur
as they meet and there is nothing left to tell.

FOR ANDRÉ KERTÉSZ

Two Aunts Appearing

An old woman in an empty square:
a man approaches her at the far corner.
It is the winter of the year after the commune.
The trees open their mouths and gasp for air.

An emptiness is working through her bones
like acid through a zinc plate, drawing
a blueprint of veins,
lost clear shapes, skin-scaffoldings.

Two heavy black aunts flap free
from under her black scarf, a generation
of brittle bones and headscarves,
part of a conspiracy

to colonise the squares and streets of the mind
with remorse. But they are tender:
their legs are thin glass monuments that sway
with the gentle nudging of the wind.

The Accordionist

The accordionist is a blind intellectual
carrying an enormous typewriter whose keys
grow wings as the instrument expands into a tall
horizontal hat that collapses with a tubercular wheeze.

My century is a sad one of collapses.
The concertina of the chest; the tubular bells
of the high houses; the flattened ellipses
of our skulls that open like petals.

We are the poppies sprinkled along the field.
We are simple crosses dotted with blood.
Beware the sentiments concealed
in this short rhyme. Be wise. Be good.

Hortus Conclusus

A woman feeding geese might sit like this,
in a walled garden with rabbits and birds,
and an angel come and purse its lips for a kiss
speaking air instead of words.

And so the child was born, out of the air
and a scroll flew like a pennant to proclaim
the kingdom to which he was heir,
where everything was white and had a name.

Now languages dissolve I'll start again
with shadows, touch and sight.
I'll reinvent a world of geese whose reign
will seek new synonyms for white.

The Voyeurs

What are they staring at? Haven't they seen enough?
Perhaps it's natural to stare at backs.
Just as we pass a lighted window light makes
visible that wealth of alien stuff
of which half our minds are made,
leaving us lustful, lost and afraid.

They too are in transit. Look at his hat
(a straw boater), her headscarf (a long
inverted flame), the way their clothes hang.
There must be a hole in the wooden slat
and beyond it something perfectly new
and terrifying that light will not let through.

Voluptuousness

I think of a child dancing along a faint chalk line;
the sound of his feet, the flop of his hair, and his breath
a short skipping rhyme of tumbling aspirates.

The small knotted belly, the slightly sweating thigh,
the damp neck and palm, and nearby on a bench
a mother or elder sister rich in voluptuousness.

My sister is an enclosed garden. In the garden
the soft wickerwork of worm casts, black earth nipped
into buds, scored into clefts and crevices.

On windy ways a dancing underground.
Inside the bones unsettling swathes of thought,
the mind exposed to crisp surgical fingers

that pinch it into song, the local floods
of swollen veins whose banks cannot contain
their discontent. I think of my two children

swept along those waves, arriving where they are
at pianos and computers, before their mirrors,
their eyes illegible, a foreign writing.

I was once a child too, leaning over the edge of the pram,
examining my brother like a specimen, with my mother
behind the lens, her face hidden, rich in voluptuousness.

Passenger

A long stop at a hot provincial station.
Heat turns to dirty water, little jewels
of smut, rivulets of perspiration.

The light crowds close, concentrates in pustules,
drops of poison, off-white, plump, opaque,
suspending grit in a soup of molecules.

The trees too are hemmed in. Their heads ache
in deserted railway yards, among lines
of empty wagons in sidings. They bake

in powders, asphalt heaps, among faded signs
announcing factories with broken windows,
wreathed in smears of smoke, in the confines

of yards with scatterings of scrap iron, rows
of used flasks abandoned years ago
to trucks blocking gates that neither open nor close.

                    *

The girl is far too smart. Her wrists are bare,
uncluttered. She wears four finger rings,
a thin gold anklet. How clean she is. Her hair

is neatly bobbed and shining. All her things
declare a certain distance: the delicate shoe,
the lycra top, the jet black pants' rustlings

and foldings. Even her scarlet nails look new.
But not her book, the *History of France*,
an ancient faded copy. She's half-way through

and turns each page with an impatient elegance.
Despite the carriage's wild jolts and swings
the book on her knee maintains its precarious balance
and this, as Holub tells us, gives her wings.

FOR DIANE ARBUS

Paragons

Those with two heads know something you don't
DIANE ARBUS

Distrust everything – especially the happy face,
the successful face, the face with something solid
stacked behind the eyes. Locate instead the scapegrace,
the lost and the squalid,

those who have nothing to say with the eyes but the eyes
are open and inward or are lost down a well
where you look down the shaft to find them and their faces rise
like your own in the circle

of water, with lips large as dinner-plates: the man with a tail,
the man who smoked cigars with his eyes, the Siamese twins
in Hubert's or Huber's where there is neither male nor female
but paradigms and paragons

that tickle your guilt and your pity. You say: I don't want
to make you cry, but when the button's there you press it.
And it's true that those with two heads know something you don't,
only you guess it.

On a Young Lady's Photograph Album

*The parents seem to be dreaming the child and the child
to be inventing them*
DIANE ARBUS

We don't finish smaller and clearer as the years go by
but blurrier, vaster, ever more unfocused, full of grains
that dance before the face, evaporating in a sky
of rising cloud, and what remains
is perhaps a voice saying (for instance) 'mother'.
Even appearance becomes something other

than imagined, something between the atoms, like a rift
between lovers, one that must be filled with bodies or words
and a peculiar tenderness. We watch as clouds drift
behind the face, and afterwards,
as the face slowly dissolves, the contradictions
settle in to be resolved in gentle fictions

of families, of children with their pets, and of spaces
with the smell of the past trapped in their unstable walls,
of doors that open on nothing in rambling palaces
where Disney's Sleeping Beauty falls
asleep and the ivy is your mother's long hair
blown into tangles that strive against the air.

The Baths on Monroe Street

> *You're carrying some slight magic which does*
> *something to them. It fixes them in a way*
> DIANE ARBUS

At the baths of Monroe Street two women are crying.
The walls are patched and blistered like Eliot's Jew.
Decades of steam. The carpet is wet through
with feet or with tears and the matrons are dying
of cancer or disappointment, their hair crimped in sheets,
their broad bosoms swaying over stomachs arranged in pleats.

In a sudden fury Alice begins. She launches a volley
of clicks at the mist and the leery disappearing
smiles of a hundred Cheshire Cats who may be hard of hearing
but know an assault when they see one. Like a reveille
the cry goes up to wake the dead, and the dead rise
out of the walls and the water with terrible answering cries.

Ah love let us be true to one another! they wail in the steam
of the baths, remembering their Matthew Arnold. The towels snap
as they descend on the savage intruder, the teeth also snap
and the air's full of flesh. They can see the gleam
of the lens, which is Alice in action, and they close in
as all nightmares do, on those who are rigid or frozen.

They take the instrument from her (and who after
all can blame them? Because theirs is a life not to be opened
like a tin of sardines, because they feel they own what has happened
and goes on happening to them as they totter and fall
on the slippery carpet) and by the time their energies fail
the camera is drowned in a cleaner's convenient pail.

Bichonnade

– that we may wonder all over again what is veritable
and inevitable and possible and what it is to become
whoever we may be
DIANE ARBUS

The Mystic Barber teleports himself to Mars. Another carries
a noose and a rose wherever he goes. A third collects string
for twenty years. A fourth is a disinherited king,
the Emperor of Byzantium. A fifth ferries
the soul of the dead across the Acheron. There's a certain abandon
in asking, Can I come home with you?

like a girl who is well brought up, as she was, in a fashion,
who seems to trust everyone and is just a little crazy,
just enough to be charming, who walks between fantasy
and betrayal and makes of this a kind of profession.
It takes courage to destroy the ledge you stand on,
to sit on the branch you saw through

or to fly down the stairs like Lartigue's Bichonnade
while the balustrade marches sturdily upward, and laughter
bubbles through the mouth like air through water,
and the light whistles by, unstoppable, hard
and joyful, though there is nothing to land on
but the flying itself, the flying perfect and new.

THREE CHANDLERESQUES

The Big Sleep

A perfect bubble of space floated above him.
A pool opened
at his feet and he dived in.
Eyes of glazed terracotta swam in dim
wreaths in a building like a church. What had happened
to Marlowe? Some Mickey Finn

been shot into his veins. The stillness froze
to further stillness,
the cold grew jaws.
A library like Michelangelo's
stretched its long neck before him. A stewardess
showed him through doors

into a courtyard where the statues talked
in stern-sweet voices,
an orange tree
fountained at the centre and a baby milked
its mother's breast with gentle and precise
movements while she

glanced sadly up at him with the sea in her eyes.
You're doing fine
Marlowe. Now do
the difficult thing. Get up and walk. To his surprise
the ground stood firm, longing to be defined
by his feet, so he walked through

into his own heart's aching and felt strong,
a youthful Marlowe
like a tune blown
by a child on a whistle. Then what sounded wrong?
No more perhaps than a strange voice in his window.
Maybe his own.

The High Window

White light, grey stone. That solving moment when
a thought appears
and settles on
a landscape, amplifies some hidden pattern
of trees, unscrambles the clouds and clears
the face of a pale sun.

Windows divided between transparency
and reflection,
the giving back
and the absorbing of vision, the hard currency
of what exists and what remains unknown
between white and black.

Winter sunlight on walls, light frost on grass;
the dripping distant
call of birds in leaves
in a bare forked garden behind glass,
perfect, lost, and no more important
than passing waves.

Daydreaming, Marlowe? Better than nightmare
this lit column
between annuncee
and angel, in a perspective of the air,
with blue hills, quaint flowers and a solemn
Latin delivery;

better sanity than madness, at least to be saner
than we sometimes are;
better the calm
rules of proportion, of *pietra serena,*
than the preaching of mad monks or the dictator
with his long arm.

The Lady in the Lake

Their bodies were straddled along the road:
not spartan men,
their spoils of war
were bodies taken out and spoiled, a heavy load
of shopping in a drift of plastic bags, a bargain
from the big store.

Black warriors in Pompeii skins, black holes
in further space, holed
like ships, not sinking.
One death is a thousand deaths. The rolls
of honour are full of names that grow cold.
You are thinking

too much, thought Marlowe as he waited for the car
to rise from the lake.
One death is all you need.
The face is washed away. The particular
becomes the general. Easy to mistake
the pretty head

for dough, the upper for the nether lips.
Too Jacobean
Marlowe. Consider
the fate of Marsyas whose narrow strips
of skin wailed like a high-pitched organ
over the ladder

of his ribs. Consider even that woman
filling her mouth
with pills, going down
in her holed ship, still trying to summon
the images that sank her, a truth
with which to drown.

*   *   *

TRANSYLVANA

(for Peter Porter)

Sylvan meant savage
W.H. AUDEN

We're here to look for something, perhaps a house
buried half in the hill, with damp walls,
a jutting terrace and a long view across

the park to an artificial lake. Snow falls
on the branches and a surface of sheer ice
where a mob of skaters wheel and weave white petals

frilled with crystals, Transylvanian lace.
My mother's home town. The trees are thick with green.
Summer. Somewhere, in another place,

the skaters move to a frozen music between
the trees, performing a slow dance along the brink
of a precipice that cannot be seen

from where they are. They are lines of ink,
impossible to read now. A fountain jets
snow. The bandstand is a skating rink

full of toy soldiers. Above them the sun sets
and rises and sets again. My mother leans
on her elbows. Her brother pirouettes

across the lake. She is ill. A tree screens
the hidden steps which lead up to a hot
clear patch of sunlight. The ice queen

melts in a derelict house. A flowerpot
dangles dry stems in the porch. Where are we?
The skaters move in the distance, shot

through with dead light. Their translucency,
their quick black feet, remind me of birds.
The house says nothing, staring vacantly

into the bushes. Above it vague herds
of clouds meander like soldiers on patrol
at a border station between two absurd

countries, watching empty wagons roll
up and down the track. The skaters rise
from the pond. Families stroll

among the trees. The fountain dries.
The city is full of unshaven faces
darting round corners, quick evasive eyes.

*

Our Virgil is thin. He waves a red carnation
in his outstretched hand. His mouth is sad.
Urine and darkness. Taxis hover at the station

like flies round rotten fruit. Roads being bad
we skate and bump along, juddering on scarred
cobbles, loose flakes of tarmac, past semi-clad

seventies blocks. The driver brakes hard
as we shimmy round a tight bend then lets fly.
Here only patience is its own reward

and patience is unending, numbing, sly,
deflated, almost anaesthetic in effect,
sensations slowing up, the batteries dry.

*

Virgil's wife is not long dead. He hankers
after her. Hence the obsessive tidiness.
Hence the old clothes queuing up on hangers,

a line of ghost wives, each in a different dress.
Hence the suitcases of old shoes, dead soles,
dead arches, metaphors of emptiness.

Waste not, want not. Words. Each word controls
a complex microsystem full of shoes.
There are housecoats, jackets, carefully packed rolls

of stockings, handkerchiefs. Someone might use
them sometime, these ritual cerements
whose buttons bless, whose broken straps accuse

the world-of-what-remains of innocence,
complicity, not knowing. The wardrobe
boxes up its knowledge, stores an intense

237

thickening, a denser universe. White globes
gather on shelves with the familiar stifling
smell of disease: bacteria, microbes, grubs.

*

Rainy mornings. Virgil unwraps a packet
of cheese, carefully slices it and lays
it out in a pattern. He is delicate

in his dealings. He fills whole days
with wrapping and unwrapping, making neat
divisions. He must go easy, paraphrase

the given grammar of each slab of meat
in simple sentences, short words, with stops
and dashes. He must become an aesthete

of necessity. In dark empty shops
he exercises taste, brings grace to bear
on grease, on cooking oil, thin chops.

*

Here are new apartments. Floors rise in austere
towers. The rubble remains: a long ditch
fills with rainwater the colour of flat beer.

Panels drop. The lift is stuck. This is a rich
country. It has silver, gold and bauxite,
natural gas, a seaboard. It can afford a hitch

or two, a twenty-watt bulb on a winter night,
a telephone exchange like a starved behemoth
straddling an unlit street. Basically it's all right:

you can have people or food but not both.
The building stutters, blunders to a stop.
The ditches breed defiance first, then sloth.

*

It's spring. Virgil negotiates the hill
above the city, steep, up crumbling steps
with a view out over spires, an idyll

from his childhood. An orange river creeps
below him, escaped from a paintbox and spilt
across brown paper. Beside it, small heaps

of rubble wait for houses never built.
They shrink to miniature pyramids
of powder. Sunlight reveals a soiled quilt

of roofs and walls. Cars scuttle like invalids
from block to block.
                              Enough of looking down,
of light stored patiently under the eyelids,

time to look up to the spectacular crown
of the city and the vast five star hotel
moated in mud, a petrified eiderdown

of cloud squarer than the rest, parallel
to the flat streets below, sheltering
its nightflown and exotic clientele

of representatives (who knows what they bring
or what they take away). It can't be much,
thinks Virgil and keeps clambering.

                              *

Virgil leads his visitors to the only
reliable eating place in town. He smiles
with sad sharp eyes, a smile both lonely

and endearing. High summer reconciles
hill, hotel and river in an embrace
of light. Light drips from guttering, from tiles,

pours down steps, down the green carapace
of copper domes, shimmers across bushes,
tucks itself into leaves, settles like lace

on last night's puddles and webs, rushes
down streets, bursts round corners in wild beams.
Busy times. The proprietress brings dishes

of soup specially prepared. The bowl steams.
A terrace with a tree. A cabin proclaims OASIS.
Cola labels. Plastic. The whole place dreams

of order, is a kind of synthesis.
Its cheap and easy kindnesses must prove
something to someone, provide a basis
for argument, a point from which to move.

*

The ticket hall. Two bare bulbs burn. A third
has given up the ghost...Ghosts stand in queues
at holes. Ghosts bandy words

behind the counter. Successive greys infuse
a solid glass curtain. Beneath its waves two ghosts
engage in a discreet and aimless exchange of views.

*

The traffic lights too have given up. The dead
drive dangerously among the living. A policeman
flourishes his red stick like a neatly severed head.

*

The trams have sagging bellies. They drag their heels.
They've eaten too much rust. It takes four men
to steer them straight with four bent steering wheels.

When soldier meets driver he makes a proposition.
When driver meets soldier he makes a contribution
thereby maintaining both in honest apposition.

Two old men meet. They shake hands. One has lost
a leg. Friends of different tribes, they speak
the ruling language. One waits till the other has crossed

the road before moving back into his own ethnic
group. The other hobbles on, part of the great
majority; amiable and sick.

*

When patient meets doctor an envelope
passes betmeen them. One offers obols
or collateral, the other offers hope.

*

240

The central square. The statue of the just
king (old dispensation). About him six
flags of the new salute in a strong gust.

The tiny local leader (new dispensation) kicks
his hind legs up, lets fly a leader's fart.
The old leader once kicked against the pricks:

the rough provincial redefines his art.

*

Virgil has friends. His contemporaries
remember everything, keep each other alive.
Everyone has his or her list of stories.

So does everyone else. People arrive
at individual outstations and make their peace
with consciences, authorities. They survive

as long as possible. Their numbers decrease,
their books smell ever damper, their pictures fade.
Some die on operating tables. Some piece-

meal, by stages, head downward, their bills unpaid,
their buttons undone. One falls under a train
after a drop too much, one having made

her bed and put on nightclothes. Their pain
is stored in umbrellas, overcoats, magazines
with half-solved puzzles. It remains

to be tidied up. Tidiness means
control and end. The pernickety
scuttling, the counting out of spoons,

the final indispensible dignity.

Virgil's Georgics
(after the illustrated calendar of Béla Gy. Szabó)

January

Moonglow. Night. Ice cold.
Trees furred like bears.
The stars have cold hard eyes.
And so have bears.

February

A frightened rabbit sprints across a field.
A frosty creature, half bat, half bear,
clings to a tree. Small flowers of frost
explode in bushes, splinter in the air.

March

A woodpecker. Trees tangled.
A nail scratching on glass.
Frozen hair on a dead man.
Shadows like soft claws.

April

A narrow ambitious branch. A bud in swell.
A herb garden. A chestnut tree. Birds unroll
across the sky. In 1954
I could put my arms around the bole.

May

Poplars full of thrushes. Sky leans
on earth. The river dreams.
Shrubs light their torches. A bullfinch
sputters on a branch, bursts into flames.

June

The cuckoo counts your years. An oil green shade.
The grass sports asterisks and nipples.
The lean black water on the pond traversed
by indolent white ripples.

July

The lake steams. Grebes cackle. A distant shower.
Star responds to star. Black clumps dither
under trees in an electric storm. Thunder.
Lightning. Changeable weather.

August

A grasshopper swings absent-mindedly.
Few days left to swing.
One sharp beam of sunlight is enough
to burn his wing.

September

On my first day at school my mother cried
but I whistled at my schoolfellows.
Around my feet the dead leaves
were dancing like swallows.

October

A leaf rattles. A bough lies on the ground
like a lost umbrella. A live branch groans
under the chattering rain and feels
a sharp ache in its bones.

November

A magpie among aspens. All things
curve in on themselves, aware
of what is still to come:
province of bat and bear.

December

A TV frost. Interference. A snowflake
breaks up in a scraggy oak.
All things given over to destruction.
A gun. A joke.

BLINDFOLD

Dancing with Mountains
(i.m. Ágnes Nemes Nagy, d. 1991)

1

Her verse was monumental. She seemed to be made of mountains.
Ottó said he once danced with her at a party
and it was all too much like dancing with a mountain.

She had a knack of creating or declaring heresies.
There were heretics in metre, heretics in stanzaic form,
but chiefly the heretics that banned or ignored her;

heretics who sentenced her friends, who sent down her husband
the critic, and when she found out that he'd been unfaithful
she ordered him from the flat on his release,

though he never deserted her, not to the end,
but called every week, helped her to edit her books,
wrote articles everywhere praising and defending her.

I met him there. He lay flat out on the sofa
because of his back, a yellowish, jaundiced looking man
to whom she had written one ravenous erotic address

she did not want me to translate, in which she wished
to devour him, to absorb him entirely. He said, Call me *te*,
the intimate form of you employed within genders.

She was dying the last time we met. We talked politics.
She asked me what I thought would happen and said if she voted
at all she would vote for FIDESZ, the party for those under thirty.

2

Between Becket and Rilke was the position she craved:
her diction was clear as spring water in sentences
simple and natural, referring to but beyond the senses.
Will-power held them together. Her images were engraved

or scratched (more physical this) into the ice.
Geysers, geology, trees steaming in winter, Egyptian
ceremonies. She tuned in her set. The reception
was perfect. Hers would have been a rocky paradise,

crystalline, more like a desert. She even looked
like Donatello's Magdalene but her god was different,
a beautiful martial androgyne sulking in a tent
before battle, her eyes fierce, her nails hooked,

while outside smaller poets ran yapping like the proverbial curs,
each of whom would have given a life to have written one line of hers.

For Graham Cable's Funeral

Death is this Dickensian flunkey, pacing along
        in his polished top hat,
the four pall-bearers bowing to each other
        like mannequins at a minuet:
the music box starts and it's bedtime and night-time.

And the puzzle's little pieces are floating in free fall
        riding the extent
air of the body whose guy-ropes have snapped
        collapsing the tent
of inner air and it's bedtime, it's night-time.

Think how many pieces the human spore comprises,
        vague scents and sharp clauses
that never will join to assemble the semblance. The actor is
        one with his ill-timed pauses,
his script half forgotten. Here is the night-time

where only the small hard seed of being can weigh down
        the body no longer
a body, but memory of memory, the unshrinkable good
        that's the only thing stronger
than bedtime or night-time.

At Table, 1964

At Schmidt's in Charlotte Street the old waiter
scuttled between tables, wrinkled as Adenauer.
The menu was opulent, the covers clean.
We ate wiener schnitzel with potatoes and sauer-
kraut chased by crème caramel, our table talk
joky-familiar or sour. We were creatures of mood,
and Sunday a family occasion, like bridge
or *Monopoly*, was a debt owed to childhood,
keeping track of lost time.

And lost time is what the restaurant suggested
with figures in shadows and rooms beyond rooms.
I can still taste the food in that arrested
development, the breadcrumbs rough on my lips,
and I find myself rattling on, as if I were an old waiter,
finding the whole thing funny and boring and sad.

That is the beauty of it: the poetry comes later,
shuffling up to you like a Low Church sacrament,
a grey-suited man with non-alcoholic wine,
glass concentrated in a bead of dark red,
serving for sign.

Eat Good Bread Dear Father

Every lunchtime they'd leave you a piece of *mignon*.
Now I can imagine the white of the paper bag
and the small yellow doily under the plate
in the afternoon half-dark. And I drag
from my memory not your room but mine
(or any room that seems to be half-dark)
to construct a world we may meet in. Here is the door
to the kitchen, here is the sideboard, the mark
on the tablecloth and the print of my thumb
on the page. Here nothing is known, everything dissolves
to noise or to music (but what is the difference?)
a music which says (so must mean) things, that solves
the pathos of cake on a saucer or the tiny

cosmic hum that rings an old woman's hand
as she moves in the kitchen like a conductor,
waving her notes into place, weaving the slender
sound of paper and footstep. We start as with lines
on a score, the *mignon* a radiance among other radiances,
with your blank childhood face and the space between lines
measuring distances.

Grandfather's Dog

His hat would sometimes precede him into the hall.
These were the bad days when everything went wrong
and the smell of leather followed him like a stray dog
across the carpet. It was a ghostly creature that slunk
about the flat, settling on chairs and cushions;
all soft retentive things would take him in,
the children, the women. The dog of course had suffered,
such was its nature, and such was theirs, the children and women.

Because failure and humiliation are unexpected
the dog was to be expected. And sometimes it haunts me,
the thought of the dog. I've seen him sniffing
at my brother's ankles. His sheer size daunts me,
his dumb perseverance. I saw him once, sitting in the kitchen
beside my mother, under her feet, at his most
persevering. He ate her slowly and left not a bone,
so I knew him to be a bitter and vengeful ghost.

And grandfather, the factory hand, was likewise eaten,
by him first, then gas, right from the beginning.
Even now as I walk through the town it is there, sharp
and pervasive, a smell of leather-tanning.

Variations on Angela Carter

1

He knows he is only an idea and not such a good one
but when he feels the black
flame in his blood his laughter sounds fierce in his mouth,
his outer skin, his shirt and his vest, hang slack

and he feels more than hears her singing in his ears.
He is thinking of her (who else) in her fields,
in her aeroplane, in her skin which is smooth,
her muscles which are tense, her neck which yields

to his breath, dissolving like a cloud which is soft,
wet, delicious, evanescent, full of strange words
which he tries on his tongue and relishes
oh years, years afterwards.

2

It is not so much in the saying
as in what a word does.
You hear it first in your mother's cooing,
in that delicate chortle, the buzz

which you feel as you touch her throat
with your pudginess, in her nipple as it roars
milk at you, in the scent of her arms as you stuff
your nose into her armpit, which is yours

and wolfish, and beyond all that, lovely,
singing with the entire self that it is,
with its history, tenderness,
self's infinite capacities.

3

The restaurant was full of seaweed. The waiters swam by
in their oriental coats. His own was as it was,
as it tended to be, a confusion of hair.
He was mesmerised by long fingers

paddling knife and fork above the plate opposite,
the shining rice as it disappeared into her mouth,
the milieu of strangers, familiars,
the electricity of truth

which, if truth be told, was puzzle and fright.
He was sitting on darkness but where
was she sitting, and who were these guests
crowded round tables? How hard it is to bear

the weight of words, to balance them on your fork,
to swallow them like fish out of water,
to test them and taste them as they come out,
gentle, neutral, sour-sweet, faintly bitter.

The Word House
(for Clarissa Upchurch)

The Word House

Here you and I are changed beyond redemption,
here we breathe doors and windows, eat
the food once prepared like a ghostly meat
for our consumption.

The past can take your breath away. You move
across the room, brittle, lithe, destructible,
and I write to hold you there in the subtle
nets that words can weave,

the words brittle, lithe, destructible.

Fugitive

She jumped clear of his clever words,
brittle, lithe, destructible,
a yellow dress in a green garden,
her eyes blue-grey-green,
her spine curved like wrought iron
under cotton, under the tight skin
and the softer, the possible
flesh. His eyes and fingers were cords

to bind her in a sentence, but she had
a monumental pathos and kept
moving. She was under

his skin and beyond it
in a place which smelled of thunder.
His arms swung at his sides, his eyelids pressed
down on his eyes, which were trapped
and delicate, the eyes of god.

The Sense of Memory

Not memories but the sense of memory,
as of a power, an enabling,
like the sun on a street with its
delicate scribbling.

To remember the sense of your beauty,
your weight, breath and movement
is enabling and powerful
as the sunlight on the pavement

which flits in and out of dark spaces in doorways
never quite filling a room that it enters
but leaving dark spaces
like pockets, like splinters.

The Word 'You'

Impossible to use the word 'you'
without you, to think of your beauty,
your weight, breath and movement,
without speaking the language

of those who have used the same words
and not for the first time:
I think of your beauty, your weight
and your breath and your movement,

I think the word 'love' with its landscape
of shadows and fires, lost rivers,
its haunted everyday objects,
its faces in windows.

We move in each other like figures
in landscapes. I think of your beauty,
the vast simple rocks of the mountains,
your weight, breath and movement.

Soil

What colour would you call that now? That brown
which is not precisely the colour of excrement
or suede?
The depth has you hooked. Has it a scent
of its own, a peculiar adhesiveness? Is it weighed,
borne down

by its own weight? It creeps under your skin
like a landscape that's a mood, or a thought
in mid-birth,
and suddenly a dull music has begun. You're caught
by your heels in that grudging lyrical earth,
a violin

scraped and scratched, and there is nowhere to go
but home, which is nowhere to be found
and yet
is here, unlost, solid, the very ground
on which you stand but cannot visit
or know.

Threnody
(for Matt Simpson)

Wipe the white beard. Let it lie across his chest.
Smooth it flat and close his eyes too while you're at it.
What is history but a beard as white as this?
Gather the length gently, ribbon it and plait it.

The breath is long stopped and the words are all fading.
The air's no longer his. His was another planet –
Pluto, Jupiter – the dear one, so distant,
a spirit floating about cupboard and cabinet,

father of fathers, a well-tempered clavier,
God in the machine in the corner of the room.
Take up his name, cut it out with reverence,
and paste it on a new page of the family album.

251

Dry mouths and dry names, shells of dead insects,
heaps of moth-wings, beetle-shards, disinfected,
no thought of flight now or crawling, they lurk
in the annals, sad husks, untongued, undetected,

in rooms of faint darkness with the sound of ghost feet
across halls of vague carpet and trousers in a chair,
in long-distance calls and buckles in the mirror,
faces of children: thick dark hair.

István Vas
(1910-1991)

1

When your best friends are taken away;
when your mentor's daughter (forbidden,
you live with her in secret) dies of a tumour;
when you're constantly hiding
and the love of friends protects you
from starvation or bullets,
and you return by secret corridors
to Byzantium not Rome,
then you'll know at times of suspicion
that all is suspicious and everyone's done time,
and it's only the wind that blows
between words not through them
that constitutes poetry,
so you practise your craft
lightly, assiduously,
and when that world vanishes
you too take care to vanish
with the beauty and intimacy
of a secret friend, tumour or lover,
sensibly, quietly, silently taking cover.

2

Candles in the window on All Souls' Day,
October wind gathering at the glass and rain
softening dead leaves. The tanks are rumbling again,
lorries are taking a whole town away.

We've been here before, whatever the season or year.
Your hesitant voice in mid-sentence, stopped in my ear.

PORTRAIT OF MY FATHER IN AN ENGLISH LANDSCAPE

(1998)

Rabbits

The rabbits are about their business
of softening. They congregate in gangs
by hedgerows as if waiting for an event
of greater softness to overtake them.
The clouds overhead grow rabbit scuts
and bolt across the field in evening dress.
The whole sky is purpling with the scent
of evening. A clock opens and shuts
time out. Flowers bend on a single stem
and wind plumps leaves to wings.

Rabbits flicker into open spaces
all by themselves, exploratory, vague,
bristling in the wind, apologetic.
Out of sight, they settle
delicately then hop away, their faces
dreamy and purposive. They are a thick-
ening in the dark, a curl of soft metal,
a wholly benevolent plague
for which woolly words have to be invented,
something earth- and dropping- scented.

They lollop about in silence for a while,
shiver and bob, consume, dart back
into their holes, peek out. Soon the field
swallows them whole. The clock claps
its hands. They run off scared. The wind
bursts from a hedge and over a stile.
Leaves mumble, their lips are sealed.
The train swoops down its sinister track,
and the clouds make dramatic shapes
in the sky which is dropping like a blind.

Something of terror remains in the grass
where the rabbits have been. Night
comes on as the negative of daylight. Where
is the bristling gone? Something is shaking the train.
An old man holds his cup in trembling fingers,
waiting for the tremor to pass.
Insignificant stations swim through the air
in a fog of names. Some warmth lingers
in them and hovers there like a stain,
or a bird or a figure caught in mid flight.

Golden Bream

It may be nature morte *but it's still life*, said the joky sixties poet
and I'm sure he is right, because there is death in it,
not just in the codified clutter of skulls, books and bubbles
but in the whole enterprise and so particularly
when plainly dead creatures, like pheasants and hares,
quails, sparrows, orioles and trout (but chiefly the birds)

do so much lolloping and hanging, neatly shimmered up,
displayed with the instrument of their final bringing down,
and garnished with a few tasteful etceteras such as flowers,
and yes, they are beautiful, in every scale and feather,
and honest enough – they actually taste good
(those wonderful spices, the garlic, red onions,

the wine-water tinctures, the eggs, the pimentos and lemons) –
and despite what Berger says it's probably better
than owning the genuine things, somehow more touching
and dignified, almost transcendental, beyond material
through the material, a kind of sanctification
of the sensible world, moving in beatitudes,

with death in the centre (and what could be better?)
hovering tactfully beyond the sumptous canvas,
death with all its unlimited readings – a child in a fever,
the soldier in his trench, the burning villagers trapped
in a hut by the military, the grinding bastard that simply wears down
and exhausts you, all of which is in the nature of things

and you don't need to prove that, just look at these bream
who have clearly not survived nor ever could survive
the peninsular war or the hook, their furious
disappointed eyes telling you it's over, that the cold
has come too suddenly for even half-way reconciliation
between stillness on the one hand and life on the other.

Daffodils

I am bothered by the nagging translucency
of these daffodil petals in their Busby Berkeley outfits
of six yellow skirts around a frilled bell
darkening to its centre, their stern stalks bunched
in the glass on the sill by a warm brown wall,

and I'm wondering if I can make any sense of daffodils
(or Diaphenias or Daffy Ducks for that matter)
or of any of that unwonted clutter of names
which has done nothing to force them into flower
quite in the way they do here or to gather

those pleated petals to such concord of dancing
or stillness, recalling the skin of my mother
at fifty, slouched, puckered and dying,
her flame indrawn under bruised plums and purples,
or my skin, for instance, in its cold variations

on one theme of pink, full of cracking and byways
that grasp at the sunlight, almost transparent,
opening on something that passes them by
or cuts a swathe through them, not quite the sun,
but having the nonchalance of sunlight.

Mouth Music
(i.m. Harold Woolhouse, botanist)

Emma Kirkby is an expert on ethylene
we must get someone in to talk avocados
Burnham Beaches are down, the birds are protected
    said the dying man in gaunt profile on the bed

Così fan tutte is a fine work of fiction
one must hear the boom of the bittern, a bassoon would
probably do it, or a cello if it's cold
    said the dying man, his hands twittering twittering

Binsey Poplars with all its tall beeches is wailing,
the garden needs a good prune, a thorough dactylic,
the sumach has pinnate leaves much like a rabbit
        said the dying man, his head battered and fossilised

But we love him, said the visitors, and his words are disturbing
the bastions are down, all the high scaffolding down
the language is folding in on itself, fold down the covers
        said the dying man in his pride and withering

Between words grow the senses one hears in the night-time
or smells in the daytime, that lodge in one's tonsils
like airy cabbages or clouds full of antonyms
        said the dying man to the living in his wisdom

But we want him here with us, just as he has been
just as we hope that we ourselves will be, where the wind
sings in the attic and the water seeps through the stones in the cellar
        here where we sit and make noises of talking

The noises of talking, a botanical opera, the sound of a number
on the way to becoming, all this amounts to a kind
of affection which has its own logic, the visitors protested
        as the dead man lay talking and the furniture listened

as furniture must by its nature having no tongue
to tell of its sorrows, having no lexicon, language or logic
and incapable of becoming by simply changing position
        by booming or bawling or bursting into childish tears.

Gunsmith

All day the gas-jet glows in the gunsmith's window.
His long slow face is yellow with it. He smiles
like a shy man, even his moustache is shy.
Plainly he loves his work, he takes so much care with it.

Chiefly it's polishing, soothing, easing the barrel clean,
rubbing down abrasions, filing out a scratch,
straightening sights. He is making an object,
himself a part of the product of his skill.

Thoroughly gentle, almost apologetic,
how difficult it would be to dislike him
in his honest endeavour, his modest demeanour

as he turns the barrel over, blows hot dust away,
as he makes space for himself in the glow of his window,
in the soft detonations of light when somebody enters.

Tinseltown

Nothing but a glittering you can't describe,
nothing but names and smiling at faces: no
jewels but plastic beads, no tiaras but card,
no face but that which fits you, a tall mirror
hung by the magazine rack, some pearls of frost
on the window beyond, dripping elegance,

full of December, and rain starting to dance
on the pavement where a woman has just crossed
this busy road to push through the double door
to where you stand by the counter, working hard,
totting money at the till in a green glow
of figures, servant to that commonplace tribe

queuing for papers though it's nothing to do
with you what the tabloids blaze across the front
page, you simply read it along with the rest
and it's good for a giggle, just like this crown
of tinsel you got wound into your hair, which
catches the lampglow all the way down the aisle

and slips occasionally forward, so while
you are counting you're always having to switch
hands and flick the thing back so it won't fall down,
but sits perky and sparkling, a silver nest
of light, frivolous, and when it falls you don't
stop to pick it up, it means nothing to you.

The First, Second, Third and Fourth Circles

1

Most cities approximate to a circle and so does this,
curled about the double bend of its river, on one side snuggling
to cliffs and hills where the cool air shuffles through a park with cedars,
a cogwheeled railway, a deserted tram stop,
some concrete tables for ping-pong or for chess,
and benches where migrant workers from Romania
sleep to shave in the morning by a working fountain,
hearing at night the wind in its mild cups
stumble up stairs between gardens, trailing a cloak
of lightbulbs and shopsigns over the gentler slopes
which are peopled with villas and baroque excrescences,
belvederes, weathervanes, cherubs and furies, cupolas and turrets,
a wrought-iron gate with doorbells and nameplates
which allows a visiting wind to drift through the hallway
between two apartments whose front doors give on to
large Ottoman carpets and rugs hung on walls,
and endless shelves of once-subsidised literature,
to say nothing of rattling East German spin driers,
expressionist plumbing and between-the-wars pictures
such as are found even in bedrooms of fifties estates
where no one's disturbed except for the sheepdog
slumped on a doormat, listening to its owners
snoring aloud in partitioned compartments
stuffed with old furniture intended for bigger rooms,
or howling to late cars or the crumbling glass
shattered on the high street where two drunks are fighting
and the police pick up girls from discos just for the hell of it,
doing handbrake turns by domed Turkish baths
sweeping down the embankment, past the olympic pool,
the chain-store installed in a reconditioned cellar,
the emptying restaurant with tables in the yard
where a few stray napkins float between chairlegs
in this mildest of weathers down in the square
or up at the museum-palace with its soaring prospects
and prancing statues of princes pulling faces
at the black of the night-time Danube, surveying the far side.

2

Cars are creeping round the portico of the Prussian style Academy,
the Westminster gothic of Parliament and the fifties modernist
White House of what was just a few years ago
the party headquarters, and beyond it the boulevard,

Angelfield, New Pest, and the distant industrial suburbs
beyond the third of the ring roads, the third arc shielding the second,
and the second haunting the contours of old city walls
embedded in tenements of the innermost ring,
pierced by radial highways, cafés, department stores.

3

Nineteenth-century grid-maps where everyone lives
but wants to move out of, in one room or two rooms
or one and a half-rooms, ranged about the communal courtyard,
the sound of a tap or a radio, a beggar or busker,
under the residents' own square of sky, towards which climb
neglected stairs with blown away putti,
untrustworthy lift-shafts which back in the dark days
brought terror to everyone, when in the dawn hours
the lift started up and a car was seen at the entrance,
and a single shepherded figure disappeared off the grid-map
into uncharted country beyond the reach of the suburbs.

4

The local girls are offering rides in a handy apartment
to the accompaniment perhaps of a video,
while next door, behind secessionist doors,
the lecturer types out his lecture and the German quiz host
slides down a cable which the whole block has paid for
and a lost voice interrogates itself at the mirror
or sips from its little black cup of resentments
which keep the heart beating all through the night.

The House Stripped Bare by Her Bachelors, Even

The outer layers are gone. The houses shiver
in brick underwear. They feel the shame of it.
Their iron bones embarrass them. The river
has worn them down and left them bare,
all edges and splinter, wispy as maidenhair.

They are softer than they think. Fingers of lead
have probed their sides, shells dug them in the ribs.
Friable earth, they crumble into gutters,
shower with white dust the blind head
of the man in the doorway, wave broken shutters
at each other like so many soiled bibs.

The bachelors who stripped them bare are blowing
about the street with sweetpapers and other ephemera,
seedy old raincoats lost in a dust haze,
who hesitate, vaguely aware of where they are going
humming an air from a pre-war opera,
if only they could think of the name of it.

The Idea of Order at the József Attila Estate

The lawns are in order, someone is keeping them neat.
No one has yet tipped rubbish down from the tenth floor.
People are walking their dogs or waiting for buses
As if they had taken to heart the architect's fiction of order,
And saw their own lives in exploded and bird's eye views.

It all has an explanation. The woman once sentenced to death,
The silver beard of the courier-spy, the pentathlete,
The shrunken delicacy of the woman with the zimmer frame:
These lives fit together as if in a programme, a drawing
In a department, one all-embracing stroke of genius.

The lifts rise like zips. They do up the block which maintains
The sealed and communal weather of its residents.
It is peaceful and calm in their versions of being,
A dream of files and cabinets at uniform temperature
Where death entails merely a comfortless distancing,

Something diffuse, clouds seen from the roof garden,
Thousands of breathing cells misting up windows,
Waste materials flushed down arterial pipeways,
The voices of children scrambling upstairs,
And the distant suburban railway coming and going.

The Manchurian Candidate

Imagine your own thoughts are not your own,
that you're a puppet waiting for a sign,
some secret signal, which will set you off
down preordained paths along a narrow line

unrecognisable to you, a way unknown
except within your nerves. This is the stuff
of nightmares, and your Laurence Harvey face
stares strenuously back, half out of place.

Imagine a small town in the Midwest:
one day you are confronted by a mass
of slimy matter, a blob that comes and eats
folk's innards out and monstrously can pass
through windows, walls and doors. Perhaps it's best
not to think of this. And soon the thing retreats
into its hidden spacecraft, disappears
for months at a time, or even a few years.

Imagine a place, a clean white house, some chairs
set out on porches. This place belongs to you.
It's like a mind, fresh-washed, hung out to dry.
It smells of comfort, offers a fine view
of lawns and streets the whole neighbourhood shares.
Somewhere a neighbour's child begins to cry,
a radio blares, or you hear a woman shout,
then rain comes down to wash the memory out.

Variations on Radnóti: Postcards 1989

1

A wicked cherub perched on a pilaster
(His torso only) portending disaster
In somebody's gateway.
He grins and winks: half menace, half play.

2

The bustiest blonde in town some six yards high
who smirks behind sunglasses on a fire-wall
advertising the state lottery, may be a spy
but is in any case far from impartial.
If only I could squeeze her mammoth four-foot tits
I too might manage on state benefits.

3

Mother and child on a balcony.
Behind them the river stirs and shifts.
Parliament looks on and creaks
down delicate buttresses and broken lifts.

4

The miracle of the statue's foot which leaks
medicinal water. The miracle of the boutiques.
The miracle of *wirtschaftswunder*. But now we are
talking one miracle too far.

5

This is more like it, a balding middle-aged man
feet firmly planted, a mild pot belly, dressed
in quasi-military gear;
in his hand a peaked cap and a thirty-year plan
to confound both east and west,
give or take a year.

Busby Berkeley in the Soviet Union

1

It's the Ministry of Culture Symphony Orchestra,
a sly and dangerous band of men
living in Stalin's greatcoat, with Dmitri
Shostakovich jammed into one pocket, Beria
into another. Distant echoes of glittery
ballrooms and a harvest moon

where a silent snake of Conga dancers grinds out figures
of eight to routines impeccably
transferred from Berkeley in true Soviet spirit –
sinister choruslines consisting of beggars
and blondes in collusion, employed by the KGB.
Together yet separate

in each square of space, they spin to light froth, coagulate
to stiff geometries, symbolic
of the will of the party and people. With set
expressions of joy they're working to liquidate
whatever is louche, undisciplined or chaotic.
Forests of arms and legs float

or crystalline marble. They're playing a waltz in the pit,
terpsichorean labourers, miners
of melody, glossy anonymous ranks
of Stakhanovites, brigades of polish and spit.
Light, anaesthetic, sexy, a row of binliners
in satin rises and sinks.

The girls flash thighs and high pale knickers, ingratiating
and threatening at once. We dance on
brittle but enchanted legs. The nightmare years
are back, more seductive than ever, aching,
lyrical. Outside, undesirables have begun
to gather. The walls have ears.

2

This music is in your blood, slithering through your arteries.
It's no longer 1934
but whatever you want. Call it today if
it pleases you. You're watching TV, some series
about hospitals or cops, an investigator
on the scent or a plaintiff

in a court case or a documentary about fish,
it doesn't matter what kind of tripe
you fancy, you get it all, good quality.
So you think you are safe, but under the rubbish
it raises its head. Sweet music. Suddenly you wipe
your face. Electricity

courses through you, or is it nostalgia? Insidious
and creepy, you hear it mount the stair
like desire. It makes you feel horny, childlike,
delighted. It's like going out to the pictures
on a rainy night when water catches in your hair
and the yellow streetlights strike

along the puddles. You shut your eyes and see regiments
of soldiers or dancers shuffling by
and know they're beckoning for you to join them.
The glamour's irresistible, the sounds and scents
of the crowd, you're taking your part in a tragedy
or marching to an anthem

drunk yet disciplined, Dionysiac, in the triumph
of your will or somebody else's,
the people's, the state's, the zeitgeist's, direct
and certain, carried along in the mighty oomph
of the band as it marches past familiar houses,
impeccable, bright, correct.

Four Villonesques on Desire

1 *Obsessives*

Some can only lust for what is gone, for the grey
in the green. There are those for whom beauties in their graves
exude a legendary perfume in which they can play
out their mortality. Some sing about desire in waves
of the sea, desire at the all-night raves
of the energetic young, desire in the emptiness
of mid-morning, desire in warm salty caves.
The well-dressed body, they say, needs sometimes to undress.

There are those, they sing, who cannot drive demons away
however they try. Men who prefer close shaves.
Women who itch, people who spend the whole day
dreaming of what their imagination craves,
those who are bastards, nasty vicious slaves
to hurt. Those who fall victim to a light caress.
Those who long for crucifixions under classical architraves.
The well-dressed body, they say, needs sometimes to undress.

Some cannot help but touch themselves. Some pray
for deliverance. Some, so the song goes, believe that lust depraves.
Some kill. Some die. Some prefer to frequent gay
clubs, some want to dance down church naves
in the nude. Some sit around in pious conclaves
condemning themselves. Some look an awful mess.
Some paint themselves up like Indian braves.
The well-dressed body, they say, needs sometimes to undress.

Think of all those Jims and Jos and Sals and Dis and Daves
whose numbers are constant and will never grow less.
God knows how the mind seized by desire behaves.
The well-dressed body, it says, needs sometimes to undress.

2 *Out of John Aubrey*

Where are the snows and the beautiful wanton
women? Venetia Digby for example, whose bust
John Aubrey saw in a brasier's window, or Anne
Herbert, Duchess of Pembroke? Salacious dust.
Where's Mistress Overall, married to the Master
of Catherine Hall and he much horned by her
but faithful to her beauty, unto the last.
In what air does their sweet dust stir?

266

Dear dead women with such hair... Venetian
broad-bosomed dames, objects of a poet's lust –
less lust than desire at best and not for anyone
in particular – flighty girls no one could trust
with a few glasses in them if a lover would but persist.
The Crazy Janes, Wild Alices, all flying fur
and impulse, who should have been gagged and trussed.
In what air does their sweet dust stir?

Have horses bolted? Have they fired a gun?
What have they sniffed or drunk or thrust
into their hungry mouths? Did they lie in the sun
too long? Have they woken the collective disgust
of Tunbridge Wells or finally earned that honest crust?
Did they roll in the grass, the moon a blur
of light, their eyes half closed, faintly nonplussed?
In what air does their sweet dust stir?

Has all their fine metal turned to a mournful rust?
Could danger or duty or discovery deter
them from their pleasures or did they do as they must?
In what air does their sweet dust stir?

3 *The Selfish Gene*

Where are they gone? Where are their atomies
swirling now? Where are those selves that meant
them and them only? Are they swarming like bees
in the garden waiting for an appropriate event,
or are they like ghostly soldiers in a ghostly tent
somewhere in the fields? Where is the queen
of bedroom and headroom with her exquisite scent?
What has become of the selfish gene?

Desire is a breaking apart, a great orgasmic sneeze
of pollen and dust, with no one competent
to reassemble what is lost. Where are Claire's knees?
Lolita's teenage American limbs? Girls who leant
from windows as the parade passed, the disobedient
daughters of parents who tried to intervene
in their affairs but were forced to admit themselves impotent?
What has become of the selfish gene?

What can you do once the miraculous geometries
of spirit or being are shattered? Whatever patience went
to their making, they are now blown on the breeze

which tickles other people's fancies. Kate's innocent
look was perfected over years. No one can reinvent
her curl of lip, nor Jenny's starved and epicene
quiver, her brown eyes wide, all energy spent...
What has become of the selfish gene?

All of them proper subjects for lament,
if only there were not so much hot air in between.
What was essence and what was embellishment?
What has become of the selfish gene?

4 *Pheromones*

Where is May Trevithick, sender of short rhymes
and collector of articles on the uses of urine? Where
is intimidating Susan with her list of crimes
against the imagination? Where is the spare
Elisabeth, drugged and heartstopped, with her black hair
and soft voice? Where is John McClure,
drowned in a French river, drunk on vin ordinaire?
Do pheromones die with the spoor?

Where's Derek Whiteley with his seed-times
and old roses, his institutions and professor's chair?
Where is his seed now? Where are the lost primes
of Tim the ace-guitarist and Alan Jarvis, the fair-
haired beautiful lodger? In whose tender care
is Martin Bell who finished up almost sober but poor
with his Desnos, Reverdy and Anne Hébert?
Do pheromones die with the spoor?

Where are the illustrious dead with their Guggenheims
and Pulitzers? Did they enjoy their due share
of fame and desire? Is death sexy? What agent limes
the twig their spirits are caught on when brightness falls from the air?
Beside the Deans, the Marilyns and Judys is there
a myth capacious enough to accommodate the glamour
we ourselves knew, once so close, in the bed, at the foot of the stair?
Do pheromones die with the spoor?

Where are the ones we forget, whose absence we bear
with equanimity, simply because they're not here anymore,
and we have to? Who carry our longings unaware?
Do pheromones die with the spoor?

THREE SONGS FOR ANA MARIA PACHECO

Whispers

What the old whisper to the young
which makes their hair stand on end
is what would never be told
by lover or friend

What the old ones shrouded and scarved
do with their hands and lips
is a secret they breathe through teeth
and fingertips

What beautiful muscles the young
exhibit to the old
What wonderful curves of rump
to stroke or scold

But it's secret, it's secret, a sin
to reveal except in air,
old fingers crumpled as clothes
the young won't wear

Porcupine

When the porcupine seductress
and the fat executive
sail away to happiness
and all the fish forgive

the net in which they're caught,
the hook that slits their throat
and little mermaids sport
like dolphins round the boat,

when love grows ears and fingers
and snouts incline to kiss,
and songs require no singers
then let them sing you this

let them sing their pleasure
let them sing their night,
the executive's fat treasure,
the porcupine's delight

Cat in the Bag

Always the whispering
Always the doubt
To keep the cat in
Or let the cat out

It's a dark old country
Riddled with heresy
Torturers, murderers
All in conspiracy,

Nothing you say
Will settle their hash
You stoke up the fire
They send down the ash

What earthly use
Are the mountains of dollars
And those brilliant cruel
Carnival colours

Whatever you do
Cats stay in their bags
The rich in their villas
The poor in their rags

The poor in their rags
The dogs at their vomit
What earthly good
Can ever come of it

Directing an Edward Hopper

Life is like this, only more so,
life being what life was and was dreamt to be
to music in the cinematic glow
of streetlights, a barman stirring a daiquiri,

a plate-glass window, the wind cautious,
raising my hair above the railtrack
where a train is expected and rushes
below, tugging purple shadows at its back,

a reassuring sinister sense of the dark
warehouse at the back of the mind,
the boredom of the bench in the park,
and those extraordinary blind

silences we collapse into on hot days
where all we want is to shut our eyes
and stretch out on the bed in a blaze
of floral wallpaper, while the suitcase lies

at our feet and we are half packed,
ready to go, as if the script
of our lives demanded it, our soundtracked
conversation tightly gripped

in the safe hands of the future
which is pure nostalgia. That is where
I am headed now, that miniature
version of our elsewhere,

and when we love we shall look as dated
as imagined childhood,
a childhood I myself have created
and would escape from if I could.

Day of the Dead, Budapest

Down the main arterials, on ring roads, in alleyways,
The dead stand perpendicular with heads ablaze.
And some of them blow out, while others burn right down
And leave small patches of darkness like footsteps about town.

Sap Green: Old School

The copper dome of the old school had turned
into the colour of soup they used to serve
on certain Fridays. The dining-hall lights burned,
low in the autumn gloom, You boys deserve

all you get, muttered the head into his gown.
A desperate smell of tobacco. The old man
had a bad smoker's cough, his fingers brown
with age and decay, faintly reptilian.

Retreating backwards into the fog, the class
of '65 were entering the pool
of memory through dark translucent glass
the colour of sap. It was time's own school,

uniforms languishing in cloakroom showers;
the loss, the charm of wasted after hours.

Prussian Blue: Dead Planets

The dead planets have gathered a deposit
of Prussian blue. The moonlight leaves them cold,
the sun has moved to other regions, their old
friends have deserted them. They are content to sit

in their dust, while under the dust, a mild ash
is still cooling and will go on cooling for aeons.
Out at midnight, children observe millions
of dead stars or watch a passing aeroplane flash

its wingtips at them. There is music in space,
a deep thrumming between plane and cello
that settles in the stomach and helps the digestion,

a pulpy, smooth, emollient interface.
It is absolute, abides no question.
It sings to crimson lake and lemon yellow.

*

Sometimes, under a tired eye, you see
the faintest ring of Prussian blue and think
how sad it is, like the faded ink
of a dead uncle's letter or the shadow of a tree

or a peasant's skirt, and you wonder what
it's doing there, under the eyes. Can one believe
in beauty like some simpleton and leave
the rest to sort itself out, rely on the gut

with its weakness for violins and sentimental songs?
The very idea is absurd. But listen! Do you hear them?
Bells! Bells across the street. Deep Prussian souls

muttering to puddles and cars. The world belongs
to perceptions of the world. The mice in their holes
creep out to sniff the cats but don't go near them.

Chalk White: The Moon in the Pool

(for Clarissa)

1

Between classical columns the water lies
rippling its faint skin to the sexy moon.
Breast fills with milk, eyes roll and weep, wind tries
to creep between damp petals. Dawn soon.
Between time. Not sleep but a kind of dull
zombie wakefulness. I float like a ghost,
knocking against the hard walls of my skull,
uncomfortable, dissatisfied and lost.
You breathe. Breathe and rise. Mumble. Stir. Hover
in the darkness that is on the point of breaking.
Your flesh is sweet warm dough under the cover.
Light begins to slide over you, aching
with a kind of passion. It speaks. My dear,
it says, its voice unexpectedly near.

2

My dear, says the moon, says the water, say
the classical columns. Their tenderness
surprises me. It is not like them to display
such human frailty. They usually dress
like dandies or symbols. In any case
there are no columns, no moon, only sounds
made by words whispering, a mouth, a face,
lack and desire, language doing its rounds.
O, says the moon and nothing more. And O
replies its reflection in the dark pool
under the eyes. What else makes such a glow
in the night, or echoes through the locked school
where we learned to love each other and talk
about love, diagrams drawn in moon–chalk?

3

Let's bring it down to real time. Almost three
in the morning early in the new year.
I've been awake an hour, can faintly see
your hair, could easily whisper in your ear.
But you were tired last night. I move with care
as I search for clothes. The word 'beautiful'
comes to me as I look at you. And you are
beautiful. It is as if a bowl full
of water were carefully balanced on a tray

and I were carrying it through the closed door,
desperate not to spill it. And a ray
of what could only be called moonlight or
felt like moonlight touched it and the door
opened into the hall with its cold moonlit floor.

4

Try again. I want to make the moonlight
vanish. I want to hold your face without
its glamorous appurtenances, to write
the moon without anything to write about
except the weight of your face in my hands
which has a meaning I will not have made,
which language itself broadly understands,
which is what you too would see if you stayed
in the white noise of the mirror, or ran
into a dream full tilt to emerge whole
and awake. But I am only a man
whose presence prefers to call itself a soul,
and you are asleep, and there's no moon
except this one in the pool and soon it is gone.

Cerulean Blue: Footnote on Wim Wenders

Angels do exist. Wim Wenders almost
had them right with that slightly shop-soiled look,
neither pure spirit, nor pure intellect, lost
on some level of their own, their eyes in a book

but raised fatally in a cool engagement,
and there they hold you and you feel looked through
but with a vague and troubling presentiment
at the colour, somewhere between grey and blue

intensifying to clear sky which is
merely a form of seduction, and you sigh,
already smitten, and get on with your business

which is what it always was. You start to count
the coins in your pocket or the spots on someone's tie
but keep losing track of the amount.

*

Just as, for example, you might sit down
at a table and begin to swim in pale smoke.
The sun floats in the window. Whole years drown
in your coffee and you start to remember a joke

without a punch line when an angel rises
from your companion's mouth and calmly hovers
above her head but your self-possession surprises
even you, and the thought of becoming lovers

solidifies like a screen on which is projected
the dream-film of all those other lives which are
not yours, and before you know, you've interjected

some ambiguous remark the angel hears
and sniggers at, then moves off to the bar
with his transparent head and disappears.

Romanian Brown
(for Irina Horea)

Political crises, shortages, rising crime.
The dictator's palace is unwittingly postmodern.
Life proceeds under the now-benign, now-stern
paternal gaze of Freudian Father Time.

If looks could kill… In high-rise flats the click
of keyboards. The gentle sea-sigh of computers:
fingertips of neighbouring literatures
touch across the corpse of the body politic.

Editors and translators conspire in the cold.
A chill runs down those delicate hands.
The TV spouts videos, foreign rock bands:
nothing now can ever again grow old.

Beggars are drifting through deserted squares
like paper sacks or ghosts of dancing bears.

*

Under the eyes a deep raw umber opens
into the warmth of the self like a letting-go,
and one slides through it to the marrow
in the thigh-bone and the thick translucent lens

of the joints. It is as strange as the world;
as disturbing in its brilliant intimacy
as the metaphor of the heart, that literary
device; as odd as the drowned sailor's pearled

and erotic eyes; as peculiar as the voice
you hear when you speak. No one who lives
in ordinary rooms with the great imperatives
of work and need lives there entirely by choice.

To sit in the dark settees of the eye is to know
the heart as literature, to suffer and let go.

*

Warm greys and browns. The softer certainties
assume jumpers and skirts, melt into tights.
The world must be civilised. Each colour invites
a cool intimacy between intelligent entities.

Long spatulate fingers stretch across a web
of nerves cocooning the fly of desire
which must nourish us somehow. But we tire
of its endless demands and night too starts to ebb.

The night is dark as coffee. The bushes outside
move in the wind, both hot and cold at once.
The trees are tossing their heads with impatience
and the whole sky begins suddenly to slide.

A kind of desperation runs through the deep
brown of the eyes and judders into sleep.

*

Solitary climbers sleeping at the tense
edge of precipitous forests under a dark brown
shower of needles stolidly arrowing down
into the earth can feel a bear's presence

(there are still bears in Europe, and wolves too)
in the soft pad and roll of the wind as it treads
towards them. The early autumn sheds
furred leaves which gradually form a thick glue

and a bird sings on the sharp snow-covered peak.
A woman lies in her tent, her dark brown hair
spread beneath her like the claws of a bear,
and all the bears and wolves begin to speak.

In a clear glass of Irish whiskey a train
pulls away from the platform through dawn rain.

*

A deep smudge of brown, something like a forest,
suggests an entrance into a possible past.
The dead come and go there like the forgotten caste
of an old religion. A woman offers her breast

to someone frail or a wolf or some kind of bird
in a potent act of charity or witchcraft.
The leaves are shivering in a delicate draught
between the pages of a book, hidden under a word.

Someone is saying: *Nature is your mother
and father* and points to a hole in the ground.
Lips meet lips with a distant sucking sound
and the hair rises, soft as a pigeon's feather.

Magic is suspect. An ancient figure stumps
between two sets of rusted petrol pumps.

*

The cloacal anteroom of the railway station. Pale
urinal yellows of the early morning.
The whole country disappears without warning
swallowed by night. The dark begins to fail.

But to think, and think…and now thin lines of steam
creep through the compartment, unfurl in grey,
briefly compose themselves before fading away.
The trains are coupling in a wet dream.

The bears are here too. They lumber across the track
in their furred overcoats. I watch them sadly.
I put out my hand to them. I know how badly
I need them. And look, they are calling me back.

And then I drift awake. And soon we start.
The train shakes like a tremor in the heart.

*

278

Blown like faint dust into the universe
whose eyes are both distant and close, this nagging pain
accompanies the sensation of being home again
as if one's own life were running in reverse.

Backwards into youth, backwards into childhood, back
into something formless yet vital, a directionless force
that stirs and disturbs. Somewhere a rocking horse
rises and dips, mouth grimaces then grows slack,

relaxing into a satisfied droop of the lips.
It doesn't last. The dust is whirling up a storm
desperate for affection, the remembered form
of the reaching hand as it grasps the bar and grips.

Raw umber, the rawer the better. The wood
receives you with its unfathomable good.

Lemon Yellow: A Twist of Lemon
(for WSU, 3 May 1997)

Nothing so bitter yet fresh as this small sun
radiating in a glass of clear liquid, be it
water or gin, fizzy or still. You see it
hanging there, doing no harm to anyone

till it hits home, when the face begins to slew
into a mask of hate, almost Japanese
in its exertions, then by subtle degrees
settle back into repose, a residue

of sunlight turning green at the gills, just there
at the tip of the nose, or in the fine
hairs on the neck, impossible to define,
soon vanishing away into thin air.

And all the bitterness is gone, discreet
as a trusted friend, and everything tastes sweet.

*

279

So one forgives everything, even time
whose bitter pill is harder to digest.
So one forgives the wormwood at the breast
which might yield milk, and the sublime

gall of indifference which drips unconcerned
from early morning trees. And one forgives
the tiny miseries and petty purgatives
one has to swallow, all that one has learned

and unlearned only to have to learn again,
the grating words, sullen as lemon rind,
with which the ungenerous reward the kind
whose anger fades after a count of ten.

Some like to suck the lemon, slice by slice
and let it slip into their hearts like ice.

*

How delicious the lemon is. It cools
the eye and settles at the back of the throat.
You shudder at its touch, at its remote
acidic laughter and its spiky molecules.

If hell is like lemons, one could get used to it.
In the vestibule café waiters like demons
proffer a trident stuck with bitter lemons
each slice so sticky the tongue gets fused to it.

But even here forgiveness wins the day
anticipating the sweetness that is sure
to follow something so stinging and so pure.
Sweetness will come: there's just a short delay.

And that wonderful light, concentrated, tense
in its yellow vest, proclaims its immanence.

*

The sponge soaked in vinegar. The feet
bunched like keys. The fingers bent and splayed.
The ragged children running in the shade
to a hot drum. The inescapable beat

of blood in the ear. Bitter, bitter. The quick
skip and twitch of the heart. You imagine
it all like drowning in pure oxygen
as the air begins to harden and grow thick.

Now the delicate tendons in your wrist
begin to ache and tears well up like drops
of the purest poison. And then the pain stops,
disappears suddenly, almost unnoticed.

The sun, bright as a lemon, sweet and calm,
trickles like sweat into your open palm.

Flesh Pink: The Face in the Coat
(for Helen at 21)

The world is full of faces. Folded behind their eyes
faces travel to work, arrive in fields, before
a whirring camera, and briefly summarise
their wisdom and desires. Where can we store
all their knowledge? On some machine with a reel
of film inside it? Such beautiful expressions
in full face or in profile are tempting to steal
or steal from, to plagiarise their confessions
and their gorgeous landscapes. Even on trains,
they leave a brief powder that fills your throat,
emanations of inwardness, faint stains
on seats where they once slumped like a discarded coat.
Hold on to its tails. We are of the same stuff
as travelled there. You never know enough.

*

Time is boredom. Children in the paper say
they are bored. They are moving at the speed
of light, which is not as it was in their teachers' day,
but faster, ever faster, till all the long days bleed
one into another, each an eternity
without dimension. Now you see it, now
you don't. Childish tedium has no pity.
Perhaps it is not to be relieved, not anyhow.
Later the process changes, though not for a while
and not so as you'd notice. The policeman

quotes Dante, the shepherd dreams, girls smile
at the camera. It is, as they say, all in the can.
The bored child is forever bored. The kiss is frozen.
Soft mouths everywhere, soft mouths by the dozen.

*

The cliché about the camera stealing your soul
is perfectly true. Someone must possess it –
a relative, a friend, strangers at a market stall.
The soul is photogenic: how to address it?
To have held a small face in your hands
is to guess its nature. You watch it grow, but what
it becomes is something no one understands.
Time excels at the editorial cut,
likes journeys and films or any kind of sequence,
but loses the plot and has to improvise,
and what it completes need not make too much sense
as long as it provides minimal food for the eyes.
Everyone is a star, for more than fifteen minutes,
more than enough to fill the short half-life of sonnets.

The Looking-Glass Dictionary
(for Gabriel Fitzmaurice)

1

Words withheld. Words loosed in angry swarms.
An otherness. The whole universe was
other, a sum of indeterminate forms
in motion. Who knows what the neighbour does
behind closed doors? You hear the chime
of the doorbell, the faint mechanical
music of the radio. It's supper time.
A window opens on a cry or chuckle,
the rest is half withheld – should it be loosed
the window's quickly shut, the door slammed tight
to seal words in. Guessed at or deduced
darkness arrives feathering words with night.
There they grow wings, like owls and nightingales,
screeching or singing till their meaning stales.

2

Screeching or singing till its meaning stales,
the cold grey light has drawn you from your bed,
the words go scuttling homeward, their bright tails
between their legs and shelter in your head.
The airport. Night. December. Rough and grey,
a blanket covers you. The windows snore
half-way between dust and snow. The day,
trying to raise itself, creeps under the door
and offers you a cup of tea. Its alien milk
enters your bloodstream like the wizened face
of the old woman with her tray. That silk
ribbon of liquid confirms your sense of place,
and winds you in, a line that anchors, warms,
and lets you enter its own world of forms.

3

They let you enter their strange world of forms
out in the playground, on the rough brick wall
where they have left their messages in storms
of chalk and paint. Their distances still call
for you, back in the classroom or a street
at some resort where you once spent the summer
among arcades, to the rock and roll beat
of neon lights, and further out and dimmer,
a buoy blinking through foggy yellow air
or the gentle drone of cricket commentary
in daytime heat which wraps you in blonde hair
and scent of oil, then dies in memory,
hovering in a haze before it fails,
like faint vibrations down deserted rails.

4

Faint vibrations of trains along the rails:
where are we now? Abroad again or home?
Between two kinds of sound. Their echo trails
along behind you (words themselves won't come.)
What did your mother say before you woke
to this? Her ribs vibrated with the thrum
of inner traffic. Something like a croak
surfaced at your throat and the hot drum
of her heartbeat made your heart dance. The slow
pulse of her blood blubbed and retreated, drove
your tongue before it with its enormous O,
and educated you to the word 'love'.
Like all words that apply and predicate
desire and loss, it brooked of no debate.

5

Desire and loss do not permit debate.
Where do the inner journeys go? They end
in trails of words, a kind of nonsense state
you cannot trust. And true, it is no friend
to kindness or reason. Words were treacherous.
Do you remember how at school they made
you catch the worms you would dissect? The fuss
as they wriggled and stiffened in formaldehyde?
The Latin names that crystallised that weak
mulch of muscle? The humours of the eye
that wept and spurted a transparent streak
of laughter between a language and a cry?
The Queen's English wrapped the pain in sound
that was articulate, in which the pain was drowned.

6

Articulate, you know how pain is drowned
and resurrected, undergoes baptism
and dies once more. The vessel runs aground
time and time again, drawn to the bosom
that nourished it. First time I saw the sea
was in December at Westgate. Huge grey jaws
snapped at the rocks, the white seethed in fury
like a pan full of fat, but cold. One word draws
the sea up, another repels it. We met
in a hut on the cliff-top, cub scouts with string
and diagrams of knots. The faint sun set
on the horizon. We were children playing
with water pistols. Food appeared on the plate
like clockwork and the clock did not run late.

7

But clockwork sometimes runs down or runs late.
The words my mother spoke were rarely home
to her, or moved at another, slower rate
which could not follow her. Somehow the room
was never hers. When she was cross, her eyes
ran before language, even before her voice,
which issued from a deep, raw, oversize
mouth inside her. We knew she had no choice,
that it would be all kindness, kisses, tears.
After the terrors (the camp, the deaths, the strange
sexual crudeness) we knew that what appears
is merely a sign and yields life little change,
that mum was a sea that ran your ship aground,
her voice a channel for that kind of sound.

8

A narrow channel. Now the empty sound
of a ship's engine, now a soft gull peeling
from the clouds, a bruise or an old wound,
plaster cracked across the bedroom ceiling.
The ceiling rose opens in a brilliant blur
and the bulb in the rose expands in purple
echoes of itself. The rain is damp fur
on the window. Your bedclothes ripple
in the night tide as you swim the sudden dark.
Your parents' voices merge with traffic. They
are arguing. Their harsh words leave no mark
but fade into the dream of every day.
The clock goes ticking on but your life runs
straight down the hill of poetry and puns.

9

Most poetry runs down the hill of puns –
that is what makes it treacherous and yet
so utterly persuasive. Mothers and sons
can mumble ambiguities and let
that rich thick soup of meaning nourish them.
The language outside meets the ur-language within
with the consistency of dream
which sits like a faint moisture on the skin.
My father's voice. A gentle coaxing lost
in the depths of his chest. His musculature
is iron swelling in his arms. Thin frost
covers him in a Russian forest. Pure
narrative lines run through him. He stands
in the street with the city in his hands.

10

Out in the street, the city in his hands,
he crosses and recrosses, hard at work.
He builds his tongue of vowels and consonants
with ifs and buts, emerging from the murk
of winter. He gathers them up like notes
shuffled through the cold hands of the dead
who smile at us from under heavy coats
of dust and snow. The coins bear his own head
as guarantee. We're at a football match
above the river. The Brylcreemed players race
about the pitch in baggy shorts. We watch
the old men on the terraces. I see his face
darkening as we walk home. The light runs
along his arm which could be anyone's.

11

His arms and mine, both could be anyone's.
We're only bodies, bodies are what we have.
We float in them among the crowd in patterns
down the tidal street towards the grave
caverns of the tube. We are a small cell
in the organism which encloses us,
lost travellers, a tiny human smell
that thickens when we rise, like Lazarus,
spectral and intimate and normal, home
among the words that mean us and reflect
our faces and possessions. We are the Rome
that all roads lead to, the dense idiolect
of heavens where we sleep and wake. It stands
in the world, half Hungary's, half England's.

12

This tiny world, part Hungary, part England,
is the macaronic my parents speak –
my dad especially. There is no bland
unbroken stream. The words seem to leak
in drips, wearing away all sensible matter,
making minute impressions, exhausting them.
I see this and am lost in multicoloured chatter
that seems to spread and deepen: spit and phlegm
and croak and fricative whose sounds mean me
and everything that can be concentrated
into the me I vaguely sense, that free-
standing monument, marble and gold-plated,
sole owner of my lexical demesne
of spotless glass where words may sit and preen.

13

A spotless glass where anyone may preen
when it is dark outside, the window throws
your image back at you. Who is the unseen
and uninvited guest in your dumb shows?
Only the skin – hands, legs, face – remain
hanging against the house opposite. Hair
disappears, clothes vanish. And now the rain
jewels and fractures till you're hardly there.
Trying to say 'you' to those smears of light
seems inappropriate. Recall the face
of your mother, that hollowed out, tight
mask in the photograph, almost a grimace
in forty-five? It creeps under the screen
of language, blankly refuses to mean.

14

The language here blankly refuses to mean
what it's supposed to. The signs are lost.
If you could only read the space between
or babble in fiery tongues at Pentecost.
What's gone is gone. Parents might be the first
to vanish but children soon follow. The winter sun
flashes off snow and the icy trees burst
with light. The world is what cannot be undone
nor would you wish to undo it when it speaks
so eloquently out of its dumbness, when
its enormous treasury of hours and days and weeks
resolves to this sense of now and never again.
It comes at you now in syllabic storms,
the words withheld then loosed in angry swarms.

15

Words withheld. Words loosed in angry swarms,
screeching or singing till their meaning stales
have let you enter their strange world of forms
like faint vibrations down deserted rails.
Desire and loss do not permit debate:
articulate, you know how pain is drowned.
You slept in beds when day was never late,
your voice a channel for the kind of sound
that rolls downhill in poetry and puns.
Out in the street, the city in your hands
lays down its arms, which might be anyone's –
Hungary, England are verbal shadowlands
of spotless glass where all may sit and preen,
blank languages whose words refuse to mean.

Travel Book

(for Anne Stevenson)

1

The ego grinds and grates like a machine.
The voyage out begins in classrooms where
stout boys in dirty tracksuits measure clean

ruled sheets of paper to a helpless stare
which pierces the heart. The teacher croons
like a pigeon, her words a soft cloud
full of light. The boys' faces are balloons
that drift below her, a bobbing crowd
of stupid gentleness. This one smells of shoes
and mud. His fingers clench and unclench,
his hair a lank mess. He did not choose
his head or body. The beginnings of a stench.
His nose runs. His nails have been bitten
down to a tiny slip on which nothing can be written.

2

Look. On this tiny slip of paper is written
the name of a plain woman. The thick lens
of her heavy glasses seems to fatten
her eyelashes to strokes made by blunt pens.
Her name is *kindness* and *friendship* and *you
will never know*. Indeed, how could you know.
Later you watch her feeling her way through
her dusty hall. This is how the blind go
into the world, resenting its bulk, annoyed
by its ill manners, its crude mischief. To live
by touch reminds lovers of the void
between beauty and desire. Can she forgive
her dead husband, her visitors, all the unseen
nonsense her eyes feed on? What does it mean?

3

We feed on nonsense whatever it may mean.
A polished grand piano butterflies
across the room, billows across the clean
floor, over the stove which crackles and sighs,
and settles by the window. Dark brown gloss
covers the eyes of Mr Shane, violinist,
now worn quite smooth, his moustache a light moss
under his polished nose. His slender wrist
is almost feminine. Art has no gender,
is an uneasy comfort zone where the mad
briefly settle and the sane diminish in wonder
at their predicament, which is a sad
and brilliant obsessession with pattern,
both raw and cooked, so soft and yet hard bitten.

4

The self cooked through is soft and yet hard-bitten.
Two tiny flirtatious girls in the back room
of a photographer's flat seem to be wrapped in cotton-
wool. An air of sentimental gloom
haunts the refugee party. I touch the hand
of the elder one: the current lifts me from
my low seat. At nine, I cannot understand
what's going on. I know there is a bomb
ticking in her flesh. Years later I find out
her dad takes saucy pictures for calendars.
The younger one bursts into tears. There is a shout
in the street that rises above the growling of cars.
One understands that sex is nothing new.
The mirror is no censor but tells you who is who.

5

What does the mirror say to the censor? Who
else can you talk to? One good friend steals
your father's stamps. Another tells you
the secrets of his parents' bedroom. It feels
odd being in a world like this. You pretend
to be handsomer than you are. Jealous
of others' success you invent a girlfriend
who helps you develop your sense of the ridiculous.
Being what you are you value romance
above sex but cannot help your hormones.
You accompany your frail ego to the school dance.
The Christmas chill enters your bones
with a special, undisguised, personal tenderness
that creeps and cools, erasing self in the process.

6

Talk like this erases self in process.
But what is self? Here are the beauties of night:
Angela, deep voiced; white-socked Brenda; Diana, no less
dangerous; Carol delicate. All of them bite
with rejection. Rejection is the law
of late childhood. Now you should sing
the beautiful teachers who filled you with awe,
of whose lessons you remember nothing
but the transcendence of their look
as it fluttered here and there, who could not reject
because their job was not to. The text book
bears witness to their names. The high elect
drift in their cold empyrean, a vacant blue
out of your range, that seems both valid and true.

7

But how do you know what is valid or true
when there is no sense of being, no fixed space
to move in, no vantage point or overview?
You don't know if the world's a human place
or some robotic jamboree in which
you yourself must appear with appropriate mask.
Weakness is your only guide, that faint twitch
behind the eyes when you are moved to ask
the necessary question. Your father's eyes,
a fat woman struggling through the rain,
an awkward delicacy under the disguise
of the poised girl, that hard-to-explain
vulnerability of the big man, the lost distress
of the body in the mirror as it sees itself undress.

8

What do you see at night when you undress,
when the conscious mask slips between one breath
and another only to slip back on? A game of chess
played by some adolescent knight with a filmic Death?
The Bergmanesque Grim Reaper? The Old Foe?
The photograph of a youthful father? The flounce
of a dress your mother once wore? Under the slow
moment, the immediate, quick, once and once
only sense of transition. The shop girl's shaking
hand as she pecks at the till. The brief smile
on the bus conductor's face as he is taking
your fare. Scrawled intercessions in the aisle
of the local church – those pregnant lines –
graffiti in the public toilets, signs.

9

Graffiti in the toilets, torn-down signs
at junctions. The Baptist minister glares
from his pulpit. Nearby, South Yorkshire mines
disgorge father and son. A teacher prepares
the next day's lesson. Peter Sutcliffe stalks
through Harehills and Chapeltown. In the pub,
girls in short leather skirts return from walks
down sidestreets, grab a spot of grub
and watch dominoes being slammed down hard
on marble tabletops. The whole world is
a dangerous romance, slowly edging forward
in the shadows, relying on memories
to get through its nightmares, meeting day
with the help of cigarettes, and cold pie on a tray.

10

Here is the ashtray's chaos, crumbs on a tray,
an empty glass. The blunt Northern accent
carries masculine warmth even in the grey
livery of garage and tenement.
Closed vowels, a rumbling in the belly.
Out on the moors harsher vowels of wind.
Spartan interiors. A sofa. The telly
by the wall. Down broken wet cobbles, blind
gropings of grass and weed. The poet in his chair
reciting Pope and Desnos. Children run
across a derelict site into a space that is nowhere
but must do. The city has room for everyone.
It does, after all, provide a kind of home:
crumbs on a tin tray, hair left in the comb.

11

Up-ended lead type, hair left in old combs:
lovers of small numbers go benignly potty;
big number men construct spectacular domes
and make long speeches. All is vanity
saith the preacher. A silver-headed man
labours among statues and word processors
turning language into an ingenious plan
to contain the universe and all its professors.
Why stop at the universe? My father picks
a stamp up with his tweezers and consults
his Stanley Gibbons. The world is full of maniacs
who hoard lost masterpieces in hidden vaults.
My mother vents her furies. The dictator resigns
after a fever, retires to a space between the lines.

12

After a fever, space between the lines
grows more attractive. Here the brittle hide
from gross events. A dazzling sun reclines
among the petals on the sill. Inside,
the cat pads across armchairs, a late fly
settles on the lampshade, the radio sings
to itself for ever and footsteps hurry by
without stopping. What continually brings
you up short? Your children trailing soft
fingers across the keyboard make their brief
excuses. Soon nothing substantial is left
except the words which offer no relief
from the bright precarious tedium of play
you read in negative at the end of the day.

13

You read in negative. At the end of the day
the light falls directly on you. Moon warms your skin
into endearments. My darling, you say
to the body whose pools you have swum in.
My dear. She catches a little moonlight
on her cheek and her shoulder. Now she dreams
of flying to her sick father, that shrunken, slight
figure in a distant bed. She moves through streams
of cloud and melts into sleep. The visitors
arrive with their negative gifts: the lamp
that glows black, cold fire, the open doors
of a closed room. It's hot in bed. She's damp
but cool – your life expands to fill the room
till there's nowhere to go. Come hope. Come home.

14

The question is where you go. Come hope, come home.
Her skin is palimpsest. You cannot read
her mind though you see it. At night, you roam
through the house watching the curtains bleed
to the floor. She is everything that holds
the pictures up, prevents headache, and turns
the world to language, sifting through the folds
of some larger brain, burning as fire burns
till you emerge like Tamino into music.
You try the word 'love', whisper 'death', and make
faces at yourself. You are growing sick
of eloquence. Perhaps you are beginning to awake
from the sleep of reason or are caught between
the teeth of words that grind like a machine.

15

The ego grinds and grates like a machine
producing tiny slips on which is written
the nonsense it feeds upon. What does it mean
to be a self, so soft and yet hard bitten?
What does the mirror say to the censor? Who
talks like this, erasing self in the process?
How do you know if it's valid or true?
What do you see at night when you undress?
Graffiti in the public toilets, signs
in the ashtray's chaos, pie on a tray
of upended type, hair left in the comb
after a fever, the space between lines
you read in negative at the end of the day.
The question is where you go. Come hope. Come home.

Portrait of My Father in an English Landscape
(for Peter Scupham)

1

The classic shot of my father is the one
in which he carries my brother in his arms
with me striding beside him, holding on
to his trousers. The past continually warms
the present. The nostalgia gap
is a pit into which images can fall
and never rise. Best to suspect a trap.
Yet there is something solid and spherical
about the figure I feel I have to build
into and out of language. He exhales
his own monument which hangs there, stilled
as the light which holds him but fails
to preserve the cells of wind that whistle through him
and could destroy his body at a whim.

2

Easy to destroy a body. A historical whim
drops him into childhood among white beards
and piety. There he stands, forever slim
and vulnerable, entranced by old men's words.
He waits at the foot of the bed. Tales and jokes,
small beaky women. Parables and sweets.
How did Jesus get to be God? Women stroke
his dark hair. His grandmother always greets
the returning schoolboy with a small gâteau.
An uncle draws a bag of squashed éclairs
from his pocket. Outside, big winds blow
up a storm. The world of tables and chairs
will never know what hit it. Soon they are gone,
preserved elsewhere but not worth sitting on.

3

Preserves and cakes. Eventually time sits on
the lot. Grandad got run down by a tram
and yet survived to claim the insurance. One
uncle opened a music shop. It closed like a clam
about him. The second grandfather died,
cancerous, still telling stories. The little beaks
are pecking in the kitchen. They provide.
There was a brother once among the relics,
a home child, insignificant, a paradox,
who died when a hill of sand came down
and covered him as he was playing beside the rail tracks.
He had a name too, a genuine proper noun.
Short words. God's scattered text. The scholar's passim.
Even on clear nights certain stars look dim.

4

On clear winter nights when even the dim
stars interject splinters of blue ice
into the conversation, dead faces swim
through wisps of cloud. Dante's paradise
glows in bright rings around the moon. There is rank
and order in their passage. Or so they say.
Ghost stories, gothic tales. A hostile tank
rumbles across the city and levels the way
to disjunction. My father in the office.
My father in the factory. In the road
with a lavatory pan on his head. His surface
is a broken narrative. He must load
his possessions onto the conveyor belt
of particularities, hard luck and guilt.

5

Particularities, hard luck and guilt
compose him. Mention his patience too,
also his kindness. His eyes are a warm quilt
to hide beneath. You can wander through
his fingers as through a wood (though similes
are not his style). You see a short man
full in the chest, thin legs, large nosed. He sees
the likeness, suspecting metaphor, can
marshal facts, add a column of figures,
size up a problem and suggest solutions.
All fathers are Prospero or else beggars
without authority. There are fashions
in viziers as in haircuts. His alchemical head
radiates a thin light which must be interpreted.

6

By what light though can he be interpreted?
He is the history I stand on with one leg.
I'm trying to peer into the murk and shed
light on my own behalf. Must Prospero beg
for interpreters? Listen, he is playing
his mouth organ in the forest. Others hum
or search for words. Something is weighing
on them. The icy wind has made them numb.
Soldiers without insignia, dying slaves
out of Michelangelo, they learn the tunes
appropriate to their sad huts and lost enclaves.
Their families are telling fortunes
in safe houses and ghettoes others have built
into chains of command, their bones cracked, blood spilt.

7

Chains of command crack bones. The blood spilt
underwrites him. One day his friends stole
a supply train. A true tale on a single stilt,
another terrifying anecdote to roll
towards posterity. One of many. What hurts
is the truth of every story, things being just
as they are, true without consequence, bit parts
in a ridiculous epic of cinematic dust.
Escape on the March Back. The First Sight
of the Chaotic Russian Army as they Spin
across Half Europe, mad Flight, sane Flight,
the Toiling Masses, Rape, Rapine and Repin.
Malenky robot. Three soldiers in a bed,
the woman beneath them crippled, maybe dead.

8

A woman crippled if not exactly dead
(his wife, my mother) offers him her cage
and he walks in. He knows she has touched dread
with her bare fingers. There is a savage
untenanted domesticity I could not begin
to measure. The reader must devote
time to getting this right, develop a skin
too tender to feel the world as anecdote.
Time to detach oneself. An overweight
man with a hernia, bad short term memory,
and need for companionship. Such late
revenges. Executions too summary.
I tell it wrong like he does. It's wrong to laugh
in the presence of a ghost or photograph.

9

The presences – not ghosts, nor photographs –
are symbols through which we walk together.
Our bodies are being resolved into epitaphs.
Outside, snow is working itself into a lather
about nothing. Language slips, words slide
and take pratfalls. I cannot quite conjure
this robust presence. Anecdotes hide
the very thing they describe in their pure
linear fashion. You can only focus
on one part of the picture, the rest shifts.
Perhaps that shifting is the true locus.
Perhaps anecdotes are frozen snowdrifts
that catch the light just so, shapes blown
and surfeited, whose centre remains unknown.

10

Surfeit of snow, the core remains unknown.
A winter park. He drags us forward, up
a slight hill. Our toboggan slithers on
and we descend. Soft landings. Now we cup
the snow in our gloved hands. A snowball.
The bus bonnet steams in the cold. The city
is an ice palace, the main street a great hall
approaching the square. His proximity
is his presence. The nearness of it. The wolf
enters his lair and asks for hot tea. The stove
in the corner warms us. Habitat and self
merge into sleep. It is a treasure trove
you cannot rob. The jewel's in the safe.
The wolf is in his lair. The children laugh.

11

The wolf in his lair, children begin to laugh
at their own fear. Kind wolf in a world of wolves.
Has father met the wolf? Wolves are the stuff
of legend. Their harsh morality revolves
about old prohibitions. One year Dad fell
from the first storey of a building site. His green
face in the hospital bed was shrill as a bell.
Poor wolf in a world of traps. Again the clean
lines of anecdote. I remember how he stroked
my face. Not then. Some other time. Just once
he let fly at me, when he had been provoked.
I had upset my mother. I felt his palm bounce
off my cheek. This wolf bites. He stalks alone
down the high street. Old solitary. Dry bone.

12

The high street is full of loners. Dry bones
in shop doorways. Here come the essences
under their layers of skin and flesh. Vague groans
of bodies in movement. Their circumstances
are apalling. We are not wolves but sheep
in the fold, gentle baas against the vast sky.
I imagine my father lying down, asleep
in that interior shelter where children cry
so faintly one can hardly tell their low
whimper from the dull sobbing of the wind.
The facts of any life are as they are, just so,
and never to be counted, stars in the sequinned
darkness, coloured sand to be sifted through
and banded, their edges neither straight nor true.

13

Bands of colour, edges just out of true,
conjure the Isle of Wight. I'm barely ten
and going through a religious phase. The blue
sky is the eye of God. Now and again
that clear sight homes in on something bright
and imposing. The teacher leads a prayer
like warm milk whose capillaries trickle right
down into my socks. No fatherly care
can ever be as sweet as this. The universe
has gentle hands to cradle a child's face.
It has its off-days too when it issues terse
directives, when it stares blankly at the place
relief should come from. I watch dad chew
his dinner, address him casually as you.

14

My father eats. I call him casually. You.
We argue for the sake of it as always,
because it is natural to argue.
I'm impatient. Some mischievous devil plays
us off against each other at opposite ends
of the table. I hate my impatience, hate
the cause of it. So hard to make amends,
impossible perhaps. It's getting late,
I look at my watch. He makes that worried gesture
with his hands which moves me. His eyes
are a warm cave swimming in faint moisture,
now turned inward, now open in surprise.
They hang there when the anecdotes are done.
The classic shot of my father. That's the one.

15

The classic shot of my father is the one
most easy to destroy. Historical whim
preserves a secret well worth sitting on,
though even on clear nights its stars are dim
particularities of luck and guilt.
He is a light that must be interpreted
through chains of command, cracked bones and blood spilt,
through women crippled, and often left for dead.
A presence, like the ghost in a photograph,
a surfeit, a core that can't be truly known.
The wolf is in his lair. The children laugh
in the high street at the old loner with his bone
and bandana, his edges neither straight nor true.
Their father waits for them and calls them You.

THE BUDAPEST FILE

(2000)

The Yellow House at Eszterháza

You find it suddenly, opening up, then
quickly closing like the entrance to any estate.
The car zips by and it's gone. You've passed the gate
before you know it. You double back and when
you take stock properly a kind of gladness
moves you to admit it, just as you are admitted
into history or heritage, something perfectly fitted
to bring about the light and giddy madness
the peasant must have felt on seeing it
finished; that life like this is an extension
of the limits of the known world, beyond mention,
incomprehensible, almost infinite,
as if it were not the chains he had to wear
but something utterly sprightly, made of air.

Today, a room stuffed full of faience stoves
so white you'd think you were in a dove cot
and the doves ready to fly. Putti like tiny cloves
protruding from stucco, part of a lost plot
in which even seasons defer to the family name.
Tendrils gilded and twining, frescoes, glass
reflecting more glass, the great room's twists of flame
turned into icing. Before, ordinary grass,
ordinary shrubs, conducting a geometric
dance, the fountain dancing, the dwarf trees
marking time, but also dancing in parodies
of local custom, then performing a vanishing trick
into dusk, and Joseph Haydn, asleep
in the music room, thirty fathom deep.

The age of elegance is short. The broad
welcome in the curving wings, enlightened
stables, kitchens, the gentle patronising of awed
visitors, the courtesy shown to the frightened
soldier make just one generation. Then the show
moves on. The Chinese hangings swell
into dust. There are no fountains to overflow
the curling brim. No major domo rings the bell
for supper. Things easy come are easy gone.
So the opera house goes all to blazes.
A machine gun strafes the precious vases.
The puppet theatre turns grain store. No one
is going to be too bothered by any of this.
Let it remain in a state of decorous paralysis.

And then a miracle. A vehicle in the drive
has grown rococo horns as living proof
of loyalty. Meanwhile, the dead arrive
on a child's bike carried on the car roof.
Like all the punning dead they want their freedom.
Enormous faience doves have taken wing
and filled the room. Where have they come from?
How could I possibly offer them anything
but some notion of elegance, of what is humane,
enlightened, thirsted for, ridiculous?
Joseph Haydn in gentle Hungarian rain,
snuffing candles out for a good purpose,
releasing an orchestra. A molehill. A piece
of metal like a cartridge case under the trellis.

Black as in Coffee

The way the spoon almost stands up. The way
the tiny cup fits into your palm, like
an amulet of darkness in broad day-
light. The way it is still as a lake
in blackest Lilliput.
                    There is in Europe
a kind of vacancy this fills, as it now fills
my own, in one black concentrated drop
as my internal barometer falls.

In the centre of the centre, at the core
of the pupil, there is a line that leads
to the centre of the heart, a tiny pool

for the last moon to sink into. There's more
of the world than this, we know, though little beads
of darkness gather there. But that's OK. That's cool.

The Lost Scouts

1

The caniculae are almost over. Cool
intermittent winds chase each other round
lush trees. Dead leaves are lying on the ground
and a light lace mantle descends on a pool
at the fag-end of the second millennium.

The wheels of the old world groan as they turn
over the bones of the dead who won't learn
their lessons and are destined to remain dumb.

The doors are open. The train empties
then fills, moves off. It is a great effort
moving towards the fire. The cog wheel railway
rises towards the woods' outer ring of darkness
without any visible means of support,
and time turns backwards into yesterday.

2

My father was a scout light years ago.
In a world of health and efficiency, he rowed
and hiked while the world was waiting to explode
under his feet, when those who could would blow
with it.

       He would leave the dark city down the river,
winding through valleys, up and down the scree-
paths of mountains in lung piercing clarity,
that could sustain a boy almost for ever.

Friends sang and played Baden-Powell games
in colonies of urban dust, wore ties
with toggles, khaki shorts and walking boots,
kept rank and discipline to funny names
adapted from wood-craft, moved through woods like spies
in a body cult of uniforms and suits.

3

They sing now, as they sang when there were many,
when the dead were young and wore vests and grins
and went diving and tramping: Mowglis, Sir Galahads,
Chingachcooks, Wolves, all of a mythical company
bound by codes and by magic, where manhood begins
with oaths and secrecy, discipline and parades.

And so they marched off, being Jews, to places
the century saved for them. Marched to the tunes
of the day that were sung in the cabaret and the beer hall,
their bodies still young but with premature faces,
my father, Akela, the wolf pack, to make their fortunes
among the lost behind a fence or a high wall,

fifty-five years ago along with their leadership,
their heroes and brothers as if on a day trip.

4

So history came and blew them apart. Their arms
and legs and heads flew off, their bodies aged
in camps. They froze in forests. Fires raged
in ovens at the heart of unbearable farms.

The handsomest, cleverest, most athletic...the fire
consumes whatever is thrown on it. Those once burned
remained burnt, but some, as always, returned
with only their whiskers singed while the flames leapt higher.

I have a photograph of six of them
straddling a fallen tree trunk. Only two
survived the time. Luck smuggled such through
prison gates, in some cases only *pro tem*.

But I can't help thinking of the lost scouts,
their songs, their chants, their ever more distant shouts.

5

Here they are now. My father among a hundred
lost boys, knights of the round table, the dark wood
glooming behind them, their faces turned red
by the central fire which signifies brotherhood.

Memory washes away the scent of ashes
and rounds off the sharp edge of broken glass,
but they keep the fire going with twigs and rushes
like decent schoolboys in a promising class.

Old men from Canada, Spain, The States, Australia,
with wives and children, gathered as if
for the Grand Order of Water Buffaloes
or the Rotary Club, wearing invisible regalia
of firelight as the night-cold clutches stiff
arthritic fingers and feels its arthritic toes.

6

They sing and tell stories. That is the role of the old
who have travelled the roads and rails of atrocity.
They sing old songs as they move through the city
in business suits, fully insured and bankrolled,
in laboratories, concert halls, cool studios,
high office blocks, respectable addresses,
their tears tucked under the pillowslips of brilliant successes
or sizzling in embers under long melted snows.

This language is too fancy for them. Let them crack jokes.
Let them remember old japes. Let them recall excursions
on the Danube or any other river. Let them have a drink
or two, let them over-eat and grow ulcers. Old blokes
with baseball caps, their peculiar foibles and aversions.
Old guys in their cups, in fine fettle, in the pink.

7

But as we leave the gardens of the hotel where the fire
dies down and move to the edge of the forest
a man begins screaming. It is now, the merest
moment, trapped in the moment, as if in some dire
prison. A single man in the wood, furious,
cursing invisible enemies, while our bus waits
like a dim lit room. There is something that hates
the world, it seems. The man in the wood is its curious
emanation.

        One of the scouts had made
a kind of a dummy he called the spirit of evil
and threw it on the fire where it fell with a long hiss.
It was a strange moment and I felt afraid
thinking of other fires, of the work of the devil
whatever that is. I prefer not to think of this...

8

What is better in early September than these
reliable trees closing over our garden
on the leafy side of the city? It is no great burden
carrying the memory of them. They please
me now, the next day, as they had the eyes
of boys my father's age before they grew
into their old age of returns. There's nothing new
in nature, not that you'd know, but the surprise
of complexity and light.

        The poet Radnóti, who died
in a ditch, wrote of his garden and his wife
on a summer afternoon drinking with his friends.

Then came history, and the wolfpacks they cried
appeared at the door and demanded their one life
and they gave it, like that, and so the evening ends.

Bruno Schultz in Amber: The Demons

There I was looking after Numero Uno,
a tiny cog in the wheels of commerce, just
a speck in the mirror eyeing a gorgeous bust.
I was like a character out of Bruno
Schultz, confined to bed, telling tall tales
of grandfathers and earwigs, with a tame
aesthetic protector to absolve me from all blame.
I can simply tell a joke if all else fails,
I thought, then remembered Schultz's fate, shot dead
in the street by a jealous officer of the Wehrmacht.
Perhaps I'd made my life up. Perhaps I'd stacked
a whole library in my empty head
and this was my life, or some of it, in print
on yellowed paper you might read at a squint.

The bed was like a page turned down. Out crept
a few demons of the conventional kind:
itches and burns, a verruca, undefined
scabs, weird discolourations, each adept
at its own mischief. A monastic scribe
might have depicted them fleeing city walls,
at the edge of the text, in shrivelled petals,
with the faces of a long forgotten tribe.
What insignificances had I given
birth to? Had they all conspired to haunt me?
One monster kept on multiplying, lost
in endless clones of itself. He'd never be driven
from my body, would always be there to daunt me
while I lay there like a child with fingers crossed.

The clothes hung on the door congealed to one
fat figure, somewhat like Sidney Greenstreet
in *The Maltese Falcon*. It was a discreet
appointment I had to make with him. I'd done
something wrong and he was to admonish
and threaten me in that lumbering way of his,
breathing and billowing in the impossible breeze.
Pointless hoping, however I might wish
for him to go. I was like Peter Lorre
but tinier still and much more vulnerable.
A bullet would find me ten minutes from the end.
I could almost hear my father begin to worry
about my lack of sleep. It meant more trouble:
a son to re-dream, one more thing to mend.

A Pink Face

1

I thought I had a sense of my own life
there in the hotel drawer, just underneath
the television, something I'd wear like a wreath
at my funeral to focus the world's grief
at my so precipitate passing at eighty-two
after a hearty meal. Perhaps I'd cut
my wrist and the blood had dried already, but
that's not how it felt at the time. Then, through
the hotel window, appeared a swollen face,
one of those stucco heads, filled out with flesh
of lurid pink, a slice of ham on a dish,
grinning violently. This was the wrong place
for such nightmares to appear. It could not last,
but I was scared and shut the window fast.

2

The pink head hung in the air, faintly burning
like a distant match. Below it the whole town
was going about its business, walking up and down,
entering doorways, setting forth, returning.
Boys were kicking a ball. A little girl
looked out of a window. At night three drunks
roared a popular song amid solid chunks
of fallen masonry. Leaves lifted in a swirl
of wind. Clouds sprinted over the rooftops
and the sun dodged in and out extremely fast
and bright. Time was doing its mad march past
in a parody of precision. The Keystone Cops
sat at the wheel and set off in pursuit.
The stucco head was slowly taking root.

3

Later I saw it again, leering through the grain
of the pine desk the hotel had provided
for visiting academics. There was something lop-sided
about the room. It seemed to fall like rain
and run away from me down through the sluice
of the street outside. Meanwhile the face composed
itself into a form of scrutiny, its eyes half closed,
the mouth set hard. It would accept no excuse,
however feasible, for my lack of sense
of life, and though I knew it was just statuary

I still felt guilty, scared and jittery
in its august, hallucinatory presence.
Whose face was it really? Out of what mould
had its features fallen, furious and cold?

4

Or was this merely fantasy, the kind you see
in architects' notebooks and harmless for all that?
The streets were full of them, curving from flat
and undemanding walls, peering through a tree
as people passed beneath. They wore the faces
of lost decades. If they had memories
they kept them hidden under the scuffed frieze
they rose above, grotesque old commonplaces
in a fallen language, a dog Latin *bow-wow*
while real life went on in the darkened rooms
they were set to guard, among the fading blooms
of floral wallpaper, surviving any old how
across the street, past curtains, in the crooks
of armchairs, in the smell of rotting books.

5

My paranoiac schizophrenic stage
was blooming nicely. Goodbye to the Me
defined by ancestors and society
(but there was no such thing). One self could rage
against another or completely ignore
its wild companions. Somebody once claimed
everyone had to be somewhere. I blamed
the world, that ticking thing outside the door
with its pink face. One day it would explode
and take me with it while the citizens
of my two countries got on with their lives
down million miles of straight and narrow road.
The self is a dead loss. The window opens
on a pale pink head. Something at least survives.

FROM

AN ENGLISH APOCALYPSE

(2001)

History

It was all so long ago that rain fell
antique yellow into the ornate gutters of the city.
Skirts were short or long, either way it was pretty,
and the whole world was frozen under the spell
of its own evanescence. I speak as a witness,
a napalm-scented ghost with a gift of flames
who even now can reel off sacred names,
the kind that glowed and terrified us witless.
I am an old soldier of the last empire, sold
into captivity by what then seemed eternal:
Brezhnev's beetling eyebrows, the sloping nose
of Tricky Dicky, bricks of South African gold.
I am an emperor, sans eyesight and sans kernel,
sans principles, sans annuity, sans clothes.

It was once upon a time, it was history,
it was the day before, the day that never happened.
The thing I am, or think I am, had ripened
to the semi-transparent spectre that you see.
True, there were consolations: when we held hands
or went driving, our hands in each other's laps,
but the car died like the other death-traps
and oil was creeping up deserted seaside sands.
People were blowing us up. The prime minister's lawn
was crowded with tanks. And as it is my dear,
I can't tell it straight, I don't think I would believe me.
It was the evening before the night before the dawn
and when we kissed we heard the ironic cheer
of what we thought was history mouthing *please don't leave me.*

I want a voice to speak this, twenty-nine
years of it, in a voice that is a hum heard down
telegraph wires from another, distant part of town,
or a train that is only a rumour mumbled on the line,
to tell us what is or was important, what made
time fly or the cat leap, or raised the alarm
about life passing with its dangerous feline charm,
morning, afternoon and night in a continuous parade
of light and darkness, blossoming and folding, you
in your girly skin, me in my own husk,
the years packed neatly away inside my purse
or so you'd think but always falling through,
the coins disappearing in the summer dusk,
my voice too straight, untuneful, strangely hoarse.

Time music is ghost music. The radio in the room
is speaking too quietly to hear so I turn it up.
It is us talking to each other across a narrow gap
at the beginning of the new millennium.
Like all human voices, we hang there a moment
as good as for ever, in a frozen frame
in a film made of frames, repeating the name
that holds us in its vague presentiment.
Those were our lips, and that noise we made
is still humming in the wires which are electric.
I am listening very carefully, my darling.
I am watching the dust swirling under the lampshade,
hoping to learn the odd useful evanescent trick
from the radio that fades a while then starts to sing.

Acclimatisation

One minded one's manners those days. The fork
turned discreetly downwards, raking and spearing,
and chewing with mouth closed, despite mischievous
hints to the contrary. England was a cloud under
which one learned the dangers of interfering
in other people's business. A distant thunder
strung the roofs together as if by metalwork
and teachers in schools tried terribly to forgive us

our trespasses. We worried away at the lawn
like blind men learning the alphabet, listened
to the grave consensus of Butskellite heads
sprouting from their collars, took energetic
part in quiz-games where ladies glistened
in sequin and varnish, heard frenetic
voices by wrecked aeroplanes in a cold dawn
huddling in frozen grey-blanketed beds.

We also misheard: *puncher* for *puncture*,
wicked for *wicket*. They were comical times,
learning fixations and the twelve times table,
the inordinate lengths short trousers could go to,
the proper droop for socks, the sound of door chimes,
the hell-hole of pet shops. Sometimes we were slow to
pick up a hint, to smile at the appropriate juncture
of a given conversation, were too often liable

to solecisms of an almost terminal sort.
But God and our teachers forgave us. Meanwhile there were
the consolations of Ealing comedies,
the *Daily Herald* and all that wonderful Britishness
to keep us going. My mother drank her
black coffee with mountains of cream. We grew less
strange by the month. The days grew short
as did our affections. Soon we were anybody's.

Pearl Grey

Holding the egg was like trying to balance
light at the tip of your fingernail. It rose
almost weightless, a bubble born of chance
and sky at the point where creation froze
to one brief statement now about to crack.
There was a pair of earrings once, two pearls
in golden corollae gently peeled back
round hard glassy mist, nestling above curls
of hair. She might have been my mother, or
any other woman of a certain time
that now seems gone (though who can be that certain?)
There were clouds and scent of rain outside the door.
It was spring or summer, you could hear the chime
of ice-cream vans, the rustling of the curtain.

All time was concentrated in that egg
and life was delicate. Birds bustled in hedges,
slurring languages. One pecked at a clothes-peg,
another tugged at a worm at the edges
of vision. Time was simply the product
of flight and language. It was saying this
quietly to itself while waiting to self-destruct.
Light stood in a cup, too petrified to kiss
the draining-board. Everything stopped in fear.
My mother sat in the kitchen. I was elsewhere.
The ice-cream van was chiming. It was grey
outside, I remember. There, below her ear
hung the pendant or maybe it was hair.
The egg was slightly rocking on the tray.

The yellow dress my father fell in love with
(for Seamus Heaney)

It was the yellow dress my father fell
in love with: skimpy in late sixties style.

My father usually works till six. Meanwhile
the garden waits. The kitchen. The terrible
last years in the last house in the last street.
History has slipped off into the bushes where
it waits in darkness like a murderer.
The whole house has grown sticky and sweet.
He looks from the window, sees you at the end
of the garden and thinks: how beautiful.
He thinks you beautiful, as she once was
but gentler somehow as if you'd come to mend
his life or mine. And she is sitting at the table
where light is dancing as it always does.

VDU

The office seemed melancholy, as do all
offices. An elderly man fingered
sheets of paper, shadows crept under tall
filing cabinets, the typists lingered
over paper cups. I was between
school and college, an adolescent bard
vaguely attracted to the Ginsberg scene
about which I knew little. It was hard
being a prisoner of the old regime,
rubber stamping, envelope licking. True,
it was closer to home than jazz and Gregory Corso
but still I worked my mischief, in a dream
of late release and looked to being through
like everybody else there, only more so.

Later I was a visitor, a ghost
at the windows, catching sight of myself
superimposed on a view of streets, almost
transparent, as if across an immense gulf
between two worlds, one inside one out,

but did not recognise the figure at the desk
with its monitors, the man scuttling about
in the background, an impenetrable mask.
Most of the staff were still there, only more so,
gentler and kinder somehow and ageless,
this time with VDUs like goldfish bowls
to calm them. Each figure had a classical torso
clad in some version of Edward Hopper dress,
all of them faintly glowing like lost souls.

Like lost souls, only more so, only more lost,
and this was my fault, because almost certainly
it was I who'd lost them. An elderly man crossed
the room. It was my father, or a memory
of someone like my father. Or even me,
reflected in the glass on the other side
of the street. He sang. It was like hearing a tree
sing to the night which was coming in like a tide.
Soon the screens would be dark and the room
washed away. There'd be just one more black window
hiding the information it was meant to light.
Someone was moving in there with a broom,
tidying things though it was all too late and slow
to make much difference to anyone that night.

Triptych for Music

Dusty Springfield: My Brother's Wedding

Dusty Springfield singing, *I only wanna be with you*,
the sound of slippers flopping forward on the floor
and a little terrier at the bride's feet signifying, *faithful and true*.
The floorboards are bare and spotless, a fragile pallor

sits on their skins, an eggshell finish, and still Dusty sings
broken words in a broken voice: *Don't know what it is
that makes me love you so*. There are very few things
in the room: a mirror, a light-fitting, a few oddities

like fruit on the chest, a signature on the wall.
Everything points to the presence of a witness
in whose honour the bulb burns and the mirror reflects.

You've got to give me some of your loving... hours fall
into an empty cup, the years are clinging to her dress.
In the brilliant window-pane no dust collects.

Elvis 1956

They are playing *Heartbreak Hotel* on the juke box.
I am not quite eight years old but the *Ed Sullivan Show*
has let a monster loose on the world. The country rocks,
blue suede shoes tap. Here, in a drift of snow,

come the Russian tanks. My parents though
are listening to Franz Lehár and the Rákoczi March.
Their eyes are fixed on a beautiful merry widow
waltzing her way round the proscenium arch.

Today, Elvis is dead, but he winds himself up
to his full height. His legs begin to tremble
and his throat has that deep catch in it. My feet

move to the jive, following his. I can't stop
for the sheer drive of his voice and the simple
throb of a damp bass, as hollow as it's sweet.

Beautiful Place

Only one beautiful place, says music as it thrums
chords to itself. When I think of the beautiful place
I imagine it with Schubert. No one comes
and no one goes in the great organic palace,

everyone is alone. My parents are asleep
somewhere in the cellars, and the wind slips
through rooms several storeys deep.
I'm in the earth with them. Something grips

my heart. A violin is scribbling light
over the dark floor. These images are
pointless, I know. Music has no need

of what we say or think about it. Tonight
my mother is dead for the twenty-fifth year.
Schubert tiptoes through the house as I read.

The boys who beat up my brother

(for Andrew Szirtes)

1

The boys who beat up my brother, day after day,
had faces smeared with snot, their skin was grey.
They cornered him outside and raised their cry:
Jewboy, the name they knew my brother by.
Jewboy, Jewboy, they called him, and struck out.
Blows were the world they knew too much about.
And when that failed they told teacher who took
delight in hitting my brother with a book.

Blows were the world they knew. They could recite
the litany of those they had to fight.
The world was rough and little of it fair,
though you could ask it questions here and there.
But with no judge in chambers and no jury
rough justice called for pity or cold fury.

2

Cold fury is what I bring them. Every night
in their cold beds. Every morning over
breakfast. Every lunchtime. Every bite
they take. May they never again recover
their appetite or equilibrium.
It's late in the day, too late and much too late.
The furies that freeze outside have made the quantum
leap into ancient past as sheer dead weight.

To be kicked in the ribs and lose your power of speech
is to be tied to someone else's bed
of pain. To feel the snot running down your chin
is like finding yourself on a deserted beach
with nothing in your stomach or your head
but waves and pounding fists, an idiot grin.

3

You come to the place by water, and you land
on salt-sprayed concrete. Cold fury is the sea
at its most melancholic. It is the frozen hand
that shoves you ashore, scrapes at your bare knee,
and claws when you turn round. A poor estate
outside the city walls: its citizens,
working in the shipyards, congregate
to welcome you suspiciously. Their kitchens

will never see you, nor their parlours. They
take stock, hang back. They offer you advice
and sundry favours. Some of them hate you now
and go on hating you. You won't go away.
You become an object of fear. You are not as nice
as they are. You want to be but don't know how.

4

London was suburbs that seemed to stretch forever,
a vast relief map of the rich and poor
divided by bus routes, streets you crossed over,
avoiding the feet of salesmen at the door,
children who aged so fast, their blasted faces
began to sag like the plastic bags they carried,
that darkened then faded to the smelly places
they lived in, left, returned to when they married,

divorced, sickened and died. There was no
refinement in this cruelty. It was broad
and insistent, a faintly robotic hammering.
Then everything went quiet. A slow
turning away and crossing of the road.
Withdrawal, sullenness and stammering.

5

Jewboy is not this island's privilege.
That shit-hatred is common currency.
Always there are those living at the edge
of self-respect who loathe the strange, the fancy
and the vulnerable. But it's not enough.
Cold fury is what you have. You spend it
where appropriate, there's gallons of the stuff.
The hatred is universal. You never mend it.

There is a kind of silence that's specific
to a place. You enter it with respect
and make your home in it. It opens up
like a heart that is almost refusing to tick.
You become it: it is now an object
you possess and love and are afraid to drop.

6

The boys who beat up my brother are living still,
Their day is gone. They're long over the hill.
I've seen them walking down the shopping street
with carrier bags, staring at their feet.

Their shoes were scuffed, cheap trainers, heavy boots.
They wore old jeans or crumpled shiny suits.
Their hair had thinned. Their scalps were peeking through.
Their knuckles wrinkled red and white and blue.

I speak plain so they hear me. I don't think
that they will listen. I offer them a drink.
They tell me life is worse than I can guess.
They tell me, and expect some tenderness
to creep out of the language and embrace
what's left of them and the whole island race.

Solferino Violet

Once he had opened his violin-case
that inner plush overwhelmed me. I know
there is a question here, an innuendo
I don't intend to answer to your face,
like synaesthesia, or something to do
with sexuality, mother, or the bowels,
that there is a power within us which howls
at the moon. And then the old man drew
the bow across and the strings vibrated sad
and dusty answers back at me. The room
was responding to him in its turn.
This reciprocity was all we had
between us and it had begun to bloom
Judaic flowers: Oistrakh, Heifetz, Stern.

Get real, I said. These are the grandfathers
you never knew and felt no strong desire
ever to meet. Old schlocks gone to the fire
with their doilies and candles; infrequent bathers
in the Protestant sun, solemn upholders
of precedent, given to self abuse
and cancer, eternal bearers of bad news.
I was an unwilling fly on their shoulders.
I believed my own propaganda like
anyone might. I didn't want them, wished
them gone. With the floor vibrating under
my feet, I was waiting for the music to strike
some respect into me so I should feel ravished
by its omnipotent *yes* of squeal and thunder.

When thunder came I let the violet seep
into my bloodstream along with all that
ravishment. I was in a shallow sleep
where dreams move in insidious flat
planes under the watchful eye of a mind
left unattended. And then cherries! A wood
full of cherries appeared somewhere on my blind
side, disorientating, the colour of blood.
A memory of rolling down the hill
gorged with black cherries, my mother looking on
then rolling with me. And so everything
kept rolling. I could imagine being ill
with too much sweetness, finding myself alone
with a stretch of wire, a single metal string.

Resin along horsehair. My brother stood
in front of the open window, tightening strings.
A G-Plan coffee-table, more glass than wood,
supported an ashtray and some tea things.
The suburbs were singing. He wore a quiff,
Cliff Richard style. Felix Bartholdy
waited on the stand. There was something stiff
about the day, stiff and melancholy
as the furniture. Slowly I was waking
from nightmare to a kind of lovely music.
My brother played. He really was good at it.
I accompanied him, my fingers aching
with tension and all the summer air thick
with the sound of the colour violet.

Rousing those violets, the old man ran
a couple of scales through his withered hands.
Light from the stained glass window threw bands
of colour across his fingers. He began
some other piece whose name I now forget.
I felt like leaving. I didn't want to be
wound into this, not here, in Kingsbury,
North London, staring at that violet
plush in the open case. I felt, as they say,
strangely moved. It was a long time ago.
Some thirty years. Even now the faint buzz
of the lower strings can give me away.
It's nice to think of a colour called Solferino.
Of course, I didn't then know what it was.

All In

1

At fifty I recall the *Best of British* like pork
set out on a slab. There is the ringside and there
is our friend, Tibor, the wrestler. It is hot work
being thrown about. My father and I stare
horrified at his violent transformation
into gristle. Bruise after bruise appears.
We feel indecent in the foreign commotion.
My father shakes. I'm on the edge of tears.
This is the empire, the gladiatorial
climax of something tough and full of spit.
We don't recognise it as such, but a vast
weight is collapsing in the inquisitorial
balance. We can't bear to look at it.
When the lights come up we disappear fast.

2

We disappear fast, much as we always do
at times like this. A sexual drone begins
as on a distant bagpipe. Someone is falling through
the ropes. A woman adjusts her dress. Light thins
to dust. Bodies move as if in a mirror.
There's too much flesh in the world, too much blood
in the veins. Beckmann. Balthus. Burra.
Heavy thighs push through a field of mud.
There is a language for this and I am trying
to speak it. It is an old clock that shudders
in the corner of a boarding house: *glug, glug*
it says. On the window-ledge flies are dying
on their backs. Inside it, cloud shadows
billow across the bathroom shaving mug.

3

Big Daddy is about to splash from ropes.
His enormous belly sways as he climbs up
straddling the post. The other man gropes
the air like a crocked spider, waits for him to flop.
The sadness in their eyes crawls out with them,
emerging from headlocks, nelsons, shoulderpins.
Their strangleholds delicate as the stem
of a wine glass when the big party begins.
They are nobility in the abstract, bodies beautiful

cradling wounded minds. Their lovers touch
their hidden softness with solicitude,
turning them into butterflies, light bulls
in lost china shops. Nothing is too much
for them to ask, no single touch too crude.

4

My father and I recoil from violence.
He hits me once and there's an end of that.
I don't hit back. We're living in a tense
empire that could fall and squash us flat.
It's slowly falling now but there is time
to roll away in one well practised ruse.
The map beneath us shifts and burns like lime,
its scarlet territories are a bruise
that will not heal too fast. But here we are
and here is Tibor flying through the air,
a human projectile about to crash.
The sport is low, but he's a shooting star.
He hits the ground, he brushes back his hair
and waits to loose his trademark forearm smash.

The Umbrellas

Even now I cannot help thinking of them
as historical. The noise they make drowns
out the radio static of the street. Grey gowns
of rain flutter or run away in a million gem
spectacular but these dark suns expand
and guard us from the present danger which
is simply a drench of brilliants, rich
as the flood. Look, children, I hold out my hand
beyond its perimeter fence. The fine
spray gathers in my palm then dies away.
I close the black sun and hobble off with it.
It sighs as it closes, approximates to a line
or a stick, like the day before yesterday,
or the meetings of a wartime cabinet.

White Hart Lane

(for Francis Gilbert)

It hardly matters now. But it was there:
the stadium with its single focus, and you,
fragmented, anxious, someone they let through
with gestures of diffused paternal care

because you too were to be initiated
into what they were, which made you proud,
yet careful. You were and were not the crowd,
its passions high, ironic, understated,

brutal, like an earthquake just beginning
with a drumming of feet and the small roar
rising as teams appeared on the far side

dappling the pitch. You watched the notion of winning
and losing harden into focus and kept score
of everything, the small matter of pride.

*

It's premonition. The whole thing's premonition
and there's the poetry. The lilac team
is (phonetic) Dózha. Do you remem-
ber? Time is fracture and compression,

like this line. They're only names you recall
with a certain vividness. But later
when the ball came your way, like rainwater
in a winter pantomime, like any ball

a challenge, a threat, something personal
and you practised juggling with it or ran
zigzags between markers, you were chosen.

The hours you spent by a suburban brick wall
in northwest London! You were already a man
without a future, as if all time had frozen.

*

It is what dance is, only with a brief
dumb purpose: courage, grace, power, speed and guile
at the service of pride glimpsed through a turnstile,
accompanied by the sharp, interim grief

of any loss. Even a dull game will serve
to keep things ticking over and the great ones
survive in fragments beyond their seasons
in a leap, or run, or tackle, or body-swerve...

But I'm dumb, like everyone else. It is the way
it must be, that you must understand:
it's what we are, who can't speak or dare to think

that it or we matter. It's just another day
in the league. I hold my father's hand
both of us pitched forward, on the terrace brink.

Spring Green
Three apocalyptic grotesques

Think of it at the feet of a young dandy
in emblematic Tudor costume: part
nature, part intellect, much like the heart
he wears on his full sleeve. Romantic, randy

and common as grass painted by a child
in her first school; look, it runs down the page
and dribbles onto the desk, an image
of everything that is innocuous and wild...

White rabbits, mushrooms, snails, blackberrying,
the sherbet dip with liquorice stick, pence
in purses. He is dreaming of her hand

white as a sugar mouse, of burying
his head in her breasts in a green nonsense
of lawns and roses, somewhere in England.

*

The floral clock moves round from light to shade.
The boarding houses rattle with visitors.
It is *Brighton Rock*, Sid James, Diana Dors,
Brylcreem and Phyllosan and Lucozade.

Dirk Bogarde kills Jack Warner. The Duke of Squat
dances with Miss Fiona FitzFollicle
at her coming out party. A spherical
moon is lightly balanced on the scout hut.

The grass in *Genevieve* glimmers like yards
of cloth in a tailor's shop. Kenneth More
perspires gently in the August sun.

Along the sea-front men are buying postcards
of the promenade. West Indies score
freely on a green wicket. Time moves on.

*

A perfect greenness, everything is neat.
I'm back in the springtime of a realm
of primary colours which overwhelm
desire, back at the young dandy's feet

among earthworms, beetles, between the blades
of individual grass from which depend
bright beads of dew. It is, I think, the end
of the world. Birds are singing serenades

to the great chain of being for the last
time. Someone is slicing up a cow.
Someone bottles the spaces between things.

Life is kissing and telling, but telling it fast
as if there were always and only a single now,
a spring to cap and end all other springs.

The Ropes

There was a hut a mile along the cliff
where cub scouts gathered. Here they learnt the ropes
and how to tie them into useful shapes.
It was a chapter in their faux-naif
childhood, since time was passing and quite soon
there would be no more children. The adult
winds, the massive grown-up sea, the old salt
in the mature parlour; late afternoon
for a Phyllosan culture in climacteric
decline. The ropes were only the words
anyone used, sagging a little, loose
as old clothes and the ancient air was thick
and hoarse, the cliff crowded with blue birds,
sheepshanks and reef-knots tightening to a noose.

Sepia: The Light Brigade

A late spring rain has washed the field away.
Skin shows beneath the skin. A pallid smudge
of earth turns into marsh, to a dead language.
Under the grass long smears of human clay
lie down and rise, lie down again, and walk
into low cloud as if into lines of fire.
A couple on the path. A woman. An entire
family out for a stroll. The leaves talk

in ghost whispers and a bird reiterates
its single warning that life attends on fear,
that every green must turn to sepia.
The future looks on patiently and waits
clipping its fingernails, tugging at its ear.
The landscape yawns, grows steadily sleepier.

Copper Brown

And when it was worn smooth, a Victorian bun
with all its features drowned, obliterate,
a kind of pessary or wafer, without date
or motto, when it could hardly hurt anyone,
under a garden clod or in a forgotten tin
along with buttons, old stamps, bits of lace,
with its horrendous apology for a face,
a half-cock ghost next to a rusty pin,
it still disturbed, if only for the hands
you knew had touched it once, its princely sum
part of a historical continuum
that would eventually present its strict demands,
when it would stand there pounding at your door
like death in the simple annals of the poor.

In the Greek Restaurant

Sometimes I dream I am swimming. Afternoon.
The sun shines in the window across the bed
which still has not been made, curiously slanted.
And from downstairs comes the sound of a cartoon
with jerky music. My tail goes *twitch*, *twitch*, *twitch*.
I am a big fish in a small pond. And then I wake.
It's time to start cooking, get the plates out, make
the tables ready, prepare another rich
but neutered stew. The kitchen grows quite hot.
We swig a little wine, keep working till six
then relax a little. Great big gouts of steam
hang by the ceiling over the open pot.
A distant radio plays. The wall-clock ticks
inside my head, the kettle emits a dying scream...

To have come so far and then to find the street
reasonable but no more, the weather dull
with not much passing trade when pubs are full,
a market nearby, occasionally to meet
old friends who might help out, the children set
for business or professions at some school

326

and your hair thinning, your eyes like cat's drool,
saying hello to the old girl with the hairnet...
It isn't good enough. But then your countrymen
drag their ghosts in, pour out a few drinks...
a bit of *folklor* for the visitors...
the odd loud fight or quarrel now and then...
and deep in the night the darkly spreading inks
of squids across vast glimmering kitchen floors.

Coolidge in Indigo

There are bad scenes. The film with the jagged
edge between two murders when the curtain
moves and the child stands lost and uncertain
staring at shadows, imagining the haggard
face of his mother opening her mouth wide
and the sound of a fly, the simmering
of a pan and the distant clock glimmering
like his image in the window, multiplied
as if for ever between two moments. So
into that dusk came Coolidge, its shuttered
general store and desolate garage
trailing off into dust which seemed to blow
from nameless places where nothing had mattered
for years or suffered some terminal haemorrhage.

Then Anthony got out to check the map.
Three or four men glanced over. They were poor,
the kind who lend themselves to metaphor
with nothing else to lend, caught in a trap
which had closed over them. Their mouths closed
over each other in that twilight, stranger
than cinema. Each one smelled of danger,
of damp but flammable rooms. They posed
in their dreamscape like symbols, long detached
from anywhere but the desert and the long
featureless road where station-wagons rusted.
This was a bad moment. My foot gently touched
the gas pedal. Something was wrong
with the map in which we had naively trusted.

And then the road trailed off and hot dust threw
itself against the tight window. A road sign
pointed to towns way off the marked line.
The thin Arizona wind gathered and blew
vague traffic past us, and later we arrived
in some lit town, and later still in Scottsdale,
in time for our dinner date. The night was stale
with relief. We felt we had survived
some insignificance. Our host waited
in the lobby and we drove off to a vast
inedible dinner. The sky was indigo,
with many stars like something inflated.
Our host was counting his credit cards. At last
he found his preferred option and we could go.

Kayenta Black

Some time through dinner Freddie Ganado said
he'd worn black for six years but recently
gave all that up. His clothes looked black to me,
but no, he said, they were dark blue. We had
arrived in Flagstaff, having left behind
the reservation with its thick despairs.
Kayenta, torrential rain. Rows of school chairs.
One attractive girl had made up her mind
to be the first Navajo US president.
Sharp as hell but suicidal, our host
informed us as she drove us down the road
to Monument Valley, herself a monument.
After seventeen years she resigned her post
from sheer frustration. And so the story flowed

as we flew on. And she had organised
a ropes project, a kind of confidence
or bonding exercise, and this made sense
right here where Indian stores advertised
trinkets and rugs next to a row of shacks.
We took pictures and read poems to a few
more students that evening while a cold wind blew
fresh and hard outside down quiet dirt tracks.
One shy and silent boy offered us discreet

gifts of turquoise. We thanked each other
effusively. He left. We talked and wrote
down names. It was sacramental and sweet,
like taking leave of a daughter or a mother,
a gentle, heartfelt clearing of the throat.

Freddie said he wanted a synthesis
between Kerouac and the Navajo religion,
it was something he could clearly imagine.
Indeed he was desperate to achieve this.
His girlfriend had chucked him. He was very young.
After the reading we all drove into town
and bought him a bottle of pale Newcastle Brown
he could not finish because it was too strong.
Sadness oozed from him, and hope. His face was
very beautiful but life was hard. Meanwhile
the leader of the pipe band was engaged
in conversation with Ian and the buzz
of the bar grew louder and Freddie gave a smile
so tired and lost it seemed the world had aged.

And I thought back to the dinner party where
Pedro's wife – a Berkeley graduate –
spoke haltingly above her untouched plate
of *vol-au-vents*. She too was in despair
and lost in this impromptu gathering.
She said it was a civilised neighbourhood
then they both left. The food was very good,
our hostess kind, and there was Freddie sitting
in black which he said was blue. Round my neck
the turquoise stone I had been given by
the silent boy in Kayenta, silent as a mouse
but six foot high and sixteen stone, in black.
So I talked on amused and flattered by
the crisp intelligent daughters of the house.

Azure

Barney Kessel strums at the smoky air
then in comes Ella. The breath she expels
has something steely about it. It smells
of perfume and aggressive hardware.

Outside: cars and the waiting universe
that catches onto warmth and chills it through,
while further up, the stars are full of blue
distances gathering to rehearse.

Somewhere beyond numbers the word *soul*
drifts with its meteor showers and dead suns,
detached from meaning like a piece of trash...

Dreaming, drifting, sings Ella, in control.
But out among the tables soul outruns
body and slowly burns down to fine ash.

                    *

Meanwhile a girl is flagging down a taxi,
a couple look through a window, and upstairs,
alone in the world of tables and chairs,
a small boy tunes in to the galaxy,

his fingers scrabbling on the keyboard. His eyes
don't need to look down. The world unwraps
itself behind the screen as he thinks and taps
out messages. Next door a baby cries,

someone is watching TV or a video.
Ella is on the record, singing this.
His sisters plays, parents get on with things.

Even the universe needs somewhere to go
so why not here? Later, the parents kiss
their children. *Drifting... dreaming... azure...* Ella sings.

                    *

Later, much later. Not Ella but Parker and Dizzy
throwing in White Christmas for Bud Powell,
and as the doomed boppers disembowel
another tune and the waitresses are busy

with the drunks on Thirteen, the boy revises
his A level maths and plays a little music
waiting for it to settle in. Bird's lick
follows some hidden line, loops and rises,

ties things together in a loose kind of way.
The soul inspects itself in a buckled mirror,
notices its eyes and its set of lip,

forgives its nose, appears a touch *distrait*
by its own standards, feels a vague terror
at any suggestion it might lose its grip.

*

Then Miles and cool. The lost soul turns its back
on the audience and blows to itself. That low
piercing dull indifferent cry moves below
the ocean surface among bladderwrack

and silence. Elsewhere dead rocks wheel
about a dying planet. The eye itself rolls
like a stone. Miles stands stiffly or strolls
about the stage like the whole gig wasn't real

but happened in his head. And the boy is reading
another text book, and the waitress serves
another table with another drunk,

and the evening goes on gently bleeding
into dawn. Suddenly the music swerves
into dance mode, the harsh jag-jag of funk.

*

Funk with the Brecker Brothers. A rapper from
Tottenham Hale in a converted garage.
Jungle's rapid displacements haemorrhage
at three-thirty a.m. under the eardrum.

A tiny luminous figure flits across the screen
collecting prizes, upping the body count.
An elder watches as the high scores mount.
Way off the pace, he's scanning a magazine

that advertises technical wizardry.
Sound, speed, adrenalin: soul food. Outside
rain is quietly cooling itself in the gutter.

331

It's what we have, our last ditch decency,
a cool hand across the street, the long slide
of water on glass, the fingers' chronic stutter.

*

Azure, sings Ella, undisturbed by this,
being herself another recording lost
in her own listening. Static settles like frost
on Fats Waller. A kind of paralysis

blights Joplin, and Frank O'Hara is as dead
as Billie Holliday. All sink in the night.
There's no such thing as satisfied appetite
in the living museum. The boy's head

contains his soul as it runs down his arms,
through his fingers, into a pool of distance.
Desire is the stars for which there is no cure,

metallic, silvery perhaps, moving in swarms
across darkness without any resistance
inimitable, dislocated, pure.

Figures at the Baths

1

Those figures emerging from the water are men
of an indeterminate period and age.
Their hair had long ago begun to flatten
against their scalps. They became pure image
almost as soon as they entered, and rising,
were transformed into a kind of secret.
The world is old to them. There is nothing surprising
left in it. Even the bottomless water is set
into a basin of marble which has always
been there. Classical columns wear the light
with a knowing patience. They know nothing of days
or hours, of wind or weather, or morning or night,
but know where they've been and know the deep
undrowned existence anticipating sleep.

2

Norfolk in January. Rain, icy cold, goes on
and off all day. The wind is like barbed wire
and the sun brings no relief. There is someone
running down the road, his hair and coat on fire.
The birthing pool, the baths, the classical
columns are consolations of memory.
You see their glowing surfaces with their trickle
of light. You hear the men move. Their furry
bodies are sleek with cold. Our eyes touch
across the room. They flare at the point of contact
as if one of us had suddenly lit a match,
as if meaning had shrunk to this single act,
as if time had begun to slip but hung there
at the edge of the pool flattening our hair.

Dog-Latin

The thing that I was was changing. Or was
it wishful thinking? The train rolled on
through a shower, spraying itself in million-
fractured glass and I was lost in the fuzz
of voices – mobile phones, newspapers, leaves
in a long wind. Houses drifted by, caught
in the rain-net, held together by taut
wires: blood, loss, distant relatives
talking in their sleep. Here day and night
made little difference. A man reading the *Mail*
adjusted his glasses. Another had put down
an empty burger-box which opened its bright
yellow mouth and breathed a pungent trail
of garnish across the fast retreating town.

Disjecta membra, little splinters of dog-
Latin from schooldays, as if all life was this,
asserting its privileges, wanting a last kiss
before the terminal parting into fog
and more rain. I looked at the ends of my fingers
parked on the table before me. The train
shook them slightly as it might shake a chain
of events. Everywhere, passengers
were becoming residents, workers, emissaries.

Something was crumbling – a people possibly,
and the flags in the garage had set up
a mad flutter under the bending trees.
It was night or morning or midday, and we
were sitting still, waiting for it to stop.

Golden Boy

Once I was the golden boy, beloved:
a woman laid me down inside a pram,
but who can tell me now whose child I am?
The years go by and who knows what I've suffered?
She brought me things once, tickled me and kissed
my plump pink cheeks. Believe me, when I cried
she came running with comforts, mortified.
Who thinks in childhood, I will not be missed?
Who thinks, *My golden age will pass away*
and turn to lead? That knowledge creeps on slow
but unexpected, when you're lying in a doorway
vaguely aware of feet that come and go.
But I was golden then and slept so long
no one was left to tell me where I belong.

The golden boy for ever on the run,
whether he runs with beasts or runs alone,
finds cold is singular, within the bone.
I look back and I can't tell what I've done
in all these years or when I turned to gold,
whether the toes came first, or fingertips
and when the transformation reached my lips,
when my poor guts were colonised by cold
which ate into my marrow with its teeth.
All I know's the heart that keeps on ticking,
its metric beat persistent underneath
the ribs that time is gradually unpicking.
I see myself in gold which might be lead,
but no one knows that down among the dead.

War Is Over

(for Anthony Thwaite)

One of those wet Junes with the skylight tapping
its fingernails on the thin drum of the house.

Yesterday, in the underground, a dark brown mouse
ran zigzag between live rails, vaguely unwrapping
the present of its small life, and when the train came,
the mouse disappeared beneath it. Along from us
a woman was writing a letter with ferocious
concentration, her lips constantly moving to frame
the words as the letters appeared. Beside her
an Asian girl was reading Jane Austen, a boy
dived for an empty seat. The war was over,
said someone's paper. There was little joy
on the faces, it was much as usual. Permanent night
down here. Upstairs, the emergence into daylight.

Visitations

As one comes in another goes out. As one
shakes out a tablecloth another is eating
a hearty meal. As one sits down alone
another listens to his lover's heart beating.

As one prays for deliverance, another
delivers a letter or an explosive device.
As one gathers the harvest, his brother
lies in the doorway. As one finds a nice

coincidence between numbers, his neighbour
sees his coins disappear down the waiting slot.
As one man examines the fruit of his labour
his shadow tells beads, counts peas into the pot

or stars in the sky and feels the night wind blowing
on his face with all this coming and going.

*

As one goes out, the other comes in. It is light
in the window where the angel bends
over the stove giving the virgin a fright.
It is bright at the top of the house where the road ends.

There's a distinct touch of gold in the gutter
running with beer. There is translucence
in the chipped saucer with its rim of used butter.
There's a glow on TV. There's a faint sense

of the luminous numinous in the alarm clock
set for six in the morning and a kind of shine
in the mirror the angels have learned to unlock
and enter suddenly and an even harder to define

radiance in the skin, in the shock of dawn
with sheet turned down and bedroom curtains drawn.

Cromer Green at the Regency Café

I used to wonder at the old ones sitting
in cars parked neatly opposite the sea
with Sunday papers in their laps, steadily
dozing near uneventful water, knitting
in silence, reading, waiting. What was the sense
of congregating here with weathered faces
beside these terminal railings in places
that signalled departure and indifference?
The sadness of the English, I thought. Odd
how they folded in on themselves at last,
something serious must have happened here
under the jurisdiction of this grey-green god
they weren't exactly worshipping, but cast
respectful glances at across the pier.

Out on the pier a three-legged dog beamed
happily at its master. Water fribbled and scrabbled
below the walkway, laughing at some ribald
double-entendre. Someone must have dreamed
all this at a time of comic anxiety.
Fisherman were casting their last lines.

Great towering hotels flashed gleeful signs.
The moon rose over the building society.
Boys were trying to surf into the stones
along the beach. Someone had thrown away
a *Daily Mail* which was carried by a gust
past cartons and upended ice-cream cones.
There were cups of tea at the Regency Café
and cod and chips on tables covered in dust.

There was nothing to say about this. It was
saying itself in the language of self-delight,
beautiful and formed, talking in spite
of us through its own generated grammars
in a kind of English no one actually spoke,
leaving behind a faint linguistic trace
like a historical essence, a lost grace
that no one act of history could revoke.
Now the wind was rising. Waves were barred
with patches of pure colour, each a shimmer
in the coming dusk with echoes of dying sound,
but clearly defined, the image sharp and hard.
A brilliant half rainbow was growing dimmer,
retreating to its source beneath the ground.

I could imagine being one of the old,
staying here for ever, staring past
the lit pier and searching the overcast
sky for the moon in the growing cold.
Nature was peopled with coherent signs
that anyone could read. The waitress brought
the bill and we stood up. It was a short
journey home and we should start it... Lines
of lightbulbs were gently swaying outside
and the wind was fresh from the north. Our car
waited, parked with all the rest in the drive
by the sunken gardens. Another seagull cried
below us. Lights were glowing in the bar
of The Ship and the old were still alive.

Great Yarmouth

The sea was black and far beyond the sand
an icy gust blew between whatever shelter
the promenade offered. Life was out of kilter
in the world and here was proof. A bright band

of amusement arcades caught the full force
of the wind. Their hyperactivity
was manic, all lights flashing, each a city
in its final throes. A tiny fairground horse

whinnied at *The House of the Dead* where ghouls
materialised and were cut down in a spray
of music. The place was empty but men lay
on stone steps, buckled and broken in pools

of flat Sega blood, and everywhere the roar
of tiny coins and pebbles on the shore.

*

Out of kilter and broken. Late winter light,
which is to say, no light at all, except this.
And it was buzzing and flashing, its synapses
wholly preoccupied, breath short, chest tight,

sweating slightly. Rank upon brilliant rank
of potential cardiac arrest, and all for nothing.
It was the latest gothic passing its dark wing
over the empty seafront on its way to the blood bank.

And here was England, shouting at the sea,
a single bent figure glaring behind the change desk,
surveying its domain, the new grotesque.
It was terrible to see it. Outside the fresh, free

silence and the barren wind, a fast car,
the darkness vast, without a single star.

Punctuation

It was a matter of language. The glottal swell
of waves as its long tongue came pitching in
lapping at land. Words were shedding their skin
on the beach to leave behind the dying smell

of creosote. It was all sadness there.
I watched amused as rain–swollen clouds swam
across the sky from nearby Sheringham
dropping a few fat drops in the thick air.

The light brimmed over somewhere at the edge,
a double rainbow sprang from a beached boat
and stopped abruptly in a wedge of dark.

There were a few cars parked along the ledge
and close to shore a bobbing bright red float
like some arbitrary punctuation mark.

Backwaters: Norfolk Fields

(for W.G. Sebald)

1

Backwaters. Long grass. Slow speech. Far off
a truck heaves its load of rust into a yard
next to a warehouse full of office furniture
no one will ever use, unless to stuff
some temporary room when times are hard.
Across the fields the sweet smell of manure.

We're years behind. Even our vowels sag
in the cold wind. We have our beauty spots
that people visit and leave alone, down main
arterials and side roads. A paper bag
floats along the beach. Clouds drift in clots
of grey and eventually down comes the rain.

We're at the end. It might simply be of weather
or empire or of something else altogether.

2

Empire perhaps. Chapels in the cathedral.
Old airstrips. History's human noises
still revving down a field. Clothes pegs hang
like hanged men. It is all procedural.
Resentment simmers in the empty houses.
The wind at its eternal droning harangue.

I'm wanting to mouth the word that fits the case
but it's like trying to roll a shadow from
the street where it has been sitting for years.
It will not go. You cannot wipe the face
of the clock or restore a vanished kingdom.
You feel the shape of the thing between your ears.

Your mouth is talking to the steady light
which listens to you and remains polite.

3

How beautiful the place is. Watch it hold
time still. I want you to tell me what this is,
this place at the back of beyond, in the sun
that retains its distance in a pale gold
mirror, minding its own brilliant business,
not in the habit of speaking to anyone.

Here is a man who loves cars. He has bought
a house on something very like a hill.
He fills his yard up with old cars. He mends things –
roofs, walls. He's biblical. He does not take thought
for the morrow, won't worry when he falls ill.
He goes swooping along on welded wings,

his children unruly, his wife losing heart.
The beautiful is what keeps them apart.

4

The WI stall. Jams, flowers. White
hair scraped back in the draught of an open door.
The butcher's. He knows you by name. He calls
your name out. His chopping block is washed bright
by the morning sun. The solicitor
down the street. His nameplate. War memorials

with more names. Rows of Standleys, Bunns,
Myhills, Kerridges. Names on shopfronts: bold
reds, whites and blues in stock typography.
Names on labels tied with string to shotguns.
Names on electoral registers. Names in gold
in the children's section of the cemetery

by the railway cuttings. Willows, faint blue
in the afternoon, light gently whistles through.

5

Too easy all this, like a fatal charm
intended to lull you into acquiescence.
Think karaoke. Sky. The video shop.
Broken windows. The sheer boredom. The alarm
wailing at two am. The police presence.
Pastoral graffiti on the bus stop.

Think back of the back of beyond "beyond". End
of a line. The sheer ravishing beauty
of it as it runs into the cold swell
of the North Sea, impossible to comprehend.
The harsh home truisms of geometry
that flatten to a simple parallel.

This is your otherness where the exotic
appears by a kind of homely conjuring trick.

6

A 1580s mural. A hunting scene
runs right around the room. A trace of Rubens,
Jordaens, a touch, even, of Chinese
in the calligraphic lines. Experts clean
the powdery limewash, two PhD students
from the university, anxious to please.

A strange dome appears, out of period
somewhere near the top. Even here
there's something far flung in the code
of a different language, another God
extolling other virtues, a pioneer
morality just waiting to explode.

Flemish brickwork. Devastation. Riders
exploring hidden walls with snails and spiders.

7

You're out at the end of the pier. It is winter.
Tall waves splutter underfoot. Gulls pirouette
and dive into dark grey. The radio is alive
with music. Its tiny voices seem to splinter
into sharp distinct consonants. You forget
the time of day. It's someone else's narrative

buzzing beneath you. New explorers come
out of the light to exploit the heart of darkness.
The world is inside out, exposed as never before.
Water and sky are a continuum.
A terrible gaiety rustles the sea like a dress
it must discard. It sweeps by just once more

then drops across the beach and remains there
in the memory, in ghosted, mangled air.

8

How beautiful it is, this silence waiting
on salt. The disused railway lines between
wild blackberries. The faint hum of stray flies
on windowsills. Time is accelerating
down the coast road leaving behind a clean
pair of heels and a whiff of paradise.

The man with welded wings roars past, in love
with reason. His wife leaves in a freak gust,
their children flying along. Dogs race across
the walls in search of a lost treasure trove.
Gently idling, vast trucks deposit rust
in empty yards with patches of dry grass.

Broad fields out of town. The slow unravelling
of a long reel where everyone is travelling.

9

Travelling through or ending. The damp house
beyond the library where an old woman
has been retreating for some fifty years,
and still retreats towards a dangerous
blind alley, towards a corner, where the nearest demon
might swallow her up leaving no more tears.

There are none left to shed in the overgrown
garden with its coarse weeds. It is as if
she had been sleeping a century or more,
without a retinue, simply on her own,
growing ever more querulous, ever more stiff
till rigor mortis had frozen her four score

into zero. Country aristocracy.
The dead fields at their last-gasp fantasy.

10

A place full of old women. Hardy, courageous,
muttering to themselves and others in cafés,
engaging unwilling partners in conversation,
accosting young men, making outrageous
advances to middle-aged couples with tea-trays,
embarassing husbands with their ostentation.

Old men in betting shops peering to check
the odds. Old men, natty in white, creaking
over bowls, with Beryl Cook elegance.
Old men tottering, sticking out a neck
at the neighbour while the latter is speaking.
Old men in the church hall learning to dance.

The old in their gerontopolis. At home
in sheltered housing, under the pleasure dome.

11

How many times do I have to say the word: End!
and still not end. You can't go further than
the sea, not on a motorway. And what
are you doing here, yes, you and your friend
from Morocco, Uganda, St Kitts or Pakistan?
Whatever has brought you to this far, flat

kingdom with its glum farmers? Surely you
don't think this is America where dreams
are the given, where you swear allegiance
to a new self? Have you somehow fallen through
the net of the world to be lost among reams
of legislature in these alien regions?

Homing. We are homing to the sea. Back
where we never were, at the end of the track.

12

On a high-cloud day, you could drown in sky
round here. You see the gentle swaying
of leaves along a wall. Something under
the water, under the skylight, in the dry
cabin under the ocean is quietly playing
a music of muted bells in soft thunder.

It is eating you away until you've gone,
like the spider scurrying up its own spit
back to its natural centre in the dark,
and the sky remains enormous. Someone
is watching the house-martin, the blue tit,
the tiny insects making their tiny mark

in the grass, and the small rain that falls far
across the field as on a distant star.

Haydn

1

No wind at all. The clothes-pegs on the line
are hardly shivering. An even grey
has closed the world off. It is Saturday
in the quiet towns of the east. A fine
distinction between two adjacent tones
of sea and air carries no distant cries
or the light dust of ground or broken bones.
There are no fresh news in the mouths of flies.

No flies at all. No wasps. No bees. Nothing come
nor gone. The day stands like an untouched drum:
Haydn on Radio Three. Letters in the tray.
It is the spaces in between that are dissembling.
The neighbours are asleep or gone away.
Nothing now can set the clothes-pegs trembling.

2

One syllable short. How does anything get in
to this stoppered corner of England where
the dust is the dust of the fields, layer on layer,
and the grass is a tight comfortable skin
in the churchyard by a ruined monastery?
The lost incomprehensible syllable is stuck
in the throat: the bones' dying industry
winds down like an old tenement block.

Until it blows. Until the fuse catches the thumb
that triggers it in the distant capital or the screen
by the wall and the fields are suddenly dumb.
Until a faint red seeps beneath the green
among ground elder, earthworms, and the lost
coins of the realm bent and scaled with rust.

Gone Fishing

Jack, assistant shopman, retired from the force,
makes fishing-rods. His Polish father's dead,
(ex-wartime flier). Jack reserves his hatred
for Uncle Joe of Russia, but, in due course

follow murderers, burglars, gypsies, queers,
Pakis, paedophiles... Oh, the lies we're told!...
he grows angry. The long-lost foreign old
are turning in their graves, giving faint cheers

for anglers by gravel pits, for the cold North Sea
lumbered with dark and fish, for winds from the pole
that blow the socks off us, cheers for summer, our sole
delight that appears, brightly, suddenly,

its pitiless eye fixed on the very spot
we're standing on. And will be, like as not.

Flash

When she looked through the view-finder she found
him changed. It was the shadow of a moment
that made the difference, one in a vast torrent
of light that seemed to have lifted her from the ground.
Perhaps the bomb had finally fallen. He
was still smiling but had dropped through a trapdoor
on the other side of the world. No more
time was left, it was all eternity.

Then she pressed the shutter and it went click
as it always does, and there he was, smiling
but elsewhere. Elsewhere was where they both were.
And it was green, attractive, beguiling
as they returned, the earth steady and pure,
washed clean, as if by hypo or by magic.

Viridian

I woke to viridian. Across the square
the rain was falling in a fleece of light
and clouds were endless. A girl with dripping hair
was hurrying across, her coat pulled tight
about her. A pair of wagtails twitched and rose
from the grass which was gradually darkening
to one deep bass note at which music froze.
Only fat raindrops were prepared to sing.

Against this the thin brightness of laughter set
itself. There it was. Someone was laughing below,
on another floor, as if all that was lost
had been briefly recovered, never to be let
go of. Her laugh was against the letting go
despite the rain that settled thick as dust.

AN ENGLISH APOCALYPSE

(for Dennis O'Driscoll)

Gladdith anon, thou lusty Troy Novaunt,
Citie that some tyme cleped was New Troy
WILLIAM DUNBAR

Prologue: The Fire Film

It was the day the cows came down in dollops
of thick snow. Sheep followed as sheep will
landing head first, their legs like lollipops

or dead matches that still fired. Every hill
on the coastline was burning. It was Bonfire Night.
I watched the children run among dead cattle

clutching sparklers, gaping at rockets in full flight
from the plastic tubes that housed them. We were going
up in smoke, but gaily. It would be all right

to run riot now, to feel blood flowing
in our narrow veins and think of carnival.
Our faces were fire-lit masks. We were growing

into our archetypes, part-human, part-animal.
One wore a calf's head, another pranced on goat feet.
We were as we had been before our own arrival

in the fig leaf of custodianship. The High Street
was blazing more brilliantly than it had last Christmas
and the wind whistled above us, dark and sweet,

from a film set in Africa or maybe somewhere else.

1 PASTORALS
(for Katie Donovan)

Jerusalem

The leaves are nodding. The traffic runs on.
It is like opening a door on a great secret,
or drawing a dusty 1950s curtain,

a passport to a country of eternal regret,
the Old Jerusalem, a forsaken garden
where the sun is always about to set

on an empire laying down its burden.
Which is what pastoral means: life in a field
of death, natural activity as boredom,

the air crowded with unreconciled
facts: dust, light, insects, birds, sheer noise,
the plants' upward drive, their fates sealed

while they blossom with disturbing poise
that reeks of drama, waving red hands
in the air with showbiz gestures, like boys

in the band, or settle in brilliant islands
of loose coral, because summer is exotic
in such country and makes peculiar demands

on the attention, but the air is thick
with the noise of the past, so it is hard to see
what it is made of, what all this rhetoric

is actually about. Something is ominously
gathering in the sky. The clouds rise
and darken like shadows under a bright tree.

Anxiety

A man and woman at a dinner party. Their eyes
entirely elsewhere. Money problems. Below:
the park, the Thames, the hopeful strategies

of mere survival, going with the flow.
Her face reddens. Little wrinkles crowd
about her mouth, having nowhere else to go.

She has the look of the wounded and once proud.
It is heartbreaking and edgy. The tiny room
is all synapses and electricity, loud

with unspoken fear. The sky is a faint plume
of smoke over London, beyond the window glass;
clouds skate along on rims of polished chrome.

Something glints in the trees and the grass,
a thin blade of water, and the first rain
sliding down the slope of the underpass.

Fragile chains dangle from the sky. There is a stain
on the carpet but it could be shadow. Tiny wires
wrap the street in silver, folding towards the drain

from long trails of stationary tyres.
She wipes her eye, looks down at her fork,
and makes as much noise as table talk requires.

The Ark

It is night in the zoo of the universe. Stars lurk
behind soft mountains and the moon dips
under water. The dreams are getting to work.

He hooks his fingers into her waistband. She slips
towards him and raises her left knee to cover
his right thigh. Her finger rests on his lips,

then moves down to his neck. He rolls her over
and traces her spine with his chin. Her head
is turned on its side as she feels him hover

above her. Her right arm is off the bed,
touching the floor. Night giggles up its sleeve.
His teeth close as if on fresh baked bread.

And then she mounts him. They begin to heave
against the tide. They are ploughing through
the waves of the sheets, steady, purposive

voyagers. Out in the field a distraught ewe
calls to her lambs. An owl hoots in the mist.
It is stormy. They are the ship's crew.

Now he's on top, his fingers round her wrist.
She strains to kiss them. The cat in the car park
leaps from bonnet to bonnet. They want to twist

round so he's behind. It takes a sudden jerk –
and there they are. Her breasts hang below her
like any creature's, in the enormous ark

they both occupy. The beasts are beginning to stir
in the hold. She plays him like a piper.
The world is pain and stars in a cradle of fur.

The rainforests of Brazil are made of tissue-paper
that rustles in her head. He is whale blubber
in the Atlantic, a well fed grouper.

Victoriana

Pastoral is a voice in the shrubbery,
the sound of a tennis ball, a lawn where croquet
is being played by flamingoes with rubbery

elegance, the arrival of a bouquet
in a cellophane wrapper. It is mud
on the boots, a hint of dung on the parquet

of the dining room. It is the English God
at his prayers in a Victorian chapel,
the compulsive criminal up before *me lud*.

It is a kind of loss. The street is full of people
going about their shopping. The newsagent-
cum-post office. The buses. The municipal

authority's proceedings. The war monument.
It is Giovanni's cafe and Faroukh's *couscous*
in the region's only Moroccan restaurant.

It is this *res publicum* of loose
alliances. The Australian botanist
meeting the lecturer from Belarus

in a garden of old roses. The narrow wrist
encircled by a man's fingers. The rough
chest his lover has delicately kissed

while sheep bleat through the night. It is the stuff
that dreams are made of, the years and hours
of which none of them could ever have enough.

Survivor

You wake. It's as if time had bound your feet
to keep them delicate. Everything seems the same,
teetering on its lightness. There is a sweet

smear of sunlight narrowing to a flame
on the wall beside the bed. How old you are
is a secret. Nobody knows your name.

You are together in a spectacular
success that no one recognises. The news,
the *Today* programme, pass in a blur.

You have survived the millennium, are free to choose
from clothes in the wardrobe. You get dressed.
You comb your hair, brush teeth, put on your shoes.

The day is waiting. It gently cups your breast
and kisses your lips. You're away in your own
version of pastoral which is compressed

into such moments. The pair of you have grown
alabaster wings. You embrace like sculpture.
You whisper the word 'love'. It is the unknown.

It is, and always has been, the only possible future.

2 YORKSHIRE BITTER
(for Gerald Dawe)

Night Out

Everyone wears drag round here. The barman
in gold lamé and a vast peroxide wig
serves pints of Sam Smith to a local Carmen

wearing the cruiser's full authentic rig
of white blouse, fish-nets, tiny leather skirt,
with three days' stubble, mouth like a ripe fig.

Richard Roundtree and Jack Palance flirt
in the corner. Norman Hunter and Pat Phoenix
are at their dominoes, quietly talking dirt.

Sniffer Clarke appears after turning tricks
down Harehills, his red handbag open,
orders a drink and prepares to take a fix.

Outside in derelict squares bad things happen,
rapes and stabbings, people are rolling round
in their own vomit, and dark pools deepen

ever deeper, ever darker, moving underground.
Meanwhile the moors are bleak and clear and wild
and the raw north wind is the only keening sound

to haunt or comfort the dreams of a woken child
as hills falls away, an escarpment drops
into place and something grips at roofs recently tiled

and lifts them away from terraces and corner shops
with boarded windows, over garages, towards the sea
where the world grows solemn and everything stops.

Girl Flying

When she stood at the top of the stairs by the door
of the college, the wind caught her up and so
she flew all the way down, as if no more

than a micro-detail on a map that any breeze could blow,
and if she could have flown of her own will
at any time she chose, this was how she'd go,

her coat flapping beneath someone's windowsill,
gone before noted, and the clouds too slopped
from side to side, sliding down some hill

in the distance, too dreamy to be stopped
or even slowed into a world with a clear face
as if suddenly a tiny penny had dropped

about her and everyone else's lack of proper place
in a motorway city above the flyover
with a bird's eye view, but not quite the same grace

as the seagulls she spotted under cloud cover
effing and blinding as she was lifted down,
almost gently, as if to hang or hover

were a privilege, like a silk dressing gown
made of wind she was wearing, whose belt was undone
and as she descended the air it was blown

out like a cord she might pull or the trigger of a gun
which went off the minute she hit the ground
with a dull thud on the surface of the sun.

Poet

He leered softly into his lapel. He listened to the sound
of bells in the distance and turned another page
of his book. It was years since he had found

himself alone like this. There was his image
in the wardrobe mirror, his jacket hung
on the door. It was the passing of an age,

the death of the New Elizabethans, the young
all gone in the air. He reached for the neat gin
in the glass. It slithered sweetly down and stung

his throat, so he filled the glass again.
The cobbled streets outside rang with pity.
It was a lost place and a bad place to begin.

It was James Thompson's notion of the *City
of Dreadful Night*, a night that was creeping up
on him now with alarming alacrity.

The dancing feet of Alexander Pope,
grotesquely blithe, tapped across his brow
in a parody of decorum, hatred and hope.

Too tired to dance with anyone right now.

Chuck Berry Live

Too tired to dance with anyone right now
after the gig, here in the Merrion Centre
where Chuck Berry has just taken his bow

with a riotous, raunchy but disciplined little number
where he mimed the wiping of seed on the wall,
and it was innocent, funny and tender

for the ancient Teds at this ugly bug ball
in their precisely dated costumes of drapes
and winklepickers, their faintly comical

pompadours with bald spots conjuring lost shapes
of threatening baroque splendour down streets
grown dull with rationing, like God's apes

wreaking vengeance for a series of defeats
after the war when fathers disappeared
and came back changed. A steady Leeds rain beats

on Woodhouse Lane creating fountains, weird
rococo pools, washing away the rubbish
with bronze-gold-copper ripples under battered

cars by lamp posts, somehow homely and British,
stabilising into damp, which crawls across
the wallpaper, with old books, silverfish.

Keighley

At night you can see the north wind as you lie
sleepless, because the net curtains bulge
with it, and the whole room seems to sigh

and billow as if the moors were about to divulge
a dreadful secret: black earth, scrub, thin grass.
The weather here is willing to indulge

its resident Heathcliffs from the deep bass
of fogged valleys or screaming tips of rock.
On a bend down Keighley way you might pass

a cannibalised Morris Minor in a state of shock,
its big end gone, its eyesockets picked bare
by scavengers, dewdrops dangling from the lock

of its open door. There is something in the air
stripping the paint away, nature perhaps
nothing more, the power concentrated there

escaping through the bleak beauty that claps
its arms around things, around trees and cars
and old men dropping ash in their own laps

in front of the TV and the latest soap stars,
with the dog by the door wanting to go out
into the wind across the becks and scars.

3 **THE PICKETS**
(for Terence Brown)

Blockade

Where ideology fails, mere livelihood
takes over, seeking its bottom line,
wherever that is, in vision or in blood

or further regions impossible to define.
The cross of St George flutters on the pole
behind men picketing in a benign

huddle, comfy, but barely in control
of the world that they are bringing into being.
They form a solid yeomanry in droll

revolt against powers that even now are fleeing
the cities they rule from. From what far regions
have the yeoman risen? Where are their all-seeing

leaders and prophets? Their everyday religions
are bottom-line affairs with few demands,
offering basic warmth for mild allegiance,

composed of mostly affordable deodands:
crumbs for the ducks, a tip for the paper-boy,
a Christmas kiss, holding a mother's hands,

comfort for the dying. I'm thinking of Joy,
Ruby, Ted and Jerry, their children trapped
in kitchens and sheds a real storm would destroy

in minutes, and Stan, hollow-eyed, flat-capped,
whose tools we inherited, and Percy Bunn
the handyman and glazier who dropped

dead at the church fête, and gangling Ron
the caretaker, whose wife left and he drank
for weeks, and every picket the son

(or daughter) of people of such social rank
as drop away now, lost in the dawn retreat,
the tankers rolling past them, faces blank.

Orators

The orators came, voting with their feet
and shows of hands. Hands were grasping fags,
clutching and pounding. I remember the discreet

look of the cabinet minister and the bags
under Ron Kosky's eyes as he talked of Paul
Robeson and of the black slaves in their rags.

Thick eyebrows were watching punched cards fall
on office desks. So Gerry Sparks would follow
Frank Chappell to the mighty annual

TUC where Jack Jones laid down the law
(Get your tanks off my lawn, said Callaghan)
while Red Robbo at BL tunnelled away below,

and I was scared of everything: the man
with the power to turn lights off and drop
me back into the chaos where I began

among mobs and bodies, the horde's gallop
towards a single figure which was me
by extension. This was England's shop

with windows broken and nothing inside to see,
and England's work as represented by
estate kids, blokes on buses, Bill and Tubby

in the painter's yard. I would not say
it was a sheltered childhood, but the loud
disturbed me, as did anger and decay.

I was a spectator, watching the crowd
wearing the faces of furious angels: their roar
was me in flames. Soon enough they slowed

back to the daily trudge, the regular shore,
their sea slapping and ebbing, their kind
gestures returning with them to the shop floor

and the parlour and the pub, fags in lined
hands, jokes and telly, the world unaltered,
as if, like me, it feared to be defined.

Orgreave

Out of the dark came the miners. Their villages
were live coals and their bodies fed the flames
that burned their love affairs and marriages.

Black dust coated their tongues and blurred their dreams.
They licked their children into shape like bears
with sore heads. At night they heard the screams

of wheels on tracks or footsteps on the stairs.
They'd rise to the surface and gradually fade
into the morning. They covered their chairs

with rough shadows that left a faint grey tide.
They drank hard and played football with caps for goal-posts,
a few turned out for a professional side

in the nearby town. They prayed for the Lord of Hosts
to lead them into a world of light but woke
at midnight hearing their brothers' ghosts.

Wheels on tracks, collapses. They only needed to poke
the fire for the coals to cave in and bury them deep.
I still remember the day their power broke

at Ollerton, Bidworth, Orgreave. The earth could keep
its darkness. It was the end of the century right now,
the end of the war. A new kind of peace would creep

out of the atom with pale hands, its brow
unlined and vacant. There was something deadly
about its frivolity, which would allow

anything at all except fire and memory.

Scene at a Conference

The kindliness of the English: a paper presented
to the ethnicity conference in Dublin in
2004. The thesis commented

on their slow smiles in a suburban garden
in North London in the early 60s. It cited
a middle-aged hand fingering a pattern

of glossy box-hedge leaves. On being invited
to elaborate, the writer mentioned the old
woman who shyly brought cups of tea to benighted

refugees waiting for a bus one particularly cold
December; three boys in a playground taking
pity on a loner in the doorway who would unfold

an incomprehensible story to them, shaking
with tears; WVS squadrons, patient
bureaucrats at office desks, their heads aching

with figures, and surprisingly efficient
bands of secretaries holding open lines,
all comprehending, almost omniscient.

The constancy of kindliness. The signs
of kindliness on rain-soaked building sites,
in electric sub-stations and down coal mines.

The forms of kindliness: terrible nights
of diffidence in front rooms, quiet
interminable minutes interrupted by flights

of fancy, the unspoken etiquette
of the lower-middle-class tea party; loss
and the coping with; desire within set

limits: all this equated with kindliness.
Warm beer and cricket, mumbled someone
at the back, who had already given his address.

And it was true, there was considerably more fun
at the Gael end of things, at the high table:
charm, invention, a recently fired gun.

Nostalgia

I recall the 70s sliding underfoot
like dead wet leaves. It was perpetual
late autumn, history nibbling at the root

of a gaudy tree. The summer had been lethal.
So many dead and there was no escape
except down cellars. It was the long crawl

to seeming safety that did for us. We lost shape,
shrank back into ourselves, turned minimalist,
steely trimmers, each with a secret tape

of fear. Russia showed us a clenched fist.
Their guns were pointing as were everyone's.
The world was tired. It would not be missed

by bodies in car-boots, fingers pressing buttons.
I don't think we were doing retro then
but who can tell? Shirley had bought patterns

from a stall on the Friday market. There were women
rummaging among hats, cheap scarves and rolls
of cotton, terylene and other off-cuts. When

did this stop, if it has? And those armfuls
of Mills and Boon in the corner? When did they
switch to Black Lace, dream-catchers and lentils?

Some decades age faster than others. We replay
them like old movies. The pickets flying high
over a ruined industrial estate have flown away

into the grey cancer-ridden darkness to die.
And these men are like a flock of starlings
briefly gathered by the refinery

now risen and gone with a lazy flap of wings.

4 ENTERTAINMENTS
(for Brendan Kennelly)

Offence

The yob in the corner with the t-shirt is laughing
at an air disaster in France. The others plead
with him to stop, but there is absolutely nothing

they can do. He's pissed, raw, gone to seed,
knackered, flushed, buggered, all done in.
You can see his head beginning to bleed

with some corrosive liquid. He's about to chin
the man beside him, picks on a girl by the bar
and tells her to suck on this. The others grin,

embarrassed and try containment. He's too far
gone, in a rusty backyard of wires and knives
he can't escape, speaking the innate vernacular

of the trapped. He's shit. Scum. He survives.
But the girl and his mates are watching him drown
in his own mire, like distant relatives

at a death-bed scene. It's a night on the town,
not even a weekend. A gallery next door
shows a drawing of sleek cars sweeping down

steep shadowed streets, a dream or metaphor
or memory of a film where people chase
each other because they're compelled to. The floor

of the pub rears up. Air hits him in the face
like a great cold wave that almost flattens him.
He is the doomed prince, king of infinite space.

The Wrestling

The Corn Exchange is a gaunt railway hall
in the Balkans. Three rows of sundry chairs
at each side of the ring are set out as usual

but you can sit on tables like other punters.
A man or woman with a face quite fallen in,
entirely without teeth; three obese mothers

with fat children; rows of elderly women
in cardigans; a bus driver, a pair
so dense with studs (a rough-cast Pearly Queen

and a King Cobra) they almost buckle
under the weight. And stolid oldies, wise
to the ways of the game, quite as fantastical

as the wrestlers themselves, their heads topiaries
or billiard balls, who know the throws and holds,
have known them for years. The strange cries

of birds, a jungle chattering, the piercing scolds
of angry deities. Anyone not from here
is hated with a pantomime fury. Scaffolds,

hanging-trees, iron maidens, objects of fear.
Two fat leotards, one in a Union Jack,
the other in glitzy blue, engage. The gods appear

and watch them with hooded eyes. Bones crack.
Pantomime turns music hall. It's Marie Lloyd
and the Great War making a belated come back,

a forlorn intimacy crawling from the void,
its grossness sweet and almost delicate,
like love between the lost and the destroyed

or a face in the blurred gallery, painted by Sickert.
The human need for blood, bone, gristle, flesh:
for Justice with her scales and lottery ticket.

Warhol's Dog

Fifteen minutes, and then another fifteen...
like being licked all over by a friendly mastiff.
You are bathed in the light of the television screen,

that slobbers enthusiastically, as if
it loved you, but you are becoming a dog
yourself, with a dog's appetites. You sniff

your way around the world, a mere cog
in the doggy universe, pleased with your place.
You watch doggy programmes, your doggy bag

in front of you, your fixed dog's-grimace
perfect in profile. You are John Bull's cur
and proud of it. Your home is your palace.

Cilla dog makes puppy love happen. Her
little yelps are blessings. Kilroy-Silk
rolls over on his back as if about to purr

then remembers he's a dog. It is the milk
of human kindness running in his veins.
Dogs know one another, recognise their ilk

immediately. Mongrel celebrity rains
cats and dogs. I have seen the chairs turned
to the telly in nursing homes. No one complains.

And when the last doggy remains are burned
in the pet crematorium you may be sure
it will be live. It is what dogs have earned

with their fidelity: a fiery erasure,
a substitute of burning glass. The dog
by the iconic hearth, framed to endure.

The Full Monty

Hen night entails low laughter down at base.
It starts below and rises like a whale
to spout from the fair middle of your face.

It's in your face, it's gone right off the scale.
Your kid is waving it in front of you.
You get it fresh before it all goes stale.

And stale it must go, nothing you can do.
That's why you laugh, to keep it fresh just when
it's started to go off. It's Danish Blue,

it's down there where you need it, where the men
can't see or reach, that source, the tickled zone.
Cheese is what you would say, but you're a hen,

and laughter's brittle as a chicken bone.
Men have no dignity, they have no grace:
without their power they're comical alone,

their nakedness is naked in your face.
No hiding place, just giggles, you're all mates.
Hen night entails low laughter down at base.

Preston North End

Tottenham Hotspur versus Preston North End.
Finney's last season: my first. And my dad
with me. How surprisingly well we blend

with these others. Then the English had
the advantage, but today we feel
their fury, sadness and pity. There were some bad

years in between, a lot of down-at-heel
meandering. For me though, the deep blue
of Preston was ravishment of a more genteel,

poetic kind. They were thrashed 5-1, it's true,
and Finney was crocked by Mackay. Preston went down,
hardly to rise again. But something got through

about Finney the plumber, Lancashire, the Crown,
and those new days a-coming. The crowd dissolves,
but we are of the crowd, heading into town

under sodium street lights. This year Wolves
will win the title. Then Burnley. I will see
Charlton, Law and George Best. The world revolves

around them and those voices on TV
reading the results. I'm being bedded in –
to what kind of soil remains a mystery,

but I sense it in my marrow like a thin
drift of salt blown off the strand. I am
an Englishman, wanting England to win.

I pass the Tebbitt test. I am Allan Lamb,
Greg Rusedski, Viv Anderson, the boy
from the corner shop, Solskjaer and Jaap Stam.

I feel no sense of distance when the tannoy
plays Jerusalem, Rule Britannia or the National Anthem.
I know King Priam. I have lived in Troy.

(for Gerald Morgan)

Death by Meteor

The night the meteor struck, the headline writers
were raising point sizes. The ten o'clock news
was brought forward an hour. In restaurants, waiters

ran from table to table. Theatre queues
were issued with free tickets. England was there
for the taking with Scotland and Wales. The pews

remained empty. Too late now for hot air.
This would be phlegmatic, immediate,
dignified, business as usual. Trafalgar Square

was full of pigeons. Trains would run extra late
until the shadow thickened sometime towards dawn
when the noise would be deafening. So they would wait

in streets or in pubs or on the well-kept lawn
of the bowling green, some tanked up with beer,
others with mugs of tea, some of them drawn

to familiar places, others steering clear
of all acquaintance. An Englishman's home
was the castle at the end of a frail pier,

the silence of a haunted aerodrome
where ghosts were running forward into fire.
Already they could hear the distant boom

of the approaching rock over Yorkshire,
the Midlands, Derby and Birmingham
the pitch rising, ever sharper and higher.

Death by Power Cut

So one by one the fridge, the TV, the iron,
the radio, flickered, shuddered, and went out.
Nobody lit a candle. Not a siren

was heard, just cold and darkness and doubt
leaking away, becoming certainty,
like a hangover after a dizzying bout

of drinking, or a desire for terminal sobriety.
Out went the shop windows. Safeways, Tescos,
McDonalds, Boots, Woolworths, the charity

stores, wine bars, offices, gyms, discos
and restaurants. It was the British winter
closing in for ever. Soon water froze

in the taps and the last of the cheery banter
died away. And the sea grew silent, the sky
fell like a pane of glass, one enormous splinter

of light, and broke across water. Not a cry
escaped their lips. They were proud in defeat.
They were a thirties movie and prepared to die

in black and white if need be, modest and discreet
as their fabled ancestors, thinking in
clipped tones. Then came a flurry of snow and sleet

that covered pavements up with dense white skin.
Lovers moved apart, as if afraid
of what touch might do. The old would grin

and bear it. It was their finest hour. It weighed
on them like history. The darkness blossomed
in them. It was like moving into the shade.

Death by Deluge

I have seen roads come to a full stop in mid-
sentence as if their meaning had fallen off
the world. And this is what happened, what meaning did

that day in August. The North Sea had been rough
and rising and the bells of Dunwich rang
through all of Suffolk. One wipe of its cuff

down cliffs and in they went, leaving birds to hang
puzzled in the air, their nests gone. Enormous
tides ran from Southend to Cromer. They swung

north and south at once, as if with a clear purpose,
thrusting through Lincolnshire, and at a rush
drowning Sleaford, Newark, leaving no house

uncovered. Nothing remained of The Wash
but water. Peterborough, Ely, March, and Cambridge
were followed by Royston, Stevenage, the lush

grass of Shaw's Corner. Not a single ridge
remained. The Thames Valley filled to the brim
and London Clay swallowed Wapping and Greenwich.

Then west, roaring and boiling. A rapid skim
of Hampshire and Dorset, then the peninsula:
Paignton, Plymouth, Lyme, Land's End. A slim

line of high hills held out but all was water-colour,
the pure English medium, intended for sky, cloud,
and sea. Less earth than you could shift with a spatula.

Death by Suicide

It began with the young men. They lost touch
with something important almost as soon as words
entered their mouths. There was not very much

they could say with them. They ambled in herds
like sick cattle, bumping into the edges
of the world. People were sorry afterwards

though some were glad. They leapt off ledges,
drugged themselves, spun from light-cords, drew
knives across their necks. Their very bandages

were infected and their mothers knew
in odd dark moods that they were bound by fate
to join them. And so it spread, steadily through

the whole island, until it was too late.
Life had thinned to a fragile carapace,
bones turned to cartilage. There was a spate

of immolations in the Fens, a case
of hanging-fever in Derby and a bus-load
of climbers cut their own ropes on the rock-face

at Malham. Whole families buckled. Death strode
through darkened living rooms where the radio
droned on, taking possession of one road

after another. Everywhere the sound of low
weeping. Some said it was mere melancholy –
you only had to listen to Elgar, the cello

concerto, to hear the national *folie
de grandeur*: all that aggression dressed
as modesty. Meanwhile the race was busily

killing itself, the sun was sinking in the west,
and one could read the experts' eyes, which were
distinctly bleary. They too were depressed.

The Three Remaining Horsemen of the Apocalypse

Then Fire, Famine, Plague, or what you will
(there was no energy left for War by then)
had drawn their horses up on a high hill

overlooking the city, to observe the men
and women below them. The air hung like ice.
The place had nothing to lose. They saw the pattern

of the everyday squeezed into one brilliant slice
of light. To them, each day sat somewhere
between desire and fear. Their paradise

comprised mere moments. A man in an armchair
was doing the crossword. A woman in a housecoat
was working at her window-box, her hair

gently fluttering across her exposed throat.
Two children were kicking a bottle. A dog ran down
an alley. The whole country seemed to float

like a vast web, unattached. They stood on the crown
of the hill and considered the course of history.
They watched as she progressed with a deep frown

along the river like Cleopatra, feeling sorry
for herself. I myself stared at the wall
of the yard trying to recall the memory

of other days like this. And then a miracle.
Time stopped and was redeemed in the faint
sunlight, the sun hazy, perfectly spherical.

REEL
(2004)

*To the ghost of childhood
and the body of the adult*

To watch is possible: therefore you must watch.

MARTIN BELL: 'Ode to Himself'

Reel

(for Clarissa Upchurch)

1

You wake to car sounds, radios, the cold sunlight
Burning holes in windows, and you sense
The missing fabric of the previous night.

The city offers you no evidence
Except the collage of the overheard,
Extended clauses of a broken sentence

Of which you recognise the odd stray word.
A car door slams. Feet scutter down the stairs.
It is the Theatre of the Absurd,

A masquerade in which the company wears
Period dress, their every movement fragile,
Negotiating brittle stools and chairs.

Eclectic, Art Deco, Secession style
Buildings multiply into a capital
Of iron, bronze, glass brick, ceramic tile.

A statue balanced on a pedestal
Is leaning over to whisper a close secret.
Two yellow trams clatter in mechanical

Circles. Dull monuments express regret
For what someone has done to them, for crimes
Committed in names they're trying to forget

But can't. Here all the clocks tell different times.
All the statues point different ways. Film crews
Shoot Budapest for Berlin. The city rhymes

With its imperial neighbour, like one bruise
With another. People converge on streets
Where there is never any lack of news.

Here is a square where everybody meets.
Here is a doorway through which troops have pressed.
Here is a yard with women hanging sheets

And corridors where boys in Sunday best
Are waiting for a housekeeper or maid
To join them on a stroll in the soft west

Wind ruffling the embankment trees. Decade
After decade resolves itself in the traffic.
The filming goes on somewhere in the shade.

2

Once you arrive in the heart of the exotic,
Which is only a transferred idea of home,
Under the crumbling stucco, the faint brick

Of memory appears. Above the lanterned dome
Of the cathedral the familiar sky
Waves back, reflected in the brilliant chrome

Of legions of saloon cars purring by.
It is as if they drove some narrative
Whose visual sub-plot struck your painter's eye

With its peculiar imperative.
Even the light here has grown eloquent,
Its language sparklingly authoritative.

The city glories in its element.
I woke here as a child once in a narrow
Bedroom that served as my Old Testament.

Like a philosopher I watched Time's arrow
Winging towards its target and falling short.
So God is said to note a falling sparrow...

Genesis, Exodus... it was a fishing port,
An English holiday town, time blew me to,
Where I could watch waves, like immortals, sport

With bits of flotsam once the wind was through.
Here I find lost bits of my heart. In these
Dark corridors and courtyards something true

Survives in such obsessive images
As understand the curtains of the soul
Drawing together in the frozen breeze.

And you, born in the Far East, in a bowl
Of China dust, carried in armoured trucks
Along Malaysian roads, and down the coal-

Seamed valleys of Yorkshire, past viaducts
And airports, can now enter through the walls
To haunt the darkest residential blocks.

3

What hope for rhyme when even childhood calls
On fiction for an echo and completes
Itself in myths, processions, carnivals,

Displays that billow down mysterious streets?
The city is unfixed, its formal maps
Are mere mnenomics where each shape repeats

Its name before some ultimate collapse.
The train shunts in the sidings, cars pull in
By doorways, move off, disappear in gaps

Between the shops. It is like watching skin
Crack and wrinkle. Old words: *Andrássy út*
And *Hal tér*. Naming of streets: *Tolbuhin*,

Münnich...the distant smell of rotting fruit,
Old shredded documents in blackened piles,
Dead trees with squirrels snuffling at the root.

On balmy afternoons you walk for miles
Trying to listen to the architecture.
It mutters continually, waving dusty files

Of unsolved grievances. It wants to lecture
Even while it sings – and how it sings,
When the mood takes it! So you take its picture

And brood upon those mouths and eyes, the wings
Of its cracked angels and draw out the sound
In terms of light which darkens as it rings.

Bells of the city chime, round upon round.
The film rolls on. A car sweeeps round the bend,
Its shadow stripping grey from the pale ground.

4

Sooner or later roads come to an end.
The tram draws to a stop beside the bridge
Then doubles back. Cogwheel railways descend

To their terminus. You reach the world's edge
To leap off or to turn around and face
The ardours of the tiring homeward trudge.

The beggars in the subway know their place.
The shopgirl yawns. A couple in the square
Seem to be locked in statuesque embrace.

Surely by now the credits should appear.
Our characters, our narratives, our themes
And leitmotifs are hanging in the air

As dusk comes on with the small print of dreams.
We get into the car and cruise away
Negotiating networks of dipped beams.

Everything snores. Even the fine spray
Of rain breathes evenly. The houses close
Their doors to the street. Bedroom curtains sway

And darken. Somewhere in the comatose
Suburbs two people chase each other through
Sequences of courtyards with black windows.

Today is history, only the night is new
And always startling. Slowly the paint flakes
On the wall. Eventually the film-crew

Pack their gear away. The darkness aches
For morning which arrives with bird-calls, gusts
Of wind and traffic just as the reel breaks.

Meeting Austerlitz

(i.m. W.G. Sebald)

DECEMBER 2001

1

The cold sat down with frozen fingers. Cars
were iced up, the pavements were treacherous.
Boys in t-shirts drifted through doors of bars

in quiet market towns. The shops were a chorus
of seasonal favourites, every one the same.
We were jollying ourselves up for Christmas

without much money and no sense of shame
because this was a time for giving and for joy.
We were all good intentions. So the postman came

and went, lorries delivered supplies, the boy
with the papers zipped about on his bike,
parents were packing the latest must-have toy,

(each one expensive, every one alike),
the butcher's whole family were busy serving
and no one had fallen ill or gone on strike.

On ungritted roads motorists were swerving
to avoid each other. Nothing had come to bits
in the houses of the whole and the wholly deserving,

nothing was incomprehensible or beyond our wits
and I myself was taking a quiet stroll
in the nearby fields when I met Austerlitz.

It was some way off the road and he was the sole
patch of dark in the bright mid-afternoon.
Hello Max, I said. And he looked up with that droll

melancholy expression. There was the faintest moon
visible in the sky. *Both day and night,*
he grinned. *It'll be dusk pretty soon.*

In Lalla Rookh, *if I remember right,*
I've not read Thomas Moore for several years,
there's a veiled prophet, Hakim, who radiates light

and draws the moon from a well. When it appears
it eclipses the real moon. Perhaps we have invented
the sad pale thing there with its terrible shears.

The air was frosty, oddly tobacco-scented,
thick grey clouds rose from his mouth as he spoke.
I could not be certain whether the wisps that entered

my mouth were frozen breath or cigarette smoke:
everything had a double or existed
in some version of itself wrapped in a winter cloak.

It was as if an enormous window had misted.
Austerlitz was looking across the field.
Beyond the window, there were buildings twisted

into macabre shapes. Some creature squealed
in the distance. A car growled briefly past.
Then silence, complete and vacuum-sealed.

2

I could not believe that Austerlitz was dead.
Though others had died that year his death was strange.
His voice had internalised itself in my head

and I kept listening to see how it would arrange
the furniture it found there. Certainly
it would improve things. Almost any change

would do that. A puff of dust from the library,
swirling like ashes, had settled across his prose,
its flavour tart, magical and scholarly,

as tired as the world. Each cadence had to close
on what remained of it. A collection of postcards,
a guidebook, a street-map. The attempt to impose

order was a perilous task, all but beyond words
while the alternative universe of flux
offered no sympathy and kept no records.

His were meticulous, a kind of *fiat lux*
compounded of atoms. My mind being a mess
I wanted his vision blowing through the ducts.

Though Austerlitz had died the tenderness
of his precision was consoling. No one
could start at quite that angle to the homeless

intellect. It was the winter sun.
His voice moved in the frozen field and I
would follow it and beg him to carry on.

3

I was writing about wrestlers. There were books
and videos and interviews. I thought
long about the body, the way it looks

and functions, the way the body fought
its enemies – other bodies, disease,
the weather, the impossible onslaught

of information, and the curious sleaze
it took to – but also its courage, miraculous
cogency and ability to please.

My half-century had passed. I was feckless
and wanted to listen to what Austerlitz
might say on the subject, however ridiculous.

I knew a good man once, of regular habits,
he began, *a doctor, who lived just there
beyond the field. In reasonable spirits*

*you'd have thought. It was a bad affair,
a long way from his birthplace. He was ill
of course, but others sicken without despair*

*quite breaking through like that. We can distil
our terrors and make them hang like a grey mist
beyond the garden, somehow peripheral,*

*and I considered him an optimist
compared to me, though that's a matter of style.
Body and mind, the way they co-exist,*

*is by breeding madness which festers a while
but sooner or later starts jabbering, and then
at last it is as if an imbecile*

*had always possessed you. Your wrestling men
are like the demons that Jesus exorcised,
playing at swine herded into a pen*

*or ring, and we pretend to be surprised
when they break free and tumble from a height.
Demons are inevitably oversized*

by our usual standards. We remain polite,
value nobility, and the poor doctor was the most
courteous of people until that night.

Things just add up, especially the lost
things. He breathed out and the air stood still
before it vanished slowly like a ghost.

4

But I was not prepared to let him go
so easily. I knew that in his mind
there was a tendency to counter-flow

and double exposure. He would unwind
the world of memory and wind it up again
a little off-centre as though it were a blind

or hedge against bad luck. *You can't explain*
history to itself, he said. *It has*
neither ears nor eyes. Humankind must train

itself to refocus or employ mirrors.
That morning I had leaned forward to shave
and thought to see myself in my true colours,

but the face was broader and I seemed to have
no focal point at all. The nose was there,
and eyes, ears, mouth, chin, cheeks, but nothing gave

the parts coherence. The face was just too bare,
I could not glimpse it as another could
in another dimension, less self-aware.

I remembered my mother's face in childhood,
my father's worried look, my children's deep
otherness, my wife's eyes, and saw the blood

that ran through all of us like dreams in sleep
in faint streams of reality, a secret plumbing
telling us who we were, what we could keep

and what we'd have to lose in whatever was coming.
But we were standing still in the stiff grass.
It was almost dusk and the cold was numbing.

Perhaps we were statues and time would pass
leaving us unaltered, or him at least.
His words were turning to silver behind glass

like any mirror, although the mouth had ceased
moving and his breath was only in my head
stirred by a wind directly north-north-east.

5

We're born in joy, we live joy and we die
into joy, say the masses crowding on the shore
of the Ganges. *You listen to the cry*

of the holy men, said Austerlitz. *The more*
they cry, the greater the joy. You speak the name
of the god and it appears in shadows on the floor

or in the seeds of a plant, everywhere the same.
But names are like dreams we disappear into
where all things seem to fit into the frame

of their narrative. It is names we journey through:
they're landscapes of what ever happens and goes
on happening as we progress, neither old nor new.

Take photographs, the way a flashbulb blows
your swollen shadow up against the wall
behind you. A momentary perception grows

into an image. It is an oddly comical
sensation. Frozen motion. Blind field. I stared
at the panoramic photograph of my old school

seeking my younger face, darker and thicker haired
lost cousin among all the faces trapped
in the moment. It was, I think, time that shared

us, not us that did the sharing, however rapt
the attention the camera gave us. We were stopped
in our tracks by it as if time itself had snapped

shut. We were part of something that was cropped
and stern but opened out again into time
that carried on either side of the camera propped

on its tripod. Look how our mouths mime
to the words we are speaking now. *It is late,*
said Austerlitz, watching the stars climb

to their stations. *The gods of joy can wait*
forever, and so can we. It was cold. I stood
trembling beside him, trying to concentrate

as the fields disappeared into the wood,
till my own image hung for a second then went
absent, not for a moment but for good.

He too watched it go, then slowly bent
his head and leaned it on my shoulder, as he had
the last time we had met, like a penitent,

and I was touched. It was terribly sad
to think of it. A car was drifting by
as in an old film. I took the nearby road

back into town just as snow began to fly.
Christmas lights dripped from windows winking
their enormous eyes at the dark sky.

6

We'd met at the station once, in the café.
It was cold then too, both of us shivering
and we said hello to each other then moved away.

I saw the crippled bushes weathering
with dead traveller's joy. At Manningtree
quicksilver mudflats and channels feathering

water with light, a water-tower, the Marconi
factory at Chelmsford. The whole train-
ride was a kind of speculative journey

into melancholy in a steady rain
of terraced houses, the imperium
of the great city spreading like a stain

across suburbs, from village to reclaimed slum
in three generations. The great hotels
at the terminus, spire and dome and drum,

were ghost planets of marble and precious metals,
metaphors for a solar system whose core
had disintegrated in a peal of bells

echoing forever along one shore
or another. Water ate away each edifice,
both centre and periphery. The roar

of crumbling brickwork and the shriek of ice
in the North Sea. Gulls swirling in a high
circle over pigeons, terrace on terrace

like slow waves. I saw you pulling your wry
face again. The place was grim. I sat down
nursing my coffee and a piece of dry

Danish pastry. You'd vanished into town,
and I waited for my train and played with the sugar,
holding a lump in my spoon, letting it drown.

7

My bookmark is a little headed note:
the Esperia Hotel in Athens. The room
looked out on a side street which seemed to float

in an almost permanent state of gloom
and only when the sun rose to noon height
did it penetrate there beyond the boom

of traffic at the front where all the light
available had gathered. The TV showed
a micro-second of hard porn as bait:

a tongue, a vulva, a thrusting groin, glowed
then disappeared. Something silky froze
into permanence, in an elsewhere you could decode

with a machine. *So a piece of silk could close
the gap between worlds,* Austerlitz observed,
quoting somebody. *The picture that shows*

*the young girl in the garden, her lips faintly curved
into a smile, is touching because she is lovely
and gone. Going is what we have deserved*

*and welcomed. The puzzled small dog on her knee,
the doll at her feet, the bent-wood chair, the flowers
behind her are silky cellulose. Photography*

*has made them into dwarfish ghosts, sleek showers
of light beating down an endless slope.
My feet are sliding even now. There are a few hours*

*left, if that. The bookmark remains. The soap
by the basin. The towels. The curtains. The name
of the hotel, which, as you know, means hope.*

Noir

With a firm hand, she dabs at two pink pancakes
and smooths herself right out. The man next door
crushes his cigarette in the ashtray and makes

a call. A car draws up below. There are more
cars by the curbside, waiting with lights on.
Everything is ready. Lights on the floor

above snap off. Whatever business was being done
is done. It's time for bed. Boys stir in sleep
to the sounds of drumming that might be a handgun.

The plot is too complex and runs too deep
for neat solutions. There are only cars
and endless cruising. There are secrets you keep

and secrets you don't yet know. There are scars
below scars and, eventually, daylight over the hill
to wipe the windscreens by the all-night bars

but shadows remain on the lung and the grille
of the sedan parked by the gate. What troubles you?
Why so anxious? Why do you stand so still?

Sheringham

When you come out of the sea, with its faint
illegible scrawl of scum like a smudged sleeve,
you hear the screak of pebbles sucked slant

under and round, and begin at last to believe
in the longer perspectives of geological
time, hearing its music as if each semibreve

of stone added up to a monumental
composition that went on dissolving
even as it sounded, out of your control;

so steeply shelving banks of grey stone sing
to one another, as if they had a voice
that was slowly but perfectly evolving

out of itself into a human face.
Once on a website I saw a man rise
out of a crowd of old scholars. It was Chris

Coles who played football with me. His eyes
were exactly as they had been, though the hair
was grey like the beachstones and his nose

seemed broader perhaps but I could see, somewhere
at the back of it, his old nose and chin
like a shadow on the steady coastal air

until a wave broke and the old face slid back in
under the new one which, I guess, had shocked me.
It shocked because both images were thin,

thinner than I had expected and so exactly
matched in the way the waves had rinsed them clean.
When I was twenty I worked in a factory

attending a boiler-sized plastic-tube machine
that spewed curved pipes at regular intervals,
which I had to file down and throw in a waiting bin.

And Chris, where was he then? On what thermals
was he billowing onward? He had been half-back
and captain too, tackling and knocking long balls

out to the wings where I was waiting to attack,
to centre or cut in, and the rain was falling hard
on the dark green and brown grass which was slick

as spittle, where enthusiasm was its own reward.
Chris was in his world, and I was stuck in mine,
except for the match after which we'd board

the school bus and go home and the rain
was still falling. We had our desks at school,
our friends, our 'A' Levels. So it would go on

changing under the rain, down a long spool
of cloud that thinned, thickened or vanished
as sun broke through. It was a miracle,

all of it, the long walls of time that crashed
about our ears without crushing us. And always
these visits to the seaside and its embellished

cuffs of water, rubbing away whole days.
I watched a toddler in a red quilted jacket
teeter down stones making tiny forays

onto the black, wet, still sucked-and-licked
lowest tier of them, seeing time itself
contract into a child in the vast derelict

expanse of the sea that swallowed up each shelf,
and the expensive beach-huts with their locks
and curtains above, one with its door half-

open to the wind, and all the silent clocks
of the digital age moving forward together
with Chris Coles and I in a mathematics

far beyond my own and, beyond us, all the other
boiled down particulars that regularly come
knocking at the skull in the blank weather

and this terrible word, love, the only sum
we can think of adding to the loneliness
to make up the difference between them.

FLESH: AN EARLY FAMILY HISTORY

1. Forgetting

Mother

The first hand coming down from heaven. Her hand.
She hovers above you. It is a premonition
Of life to come, a bird preparing to land.

Your mother's warmth. Her breasts. An impression
Of intensity as softness, and then the bones
Of her knuckles. Cheeks. Neck. The motion

Of her head, swing of her hips. The delicate cones
Of her nipples. The mystery of the navel. Heat.
Cold, Wet. Dry. Milky smells and pheromones.

Where do you begin? With fingers tickling feet
Or lips against skin ? Being lifted high
Then swung to safety? The noises of the street?

Your minor disasters? Hearing your own cry
Echo in your head? There's something lost,
Something buried deep under the eye

You try to see with, something faint as dust
Settled inside your lungs, a history
Tucked in the folds of your body like a cast.

The radio mumbles. A bell rings suddenly.
Light moving across the floor, over the ceiling.
The bird rustles. Her hair. The branches of a tree

Against the window knocking and squealing.

Sleigh Ride

You know the feeling but can't put a name to it.
All beginnings are the same and all are forgotten.
Forgetting is what you've done. You can't undo it

Now or ever. It is the cast you put on
Inside you. You have wandered about her body
All your life, are aware of it as the hidden pattern

You follow. It is as if your life were a parody
Of something she once told you. You taste her skin
First thing in the morning. It is a heady

Delicate babyish smell you must have breathed in
At the outset, when you started forgetting.
Her hands. The bird hovering. Later, a thin

Wrinkled integument with the sun setting
Inside it. Time slips away like the toboggan
Your father once pulled for you. You were sitting

With your brother, clutching him, hanging on
To his arm, everything around you white
And blurred, the sky, the trees, everything gone

Or going, slipping dangerously towards night
Where life too is slippery and you must cling
To the moon or whatever is solid. You're right

To forget this, to remember absolutely nothing.

Dead Babies
(after Canetti)

There's absolutely nothing between them. The ape
Nurses her dead child as though it were alive,
Tenderly cradles its inert furry shape

And won't let go. It's the first imperative
And must be obeyed. She examines eyes
Mouth, nose and ears, attempts to give

Her baby the breast. She grooms it. Tries
To pick it clean. After a week or so
She leaves off feeding but swats at the flies

That settle on its body and continues to show
Deep interest in its cleanliness. Eventually
She begins to set it down, learns to let go.

It starts to mummify and grows horribly smelly.
Now and then she'll bite at the skin until
A limb drops off, then another. Gradually

It decomposes. Even the skin starts to shrivel.
At last she understands at the back of her head.
She plays with furry objects. There is a subtle

Readjustment. Reverse the roles of the dead.
Turn back the clock. Forgetting is good.
You turn and turn within your tiny bed

Until the back of your mind has understood.

The Phantom of the Opera

Things gather in the back of the mind. You find them
Changed yet familiar, everything is in pieces.
Your furry toys, your games: the harmless phantom

Of childish operas is stalking the premises.
You have little idea of the world outside. The wall
Is the limits of language, beyond that the crisis

Of imagination, smashed glass, a noisy hall
Full of children you've never seen, the air
Frozen in attitudes, all too forgettable.

You push your way through the door, down the stair
To a melancholy traffic of cars and the old
Who possess the world and seem to be everywhere.

You push away from your mother but fear the cold
And retreat. She accepts you back with a fury.
She grooms you. Washes you. You are controlled

By her attentions, preserved from injury,
From infection, from your own body, lost
In her larger moods, enduring the battery

Of her breasts and never count the cost.
Your limbs are dropping off. Something dies
As you grow, decay and forget the most

Annoying, ridiculous things. Forgetting is wise.

Outside

You forget so much. Memory drops away,
its phantom limb still waggling. Wipe the slate
clean each time, scrub like there's no yesterday.

Your mother moves off with her innate
Disturbing odours. You run across the floor
And hide in her lap, aware of your own weight.

Outside are executions, show trials. The door
Opens on the operations of the body politic.
There are crowds in the street who want more

Than you can give. There's a school. There's a stick
And a carrot. A boy in a track suit weeps snot
Into his cut sleeve and feels faintly sick

While, in between, the land that time forgot
Is blossoming into enormous flowers,
Great fields you pass in the bus on a hot

Summer afternoon, the smell of ripe hours
Blowsing into poppies, corn and dark blue
Cherries, the sound of a dozen lawnmowers

In a London suburb, pastures passed through,
Wiped clean and rewritten, fields without number
Or name, like a foreign place you never knew,

The smell of flesh you cannot quite remember.

ECLOGUE: HOSPITAL SCENE

A

In the green and white light of the hospital she sat beside him
Just as her parents had sat by her own bedside.
Life was so thin and ragged it hardly seemed possible
To hold it. More than once it had slipped through her fingers
And she had to leap after the trailing string, a faint wisp of cotton,
And make herself light, almost skeletal, so it would support her.

B

The child was her first and he seemed to be slipping beyond her
Into the murk of the past that had got by without him,
Where the pale green was darker, muddier, cloacal,
A wholly internal affair like the lining of memory,
A visceral padding of flesh to block out the image
Of the war that had only quite recently ended.

A

In the green and white light of the hospital they were huddled together
Like figures in paintings of sick-beds, with much the same knowledge
That not far away in the meadow bodies were buried,
Where potato and cabbage, maize and huge sunflower
Toiled to the ticking of nature and wrapped the dry bones
In the only available form of inadequate healing.

B

And so they sat without hope or expectation
While trams came and went, and the newspapers carried
The speeches of those in authority, statistics of production,
And ghostly doctors and nurses moved through the ward
Like moths invading a larder, like leaves on the river,
Like almost anything else given to drifting.

2. First Things First

Piano

It's a baby grand with unexceptionable teeth
And a butterfly wing caught in the net curtain.
When touched it answers gently as a breath

Of cold wind, a sensualist in a puritan
Country. It is a hybrid creature with only
Three legs and a faint ephemeral grin,

With feminine curves, a gorgeous womanly
Voluptuousness. It seems almost indecent
To be sitting beneath her, guilty and lonely,

Ignorant of the role she will play. The crescent
Of her one hip is a shelter and the gloss
Of her body temptation. Concupiscent

Discords swell into proper fifths, zealous
Arpeggios clamber over her. Learning
Her vast bourgeois temperament is the cross

A child must bear as she stands burning
In the summer sun. And Chopin and Bartok
Can be enticed from her with their strut and yearning.

You must woo her carefully with wealth and work,
Until one day, like the butterfly she is,
She shrugs and vanishes into the sudden dark

Of history and other shady business.

Stove

The incinerated history of the block
Is trapped within these terracotta stoves
Grumbling and wheezing like a carriage clock

Or faintly glowing like upended loaves.
In winter our great aunts, the elderly,
Huddle beside them in fingerless gloves

Grow older, more transparent, tenderly
Beckoning us to join them. The stove sweats
And sighs with the wind in the frozen northerly

Forests we read about where dogs and cats
Are children in disguise. Life goes up in flames,
The familiar is swept under magic carpets.

Their gingerbread-brown is focus for our games.
We creep up on each other. We touch the tiles
With drops of water that glitter like tiny gems

Sizzling into silence. The stove's mouth smiles
Through its black grille. It could possibly teach
Us something, but what? Downstairs, the piles

Of logs, coal-heaps, old jam-jars, the dark niche
Of the cellar with its guttered candles. We learn
its sunken topography, its slow muttering speech

and bring our rusty buckets with stuff to burn.

Swing

Tenderly they attached the rings to the lintel
Of the door and set the swing into motion
With the child firmly in it. They were gentle

As they pushed, with proper parental caution.
The child's eyes widened. He giggled, kicking his heels
And swallowed the air of the flat like a dizzy potion.

Pendulum-wise it swung to his appeals,
Defying gravity, almost subversive:
The rings rubbed with small metallic squeals.

It was as if the whole world had turned cursive,
Leaning beyond the perpendicular
Into another edgy dimension, massive

And terrifying. His parents stood rectangular,
Respectable, as they would always stand
But ever more blurred, losing shape and colour.

Perhaps this was what they had always planned.
The swing could be hooked up out of the way
When not in use. Only an adult hand

Could take it down and make the whole flat sway.
Mother and father were gods of limited space.
Only they could willingly fade away

Like the child's own faintly breathed-on, mirrored face.

A Lead Soldier

The soldier was the first thing he could weigh
In his closed palm and feel somehow assured.
He watched it as it watched him where he lay,

Knowing he might endure what it endured.
Being a child he was aware of childhood,
Knowing the cell in which he was immured

And all the rules of being bad and good.
His nails ran round the soldier's form, the face,
The back of the knee, the plinth on which it stood

Ready to venture, glaring at a space
Behind the wardrobe or the enemy
Propped by the inkpot, where it had the grace

A child lacks, having no autonomy.
Even inside its box along with others
It held its posture with economy.

It was like having regiments of brothers
Each more valiant than the last, a palette
Of reds and blues. The child was light as feathers,

Too vulnerable. He needed an amulet
To see him through the nights his parents fought.
The soldier was the rough weight of a bullet,

A boiled-down heart, like his, more finely wrought.

Book

There is a graveyard, full moon, and, asleep,
A hero figure. Then, at midnight, ghosts
In their thousands who are doomed to keep

Appointments with the wide awake. Vast hosts
Of them whoo-whoo and helter-skelter, chill
Electric slivers of life at their last posts.

This is a story. Tell me another, until
The stories are exhausted and the dead
Retire to their grave bedrooms in the hill.

The book closes on the double spread
Of the night sky which flows for ever, immense
Beyond the page, lighting stars in the head.

A ghost fades until it is merely presence,
An aura of light-bulbs, curtains, wagging tongues
Speaking a coded semi-conscious sense.

Wake when you can. Children are singing songs
In the playground. Teacher is telling a tale.
The books lie open like a pair of lungs

Breathing words. Ghosts in the graveyard wail
To other moons. The stars have moved so far
Beyond the page they've gone right off the scale,

Small crumbs of icing in an empty jar.

ECLOGUE: FAIR DAY

A

Fair day in Budapest. Little fringed trumpets of cardboard
With barber's-pole patterns. And the man in the trilby
Is down on his haunches with his small son beside him.
It is spring in the park, too early in the century,
In these parts at least, for a snarl up of motorised traffic.
It is legs all the way, a foot-bound Futurist manifesto.

B

Too early for a child to attempt a distinction
Between joy and mere chaos and something of terror.
The largeness of things is an ongoing factor
In the tiny managerial office of his senses
Which registers hands, like his father's, those very same hands,
As the weight of a lonely order of planets.

A

Fair day in Budapest, now tucked into history
In the way you slip a bus-ticket into a book
Or it may be a postcard, or a strip from a serviette
In any case temporary and sure to fall out
When the volume is opened, as it has been, and often.
It is, after all, only a child and his felt-hatted father.

B

Everything slips from the books you are reading:
The plot, the descriptions, the fascinating characters,
And the only thing left is the smell of the pages
Or the way they turned over, and the child that once turned them,
Who slips from the book now. Look, look at him slipping,
And the hand on his shoulder, a moon with its planet.

3. Secret Languages

The Sound of the Radio

Once there were brothers tucked up nice and tight
Inside the world. Cradle, playpen and pram
Littered their double room and broke the night

With streaks of light under the door, the jamb,
The curtain, and the faintly fragile shape
Of crying like the bleating of a lamb.

One was much smaller, little hairless ape
That clung to mother, animal not child,
With eyes, fingers, mouth, everywhere agape,

Seizing just what it could, unreconciled,
Unlike the elder, to the world of the possible,
Its smelly paraphernalia piled

On a painted chest of drawers by the table,
With parents parked in the next room,
Their talk a low buzz fizzing into trouble.

But when it cried one of them would come
Immediately, alert, moving softly but fast
Between furniture, through great bundles of gloom,

The radio suddenly louder, like the ghost
Voice of an enormous world, a slab
Suddenly broad and brilliant as gold–dust

Bringing into their darkness the gift of the gab.

Early Music

The little one was a slow speaker. Not until
The toy violin fell on his head did he mutter
The word 'violin' like a minor miracle.

Language opened its doors to him. He would utter
Prophecies and curses in the vocabulary of music.
Music ran through his fingers like melted butter.

Music would be the saving of him, music or magic.
Life would exercise him no more than those quaint
Ornaments he mastered, the beginner's trick

Of sounding like genius. Women would faint
To hear him, he was so beautiful to see,
And practised night and day without complaint.

Romantic reveries nurtured the folly
Of his parents. Monstrous hopes sat on the stairs
Frowning darkly at the happy family,

(Who were they to give themselves such airs?)
But music was aspiration, they could not breathe without it.
It was the flowering of their sad affairs.

The dead, undoubtedly, were firmly behind it,
Their bloodied faces and emaciated bodies
Resounding through the child, endlessly implicit,

In scales, arpeggios and those awkward studies.

Cleaner

The daily swore like a trooper, but cleaned and cooked
While the parents worked elsewhere, back in the age
Of Uncle Joe Stalin. She was how things looked

In the early fifties. She occupied centre-stage
With her loose tongue and they acted horrified
When the children erupted in foul language.

It was comical. Grandmother would have died
To hear it, being a respectable working class
Woman, who ran to a little sewing on the side,

And as for grandfather, he was dead, alas,
The socialist playwright of the shop-floor
Swept off to Auschwitz in a cloud of gas.

Small rough hands, she had, and a pinafore.
Her nose was snub, her teeth yellow and black
With cigarettes. She would lie down and snore

On the sofa most afternoons, flat on her back,
Then give them a cuddle and some kind of sweet,
And all the rooms were clean as if by magic.

She taught them *fuck* and *fart*, their mouths replete
With her tongue and her bad teeth in their heads,
Then disappeared back down into the street,

Their bodies tucked like small flames in their beds.

Newspaper

The newspaper was faint type on pale grey,
Dissolving into dots on close inspection
As if the whole world could be blown away

Like specks of dust or flimsy bits of fiction.
The place outside was faceless. Words like ranks
Of shadows thinned to an official diction

They learned by osmosis, phalanx by long phalanx,
Until they filled you out and blocked your eyes.
Meanwhile the powdery images of tanks

And flags involved in endless exercise
Expanded over drawers and kitchen shelves
To serve as camouflage for household flies.

Mysterious as blown-out radio-valves,
The children scanned them, seeking to discover
An order of things far beyond themselves,

Another world as vast as the grey river
That ran through everything they ever knew.
They watched the delicate paper lift and quiver

In the draught. And everywhere words blew
And settled. On their skin, on their clothes. The air
Was tiny photographic dots that flew

Straight at their faces, tugging at their hair.

The Pipes

Having been born into an age of pipes
We knew integrity by its sour smell.
Our parent's friends were intellectual types

Who drew and sucked like imperturbable
Monoliths, in their dachas by the lake,
And tapped their sepia fingers on the table

Occasionally producing a dark flake
Of tobacco from their spittled lips. They rocked
In cane chairs set on porches, half-awake,

While in the darkness the clock ticked and tocked
And water gently slopped among the reeds.
Their silences were too grave to be shocked

By wars or arguments or infantile misdeeds.
The village dogs slunk by. They puffed and spat
Like monuments with barely human needs.

Tall wreaths of smoke The curious furry hat
Of adulthood, contentment, stillness. We
Respected their silence. Their empty, flat

Voices. Their deaths would be ours eventually.
We would light their pipes, enter their myths.
When the clock stopped ticking we too would be free

To turn ourselves into such monoliths.

ECLOGUE: AT THE STATION

A

It is November and snowing, like something out of Tolstoy,
Here at the railway station where a woman wearing a muff
Is waiting on the platform, while thousands of faces
Swim in and out of focus with suitcases and bundles
In a fug of anxiety that rises from their mouths
And blots out their features one breathtaking moment.

B

Here stride the soldiers with peaked caps, rifles and kitbags
That belong to a popular movie, so fiction and cinema
Seem to have entered the world, or shifted abruptly
Into the realm of the real, which has blossomed in capital letters,
Into Death, Execution, Resistance, Night Raid, and Crackdown,
All on display at the station, glamorous, vigilant.

A

It is November and snowing, much as it always does
In films of November. Families with children
Are huddled on benches, learning their lines just in case
Of Night Raid or Crackdown. The city is muttering
Into its threadbare, capacious but wholly inadequate sleeve
Its mutterings carried down platforms and carriages.

B

The soldiers are watching the woman who stands very straight
Mysterious as Garbo but infinitely dustier
As the train with its vast preoccupations draws nearer
And the film rolls on with the scene of her jumping
In front of the engine, just as we're all of us jumping
Into a film of snow, on a screen, as she coils, uncoils and jumps.

4. Her Adult Occupations

When she leaned over the light-box

When she leaned over the light-box her face shone
As though she herself had been the source of light,
A moon to a diffused rectangular sun.

Transparent bands of film flopped in tight
Orthodox curls over the edge of it,
And her hair too fell forward, black as night.

Her hands made nervous movements, delicate,
Bird-like, calculated, unerringly precise,
Her head swaying, a harshly under-lit

Mask that caricatured the familiar face.
Whatever it was she was giving herself to
Demanded close attention. The edifice

Of her presence multiplied and grew
In shadows on the wall and the dark hair
Swung to and fro. Meanwhile, her fingers drew

The shadows of light images from the air
Till the tension told on her back and wrists and eyes
And she sat up straight, as if whatever prayer

She'd been engaged on was over. The brush lies
On the table. The film curls on the floor.
The light in the box dazzles. No one dies

In photographs. Then she bends down once more.

Her knees drawn together

Her knees drawn together under the table, she wears
A pair of man's trousers and has pencilled on
A moustache. The elder of two children stares

At her, disorientated. Her voice has gone,
To be replaced by something deeper: a gruff
Stranger's on an official commission.

If this is a joke it isn't quite enough
To make them laugh or simply play along
But there is no way they can call her bluff.

Their father, engaged in talk, sees nothing wrong,
And frowns as if considering a question
She has raised. The world to which they belong

Is beyond speculation or suggestion,
Two grown-up dolls moving on a stage
In danger of spontaneous combustion.

He stands up. She rises. It takes an age.
The giants evoke a slow music of basses
And tubas. The terrible badinage

Between them comes to an end. Their faces
Burn with suppressed laughter as she wipes
Away the moustache. His finger traces

Her light skin between the smudged stripes.

Despite the heavy snow she is almost skipping

Despite the heavy snow she is almost skipping
Down the moonlit street. The children clutch
Their parents' hands. High up, eaves are dripping

Icicles. No cars. No people. Not very much
Of anything at this time. Silence. It is two
In the morning in the New Year. They watch

Their mother in amazement. She floats through
The city in their heads, an apparition
Of adult high spirits, like a wholly new

Secret. The winter is exotic, White Russian
In its dense pallour and unheard-of chill.
Minus twenty-five. They sense the passion

In her pleasure, as they did at the high table
In the feasting hall with its pig's head. Never before
Have they been up so late. They know they are still

Children, and that she's immeasurably more
Than they can understand. Their father moves
Cautiously beside her, testing the slippery floor

On her behalf. A hard gust of wind shoves
Them forward as they pass unfamiliar blocks
On strange corners with their furry leather gloves,

Their fancy trousers tucked into thick socks.

Something breathless, frighteningly urgent

Something breathless, frighteningly urgent,
Seemed to be batting around her when she fluffed
Her hair out gypsy-fashion, her mouth pungent

With garlic cloves, indelicately stuffed
With bread and dripping. She drew her eyebrows thick
In high black arches to match the rounded tuft

Of her black beauty spot. Her scarlet lipstick
Was dangerous as blood and not maternal.
This transformation was an adult trick

To scare the world out of its eternal
Terrors, and us into strangeness. She would flirt
With hard-faced men: the fat KGB colonel

In the office, informers who dished dirt.
Such representatives of outer dark
Would all be cowed with a flick of her wide skirt.

And we too would be cowed, as if the stark
Facts of existence had sharpened in our eyes
And hovered there like an ambiguous mark –

Much like the beauty spot in fact, the cries
Of distant bedrooms, the doings of stray dogs,
The deep unsettling realm of adult lies,

A sense of oil and wheels and endless cogs.

With nails filed smooth into deep curves

With nails filed smooth into deep curves and points
(Her hands had modelled jewellery in a store)
She bent her fingers back against the joints

And though the boys would plead with her: no more!
She knew these were electric attributes
To hold them still or lift them from the floor.

The body can do so much: bellows and flutes
Through which you blow, or weapons you may wield
To good effect. You wear it as it suits

And walk about in it with your eyes peeled,
But cannot see through what remains opaque
Or penetrate behind its foreign shield.

Her fingers curled into their hearts. The ache
Had found a home where it might live
Forever if her fingers did not break,

And even then the nails would surely drive
Deeper until they could not tell them from
The fabric of their beings which would thrive

On such acute discomfort. So fingers drum
On tables and the eyes open at night,
And small electric pulses lift and thrum

Through bones and lodge there like an ammonite.

ECLOGUE: MIRROR

A

Mirror into which we continually disappear. Those eyes
Are not ours, nor have they ever been, the more they have looked
For that other, the missing one. She was putting on make-up
And I was behind her, and sun on the wall was aching to speak
But all it could say was goodbye, and again, and goodbye.
And that was the best of it, the joy of the catch in the throat.

B

I saw you behind me and knew you were watching. We hung
In the air like shadows with bodies, and time was just leaving, going
Out of the door, into the dark of the hall where the coats hang.
I put on my coat and went out. There was shopping to do and the street
Extended itself in a version of central perspective.
Life was geometry, a drawing of lines with an architect's pencil.

A

Mirror into which so much has disappeared. Shop-windows
Staring back at the traffic, photographs in the album
Of lost things, almost an X-ray of bones buried under the pavement.
I was watching her go. It was foggy, my glasses had misted.
There were grease marks all over the lens as she turned the next corner
Facing the sun now, directly. She was burning to ashes.

B

You are always behind me. I am washing my hands at the basin.
I stand and imagine you shaving, your face is pushed forward
Practically touching the mirror. I hear the noise of the shaver.
An aeroplane broods in the distance above the high cloud. I hear you
Saying I love you, and watch myself move from the frame of the mirror
Into the space of the room, which is empty and burning.

5. My Fathers

My fathers, coming and going

Moustaches and grey homburgs: our fathers were
Defined by properties acquired by chance –
Or by divine decree. Standing behind her

In rooms, on stairs, figures of elegance,
They came and went in a murmur of soft voices,
Objects of bewilderment and romance.

How many of them on the premises?
Some worked twelve hours a day in an office
In the city, some placed bristly kisses

On our brows, some would simply embarrass
Us for no particular reason. Their age
Was indeterminate. They would promise

Anything befitting their patronage.
Were all these fathers one? And was it you,
My father, who pushed me in that carriage

I can't remember now before time flew
And took her away as it will take us all?
I feel myself flying. It's like passing through

Clouds in an aeroplane in its own bubble
Of air, a slightly bumpy ride down
Towards a runway as we rise and fall

Above the brilliant lights of a big town.

Their histories and fabled occupations

The histories and fabled occupations
Of their fathers lay somewhere off the map
In provinces lost to their imaginations.

The knowledge they had was fed to them scrap by scrap
And was all they ever needed. The fathers' presence
Was sufficient. They watched them through a gap

412

In their mother's eyes, beyond the fence
Of reason, arriving wreathed in smells of their own,
Some reassuring, others wild and tense

With dangers they had carried home from town.
Their fathers were the seas they read about
But never saw, in which a child could drown

However he might wave his arms and shout
For help. A singular compound figure stood
On the threshold of their bodies and looked out.

Mysterious rodents emerged from the wood
And scurried up the stairs at night to nibble
At their faces. They woke covered in blood.

Their father's moustache was a scary scribble
Above a friendly voice. His kindness shook
The world out of its endless incomprehensible

Rigor mortis like the closing of a book.

My father, crawling across the floor

He crawls across the floor. His dangling tie
Distracts the child. He hauls the child in the air
And swings it round, once, twice. He holds it high

Above his head. In the forest, a bear
Lurches towards the cabin. Almost night.
Goldilocks sits in the deepest chair

By the table working up an appetite.
Time starts up, judders and stops again
Its flooded engine refusing to ignite.

We're conked out here, stuck in the slow lane
Of history, where my father comes home late
From work as always and will not complain.

Seventy-two hours he labours for the state
Weekdays, Saturdays, doing what, why, how,
We do not ask him, but accept his fate.

Time is forever in an endless Now
Except in dreams, anxieties, and school,
Though time ticks over far behind his brow

According to a superimposed rule
We touch when we touch him. We hear him roar
In distant forests where his masters drool

And lumber playfully across the floor.

My father carries me across a field

My father carries me across a field.
It's night and there are trenches filled with snow.
Thick mud. We're careful to remain concealed

From something frightening I don't yet know.
And then I walk and there is space between
The four of us. We go where we have to go.

Did I dream it all, this ghostly scene,
The hundred-acre wood where the owl blinked
And the ass spoke? Where I am cosy and clean

In bed, but we are floating, our arms linked
Over the landscape? My father moves ahead
Of me, like some strange, almost extinct

Species, and I follow him in dread
Across the field towards my own extinction.
Spirits everywhere are drifting over blasted

Terrain. The winter cold makes no distinction
Between them and us. My father looks round
And smiles then turns away. We have no function

In this place but keep moving, without sound,
Lost figures who leave only a blank page
Behind them, and the dark and frozen ground

They pass across as they might cross a stage.

Like a black bird

Like a black bird against snow, he flapped
Over the path, his overcoat billowing
In the cold wind, as if he had trapped

The whole sky in it. We watched trees swing
Behind him, lurching drunkenly, blurred
Bare twigs and branches, scrawny bits of string,

And as we gazed ahead the snowflakes purred
In our ears, whispering the afternoon
Which grew steadily darker and more furred.

His face was in shadow, but we'd see it soon,
As he approached it slowly gathered shape:
His nose, in profile, was a broken moon,

His hat a soft black hill bound round with tape,
His raised lapels held his enormous eyes
Between them. The winter seemed to drape

Itself about him as if to apologise
For its own fierceness, hoping to grow warm
Through physical contact, and we, likewise,

Ran towards him, against a grainy storm
Of light and damp. It was so long ago
And life was then in quite another form,

When there were blacker days and thicker snow.

ECLOGUE: SHOES

A

Innocuous shape in a side street, a plaque by the entrance
With the name of the school written across it,
Nothing important, only the staircase waiting
For the roll-call of children to trample and shuffle
In some kind of order up to a classroom then vanish
Into the books in the stock-room on loose bits of paper.

B

I hear the shrill voices die as the door shuts.
I'm troubled and moved by the prospect of you in your best shoes
Entering and remaining, locked away in there for ever,
My very self splitting as I walk to the city
To where I must work but where something is missing,
The shoes you set off in that I had just polished that morning.

A

Innocuous shape in the side street, the screaking of blackboards,
While downstairs the business of everyday living
Is running itself, and a teacher holds forth on her subject
Which is Time and Behaviour: the way that the world wends
Its passage through time, which even now vanishes
Down a tight passage between sleep and awakening.

B

I hear the shrill voices of Time and Behaviour, the teachers
In thin dusty suits are loudly insistent we hear them,
The shoes that I polished are under a desk and the fingers
I checked for dirt are spread on the desktop. The dead years
Are always available, just open the desklid,
There in the books with their blue paper covers.

THE DREAM HOTEL

The Dream Hotel

As if the sea were entering through the window,
it was that close. Flecks of burning ice thrown
from the rocks it struck, each single fleck blown
sharp-toothed into the house. Meanwhile, below,
there were guests waiting to check in, a clerk
to register them, luggage piling at doors.
This was the form of the dream. Polished floors
were swimming in water, a green-grey dark.
From the top of the cliff you could see rain
gathering on the horizon, not yet ready
to fall but on its way. In one room two lips
were joined together, hands resting on hips,
the pair of them increasingly unsteady
as the flood rolled in like an enormous stain.

You wake to a light on the ceiling. How long
have you been awake? You lie next to him,
the one you always lie with. Some vague, dim
recollection. Years of memory. The song
of the sirens. The glow of the clock-radio
is green and gentle. Classical music, faint,
barely audible, oozes from it. Something quaint
about all this, your life passing on its slow
unforgiving way. The shape in the bed stirs
in its sleep, rolls over. You feel the steady swell
rising in you. You hear the sea again.
It is still far off, a slowly approaching train
down a long tunnel that leads to the hotel
and the two lovers, just as his lips touch hers.

The Gods of Tiepolo

1

Sometimes when you look up on a bright day,
the clouds have drawn apart, exposing a blue
that, for a moment, you can almost look through.
You're surveying a stage long after the play
has finished. Above you, Tiepolo
presents a weightless mass of gods and legs

418

in endless apotheosis, delicate as eggs
in a cup, or naked skin in an afterglow
when legs and arms float off into half-sleep
and breasts settle warmly against the ribcage
slipping vaguely down its slopes, while the flat
lower belly shimmers and fingers keep
curling and uncurling like an open page
in a slight breeze. But you can imagine that.

2

So you imagine it. Although this is
the soft sell version, somewhere beyond which
the world is singing at a sharper pitch,
its shrieks full of glass, crowded with casualties:
men in ridiculous wigs, women with waists
pinched to a tight ring, thin children in beds
with soiled sheets, the poor with their shaved heads
and hollow eyes, cruel sexual gymnasts
one step from madness, new forms of rough trade,
a puritan hell which no amount of light
can keep from sinking deeper into flames.
Imagine it. And through that? The betrayed
clear blue of something very simple, as trite
as touch, the sound of the most common names.

3

You listen to them. It's no different there
next door, next year. The sky is lightly cracking.
An enormous gentleness billows its wing
and you too are up aloft, somewhere in the air
on an internal flight, your safety belt
clipped shut, with a glass of whisky on the rocks
on a swivelling tray, among lazy flocks
of clouds that snuggle up to you then melt,
substantial as any god or human life.
Now you're a god. There's something piercing and sad
about this knowledge, as if there were nothing but
that rococo blue which beggars all belief,
the world below disordered, a ragged, mad
arena of blood which runs and refuses to clot.

4

In this particular Tiepolo,
The Finding of Moses,where a Venetian
beauty, dressed in the height of contemporary fashion,
stands in for the daughter of the Pharaoh,
your eyes discover a female figure, vast

thighed yet slender and long, with cheekbones sleek
as a greyhound and eyes that plead to speak
a mind so powerful it makes your own fly fast.
The even blue sky above her seems to spring
straight from her gaze which comprehends your own.
It solves the world, bandages its wounds,
ties up its severed limbs with blood-soaked string,
walks the streets of explosions up and down,
and smiles at all its terrible, sad sounds.

5

Keep flying, pilot, We're gods of air and fire,
our clay feet stuck in loam. Bring me a drink
and let me watch the clouds move as I think
of something clear as glass in the empire
of the bladed, whose agents are generous.
I'm fed up of this Rococo court, that sits
tremendous arsed, and will shortly be blown to bits
on its mountain-top five-star hotel terrace.
It's dark outside. Soon the movies come on
with hollow icons and interminable chases.
I want a woman of luminous intelligence to heal
my hypochondria. Soon we shall land on the sun
with smooth, unruffled, tanned, innocent faces,
staring at endless blue. It's no big deal.

Naples Yellow

His skin was Naples Yellow. He was wearing a suit
of cinematic glamour as if light dust
had settled on him. He was easy to trust
and spoke with a confidence that was absolute.
'Mon vieux,' he said in French, 'I think that we
are two of a kind. Nothing is what it seems.
Fiction confuses real and imagined dreams
and passes them off as plausibility.
Unfinished books are stacking themselves high
in corners: their characters have breath
but no desire to breathe. Raskolnikov
dies with an axe in his hand, not afraid to die.
Prince Myshkin is slowly walking to his death.
In every book there's someone turning lights off.'

It seemed he knew about unfinished books
but it was like meeting people anywhere,
like the man glimpsed in the café, in the chair,
in a waiting-room.
                    Sometimes the whole world looks
unfinished like that. The bed is not quite made,
the sun spreads uneasily across the wall,
and the boy over the street is kicking his ball
against the fence in an odd patch of shade...
Somebody's hand snakes out to clutch your own.
It starts to teach you something. You start to write
a sentence but the words escape. You lie
on the bed exhausted, having put the book down
some hours ago. It's the time of night
when minds move sideways out of symmetry.

'As your mind's moving now. The whole thing lists
like a doomed boat. Where are the passengers?
Who would you save from those all too tangible dangers?
Those you knew first, or the escapologists
you met much later? Remember this is fiction
and not life. The laws of the two places
sometimes coincide but different graces
attend on them. Some carry conviction,
others' – and here he snapped his fingers – 'fade
like clothes in sunlight.' He himself looked faint.
The whole café was dreamlike but he knew
that too. 'Take yourself,' he said. Light played
on his white shirt like fingers exploring paint.
'You can't play at both passengers and crew.

You hear yourself talk. Some book has it down
in black and white. And this is not just theoretical,
as you'll prove for yourself. You'll get it all
thrown back at you. And no, you needn't frown
so sceptically...' This monologue might have
continued, gone on for ever, but the voice
had almost died away. It was my choice
to make him vanish. 'You think you'll save
yourself like this?' was the very last thing
he said and smiled. The diner opposite
was positively translucent in the light.
And so I fell asleep. The story was going
as stories do, no need to tinker with it.
My eyes were blind. Whatever was, was right.

Pompeian Red

These are the mysteries and this is the house
of the mysteries. This is the red earth below,
and this is the flower we no longer know
that the woman holds. Here dancers carouse
in spirals acting out something we've long
lost track of. Here is the entrance, the stairs
that lead down into a nether place of affairs
we do not penetrate. Here is the song
they're singing in a strange tonality
which is said to move the spheres. Here is death
in a black gown sprinkled with flames and leaves
you find only under this buried city.
Here is the perfume they wore on their breath.
Here is the fabric the hand twists and weaves.

Here on the other hand is a café
with a glazed terrace. A woman is serving whatever
is there to be served. Downstairs flows the river
of plain plumbing which serves to wash away
things that are washed away. It is the Boulevard
Montparnasse and people are eating *omelettes
au jambon* and *fraises au citron*. People forget
what they eat and talk instead. It is hard
to forget this. Easier to remember
than mysteries, though this is also one.
The lava rushes down like busy traffic.
Eyes dance in their orbits, move in their limber
circuits like planets round a distant sun
that beats and pulses under molten brick.

Red suggests lipstick. The entry to a cave
that goes on for ever, a place of changes
and cast shadows. The waiter arranges
cutlery and sets out dishes that deprave
and purify. Persephone glides
down corridors of grass into the heart of Dis
and Paolo and Francesca bend to kiss
over the book they're reading. Each rides
the current that blows him or her, over
omelettes or *fraises* and a glass of red
house wine, which arrives, circumspect
as the waiter. The glazed panels cover
and reveal at the same time but the dead
keep talking as their thoughts and mouths connect.

Imagine the whole world under glass. The ash
in the ashtray. The dust in the urn. The face
at the bottom of the cup, the empty space
between more emptiness, glass one longs to smash
simply because it's glass. And yet it's lovely,
this sunlight trapped in the purring moment:
nothing will ever be better than the present,
it says, and you believe it as it moves gravely
past you. This is the mystery. This is the house
that guards it. This is the town by the volcano
which is silent as if for ever but not for ever,
the house of *omelettes* and wine and *fraises*
where everyone is free to come and go
down concrete steps into the subway river.

In all of this, it is the omelettes, the berries
with a slice of lemon, the most poignant things
that best embody the ritual. Ash clings
to them but they burn on internal batteries
recharging themselves constantly. Perhaps
that's the heart of it, nature, or the word
which stands for nature, that which is interred
with the body yet ticks on when bone snaps
under the slumped weight of earth. The red eye
winking on the dish, footprints on the grass,
the sudden movement of a ghostly head
trapped in the knowledge that it has to die
and glow like this under the terrace glass
with simple berries of Pompeian red.

Purple Passage after Nolde

1

It was how I imagined the sea to be
but it never was, not at least at Margate.
How could it match up that intensity
or resolve itself to such terrible weight
of feeling? Imagine yourself a spiritual squid
spurting ink, or pissing into your pants
at some desolate station (not the squalid
pool at your feet but the release) while your parents
frown into the fog at the back of your head.

Life squirts out at high pressure. Then the drowned
rise up. You see a red headed Christ weep
into his sleeve, consorting with the dead,
and from the sea emerges a faint sound
of relief like a man farting in his sleep.

2

You are sinking into an orchid or a tulip.
Now mother has closed her dreamy eyes
you come round by the side door and slip
inside with bees and multi-coloured flies
into the house of nature as the demon sees it,
a dark disgusting mess and far from Attic.
It's neither ideal, nor clear. You cannot seize it
with your hands. It refuses geometric
imperatives, hangs loose, amorphous, yet
is glorious and opens on dissection
on dark reds and maroons, a distinct strain
of colour like a purple passage set
in classical prose and under its protection
burning away your skin with acid rain.

Romantic Love

It was early November. The grass glowed
under a frame of light. A red bridge crossed
a dual carriageway. The train was lost
between two cities. It was as if it followed
its own chronology forward into time
which sat still watching as it watched birds
and mice, the progress of rust and the words
spoken in each carriage, all with sublime
attention to detail. Not far off but elsewhere
two people were kissing. One's hand moved
on the other's breast. A fistful of blonde hair.
The tail of a shirt. Who else have you loved?
they asked each other. Tell me, was there anyone?
But no one heard them speak. The train moved on.

*

And two girls in the next seat. One said: 'So he
went to the top of the car park and threatened
to throw himself off, but then his friend,

the one who had stolen his lover, felt sorry
and joined him and said he'd jump too, so they
came down and went to a club where there were
lapdancers and got drunk.' But we'd lost her
in the noise. The wind had carried her away.
Their voices continued lapping as at the bank
of a river, wearing it away with their tongues,
dragging along shopping trolleys, brief ranks
of refuse and the words of popular songs,
and we watched them talking excitedly, their eyes
as dazzling as the wings of household flies.

*

The man who had raped the girl at the pool recalled
his wife, how he'd bring her her morning tea
then feel her tits, and they'd fall to it enthusiastically.
That at least was his story. His listeners were appalled.
He clearly missed her although he was a brute
who had probably forced her to have sex
on his own terms. By now she was his ex-
and he'd been alone for years. That was the root
of the problem, an educated man remarked.
He talked of fucking. She referred to it
in other terms. It was her breast and not her tit
he held. Such a man should not have embarked
on a mature relationship. These sorry pricks,
he ventured, are soon hoist by their semantics.

*

They wouldn't let go of each other's hands,
since if they did they might drift apart into
the stream of the universe. And it was true,
they did let go, and there were no real strands
holding them together. But later one
entered the underworld to rescue the other
and they almost made it through, lover to lover.

Two schoolkids were walking home alone
beside the railway line with dark berries
beckoning them and marks where others had lain
among the tussocks with the blood-red stain
on their fingertips, their childhood miseries
gathering dust and weight.

   Incidentals both.
The flight path of desire. The dazzled moth.

Rough Guide

...your image destroys
itself, remakes itself, and is never weary
OCTAVIO PAZ, 'The Prisoner'

Impossible to look directly into
another's eyes. Impossible to look
into your own. You read the dense book
of being like a document you flick through.

Eyes, even an inch apart, are blurs,
clouds, like the concept of yesterday
which has an entity you sometimes stray
into beyond the limits of his and hers.

The unknown: the roughest of the rough guides,
and all it says is: you're here, you'd better make
the best of it. You entered by mistake
and so you'll leave. It's what the route map hides

and languages obscure, the magnetic pull
of all you ever see of the beautiful.

*

But I have seen the beautiful. I know
its contours and the rough guide it provides
is blissfully specific: the hand that rides
the ridge of the collarbone or moves along the brow,

the perfect form of momentary light
in this line or another. It's what Blake
saw at the top of the stair, the terrible earthquake
at the root of the flesh we think of as delight.

It's what you see when you shut your eyes and see,
the angel with the whip or a flaming sword
that burns your eyes down to the spinal cord,
the shit, blood, semen smell of mortality

you get used to because it follows you
everywhere and is both beautiful and true.

Silver Age

Rain so silver you can reach out and grasp
whole clear rods of it, and when it shatters
on the pavement it turns into a clasp
or a ring or dripping necklace that flatters
the neck of the cold queen who wears it beneath
her stately head, or so you imagine
in your childish sleep while watching your breath
sparkle and condense at the fine margin
of a legend which involves the moon,
a hero on a white horse down a lane
at midnight by the graveyard and a girl
glimmering gently like a pool or pearl
who will appear at his cold side as soon
as day breaks to the sound of winter rain.

When day breaks to the sound of winter rain
the curtains open and the legend fades
to clocks and traffic. Now the old refrain
of tick and shrug, the shops in the arcades,
the road to school, and that stranger, the queen
transmogrified into a schoolmistress.
Now pools in potholes, the viridian green,
of playing fields, corridors and emptiness.
Now a thin slice of silver at the pane
of glass above the putty and a low
mass of cloud dragging the window through
a dark infusion of thunder–bloated blue
which gathers towards December snow,
with moonlight locked into a drop of rain.

The moonlight locked inside a drop of rain
runs down the window. The hero on the horse
follows a mysterious predestined course
to school. Down by the cuttings a slow train
breathes steam across its own glittering face
before vanishing down the tunnel ahead.
The schoolmistress is getting into bed.
The graveyard mumbles in its sleep. The space
between lamp–posts grows darker and more lost.
The rails in the cuttings deepen into silver.
All images and nothing more. The ghost
of Christmas Past enters, raddled in lace,
bringing in Time gift-wrapped on a salver,
like a gesture of contrition for bad grace.

Time is where things get born. The silver salver
is the moon dressed as a handy metaphor,
an aristocratic prop and nothing more,
the moon's a prop for something else that's silver,
and so on down to the empty-handed butler.
Love, when I was a child, I thought like a child
and left out my shoes for the man who piled
up presents like a perfect daddy, none subtler
in his approaches, coming only when
I was asleep. And his bounty was infinite:
he had to lever his gifts in with a shoe-horn
(my socks peeked out, like something being born).
And so time passed, down to the very minute
I write these thoughts down with my adult pen.

Terre Verte

1

The things that grow out of earth! Weird, stunted
knobbly things with hair or other roughnesses,
priapic little gods, gods patched from dresses
the doll once wore, some knuckled, some blunted
by their emergence from the medium
that nourished them. Roots, tubers, the carrot
like a raw joke, all that wood spirit,
earth under nails, in folds of skin, at the eardrum:
Van Gogh's Potato Eaters, Brueghel's peasant
belching into a corner, calloused feet
banging on a dirt floor to a harsh pipe,
the stumpy-digit, heavy-brow, big-earlobe type.
They come with flowers to rooms suddenly neat
and scented, refreshing and distinctly pleasant.

Shall I play Priapus with you? Shall we find
the old shed with its smelly newspapers,
dead mice and dried grass? Shall we cut capers
among onion sacks, rolling on a fat behind?
Shall we cut the crap instead? Shall we get
down to it, the deed of darkness, the two
of us? Tell me what you'd like me to do?
Shall I play finial to your crocket?

428

Needle to your haystack? Camel to eye
of needle, pig to trough, horse to water,
nose to grindstone with a yo-ho-ho
and a bottle of something on which to grow
merrier still? Will you play Green Man's daughter
to the fat hog in his reeky hormonal sty?

2

Consider the texture of *terre verte*,
how it filters underneath the skin:
flesh tint is drawn across it into thin
cold layers of dew intended to subvert
the whole arrangement by a kind of pun.
It's beautiful to touch, is like a dream
of water eating away the bed of the stream
it flows through, leaving nothing for anyone.
Its lovely drowned face materialises
for one moment only under green fronds
between the bars of a supermarket trolley,
then goes off underground, down an alley
you can't enter, and surfaces in ponds
from which a stagnant round aroma rises.

The traveller in his shaggy coat: he
has it bad. And that one there with his rocking
laptop: I wouldn't trust him. The panicking
baby-boomer with his bald patch and anxiety.
They're only after one thing, all of them.
The look in their eyes tells you they're somewhere
at the edge of a joke life failed to prepare
them for, at the withered end of the stem
that leads back into earth and is terrifying.
What wouldn't they do for one moment of grace,
one leaf curling back, brash petals extent
and soft at the heart of an awaited event,
for one beautiful drowned forgiving face
to watch them in their sleep and through their dying.

Turquoise

1

Good to have reached the turquoise age. Not green
not blue but something in between, this
smoky, crystalline concentration, clean
as an iceberg, astringent as the kiss
of water on iron. So your hair drifts
across the sky where everything turns grey.
So the louring cloud-mass shifts
and colour filters into day.
So, between folds of skin your sea-grey eyes
echo the green of your jumper which is turquoise.
(Wings of house flies or dragonflies or butterflies
hover briefly, freeze into flightless poise.)
Perhaps we've chosen this very spot, this now,
and might return if only we knew how.

2

The balance is tipping. We feel the scales
go down. We live in a fortunate age.
Our teeth are still our own, our tops and tails
are in order. We need not rage
against the dying of the light. We touch
each other's skin with pleasure and trace
the lines of limbs, squeezing neither too much
nor too little. The fine bones of the face
retain a sort of tender brittleness,
their threatened beauty yields a thrill
as fingers follow eyelids or caress
the whorls of the ear with acquired skill.
But still the scales go down. Under the dress,
under the shirt and vest, it's all downhill.

3

We watch a TV documentary
on breasts, It's so bloody American,
so pathetically anxious to carry
its terrors like trophies. One thin old woman
grimaces and waves, performs a burlesque.
Her pathos has turned comic. When we laugh
it's not quite at her. Something in the mask
parodies us, part sassy and part naff,
making uneasiness easy. In the dark
my hand slides across your thigh. I sink

430

my teeth into your neck. Your fingernails spark.
Electrical appliances go on the blink.
Even this gentle pressure leaves a mark,
a turquoise, purple, blackening smear of ink.

4

Our knees are stiff, getting up is a pain.
We take care of our bowels, eat sensibly,
nothing too spicy after nine. No gain
in weight. No dope. No fags. I calmly drain
my glass of Jameson's but feel my heart
accelerate. Sheets full of cancer haunt
the chest of drawers. Minor discomforts start
long trains of thought. The mirror's gaunt
reflection follows us about the room.
Skulls in the desert open their dry mouths
to utter comic prophecies of doom.
They're desperate to confront us with home truths.
You'll turn to prose, fools! We reply in mime,
watching our shadows coupling. There's still time.

5

Turquoise. Under the sea, in slim leaves
of current the fish are brilliant repulsive
flecks of light. The predator deceives
its prey by simulating softness, gives
only to swallow. Sharp, spiny exoskeletons
form ridges to scrape a knee on. A squid
lounges, hunched and expectant. Patterns
of weed on rock form an undulating grid.
I watch my skin grow ridges. Some organic
process throws up warts, disfigurements.
Fronds of grey at the temple. Hair less thick
than it once was. We observe events
like divers in an alien ocean. But then
oceans are (it is their nature) alien.

6

Turquoise. It was an old woman's parasol
lying in the waiting room. Under its wings
the trapped air of the decade. Chirrupings
of dead birds. The half-dressed discarded doll
in the garage. I've seen one queuing up
at the post office counter, rubbing her hands
beside garish coloured advertising stands,
her complexion delicate as a chipped cup.

This poem's becoming elegiac, like her.
In Viennese cafés the waiters hum
whole operettas into aged ears. The words come
naturally, settling on a line of fur,
between the fingers of gloves. Time to kill
between the opening parasol and the bill.

7

Try turquoise once more. Turkish opulence.
Think of those soft cushions and the bleak curve
of the scimitar. The pasha's residence
is where we used to live. The girls would serve
sticky confections as we lay in bed
watching light crumple across the ceiling rose.
The petals were stirring overhead,
the leaves of the window would open and close
and air would billow through. Occasionally
we'd hear the whine of an ambulance, wake
to boys on motorbikes with their crude reveille.
Sometimes the bed itself would gently shake
beneath us. Of course this was years ago,
or never happened. It's getting hard to know.

8

Hermione, the teacher of Greek grammar,
has her face reconstructed by computer
animation. This lends a touch of glamour
to her more prosaic status as a tutor.
('A studious and meek schoolmistress
without a trace of show or ornament,'
said Petrie, another scholar.) Her tenderness
has a stern edge, that is true, but her scent
is deeply sensuous and grave, her hair
parted in the middle shows a light line
of lovely mortal skin, perfectly aware
of its mortality as part of the design.
She emerges from the photo-booth and waits
for the line of four to slip out through the gates.

9

Death is more Woody Allen than Lord Byron.
Being there at the time is the only drag.
No one gives us a branch to hang our spare tyre on
or offers to hide our face in a paper bag.
It's a bit of a joke, this old curmudgeon drone
and sneer. A Larkinesque panicky shrug.

So Mary Magdalene turns into a crone,
and Balzac to an energetic slug.
A true Lawrentian ripeness is the goal,
but somehow the body gets so out of breath
it loses contact with the panting soul
and fails to make the seasonal Ship of Death.
And all that violet eye, and turquoise gaze
drowns in a murky swirling sea of days.

10

The Shakespearian ending which turns round
to claim your immortality in words
performs a gesture. I like its human sound
and proud disdain. I like its afterwards
and quibbles, its hyperboles, its dumb
struggle with silence. And after all, there's truth
in its assertions. How many have come
to the sonnets, from the pimply youth
with his 'A' Levels, to the old botanist
dying on his sofa, mouthing the lines?
I cannot myself close a perfect fist
about the couplet which defines
the perfect closure, capturing desire.
I too am burning in the turquoise fire.

Venice

Because there's nothing that will last for ever
except perhaps ideas, I think of cities:
Vicenza, Verona, Venice, clarities
enduring for a while beside some river
rolling through them, or a crisp sour sea
lapping their feet, lost in a freezing fog,
exquisite in the ice. Something might jog
your memory of them, or any memory,

because memory too is an idea: you think
rationally but you feel your thoughts,
and watch them rise, Byzantine, in a square
heavy with cupolas whose breasts are bare
ideas of breasts that no idea supports,
canals, black water, waking dreams, rough drink.

The Breasts

She gathered up her breasts in her two hands
like small explosions, a soft outward flow,
a timing device that anytime could blow.
So life hangs on the slenderest of strands,
a lover's hunger can seem all of it,
a child, an image in the mirror, hope,
the way a back, or pair of hips might slope,
or how two closing bodies click and fit.

Time is always against us. Youth slips down
the polished shoulder like a loosening strap.
She looked down from her bosom to her lap
and ran her palms over her dressing gown,
her mirrored face drowned in a cloud of dust:
How beautiful, she thought, and how unjust.

Comical Roses in a Cubic Vase

1

There are people who grow wobbly at the knees
at the touch or scent of flowers, botanists
turned erotomanes, foiled aesthetes with spots
and bad breath, beautiful women seeking
analogies for themselves which might explain
their own bold beauty, people driven mad
or just a little queer by anything petal-clad.

Myself, I loved the way the roses could squeeze
up against each other, like a crowd of accordionists
at an impromptu party in an old-fashioned telephone-box.
I loved their funny riotous colours leaking
into the air, lost in an invisible rain
of atoms of which I was a part, the way their fall
could elicit from me something tight-furled, personal.

2

Something about the stark voluptuous thrust
of the flowerheads opening their mouths wide,
makes me think of the pores of my own skin,
and of every human orifice that allows
the world access, billowing with colour,
Alizarin Crimson perhaps, and creamy white,
like a Tennysonian chorus, dark and bright,

all with the faintest coat of luminous dust
in the light of the window, and the garden outside
yearning for access to the garden within;
outside, where there is a certain bending of boughs
and the whole earth is like a deep damp cellar,
and inside, with its carpets, tables and chairs,
and short-lived plant forms covered in fine hairs.

3

A pheasant billowed through the cemetery,
its colours exquisite but with a comical look on its face
in the blank red napkin where its eyes were situated,
and rabbits in tens panicked in small white dots
shooting over the edge, down to the railway cuttings.
It was a glorious late afternoon. The children slept
in their graves while the wonderful pheasant stepped

delicately through their dangerous territory
and everything was busily seeking its place.
Even the roses in the glass cube stated
some kind of claim, like the rabbit scuts,
to their domain in the realm of incongruous things,
their dead petals folded over the edge, vaguely edifying:
as if our own skins could be laid out like washed clothes drying.

Licorne

1

Wild flowers stream upwards on the red ground
of her garden. Their stems are curved and slender
as the handles of umbrellas, drifting away, skybound.
I wish I knew their names and all their tender
ministrations, or could feel the delicate rain
they offer protection from. The lady's expression
is gently tolerant. The unicorn is there again.
She shows him the mirror with his reflection.
She tells him his horn is the emblem of singleness
in God and Christ. She tells him about the lion
that will devour him. He paws and scuffs her dress
entranced by its softness, its busy floral design.
He know he's in her realm. His body is as white
as hers is virginal. Her hand on his neck is light.

2

These are the feminine courtesies of tapestry.
This is the welcome she provides for him
within the sliding scale of her propriety
which is ethereal and fashionably slim.
You'd think it another romantic fantasy
of control but the strict language of love stuns
your senses. There is a rigour in the lazy
turn of her neck and in the floating patterns
of the flowers that is convincing. You know
the world is better like this, your heavy horn
more bearable, your body lighter, that you'll grow
more like the image that shows a smaller unicorn
beyond the glass, who has been smuggled through
to demonstrate that this, indeed, is you.

3

His unicorn ironies are useless in an enclosed
garden such as this. This is how things must be.
It is even flattering, the way he is posed,
a compliment to his supposed virility
which is flickering, fitful, dizzying, other, grand
as Beethoven with a fragile *es muss sein.*
So it must be. The touch of the lady's hand
is encouraging and there is something fine
about her breath. Her voice is musical:

a harp to his bagpipe bellow and squeak. He hears
it summon him by name. Irresistible.
He finds himself pricking up his ears.
He hears those airy cadenzas. She is chanting verses
from a book. He throws himself on her tender mercies.

4

Why should I, *he asks himself*, inhabit
a world of allegories? I was once a creature
as real as you, whose existence you'd do well to credit.
Like the weaver, I too was a child of nature
but imagination took me, made me elegant,
taught me the rules of courtly love. I could
unlearn them all and be as intelligent
as any other beast in the wild wood,
but even the language brims with courtesy,
its syntax runs through my entire being.
I am tamed, lady. It is our joint fantasy
that brings me to you under an all-seeing
weaver-god's protection, whose fine stitching
has made you grave and utterly bewitching.

5

The garden is mine. The flowers spiralling
upwards emanate from my desires. You are,
do not forget it, a guest to do my bidding.
Come here. Lie down. I see the frozen star
at the point of your horn. I will relieve you of it.
It's what you owe me. It is the tithe you pay
for being here. Do you imagine I profit
from your existence? I who, day after day,
must feed the garden with my energies?
You can make what you want of the wild wood
that you have ruined. And you can keep those elegies
which mean nothing to me or the neighbourhood.
It is, after all, your nature to deceive.
I'll let you know when it's time for you to leave.

Black Sea Sonnets

Palm

There is the sea, we say, as the wind
pushes if to and fro, and each time it lays
another open palm before us
it whisks it away. One day is like all days,
the same phrase sung by the same chorus.
In the distance the lights and cries
of a wedding, stray dogs in loose family groups.
It is as if the night were pinned
to the sky insecurely, not quite the right size.
And what might lie behind it? Brilliant loops
of naked stars cavorting and a moon full
of bad luck growing ever more silver. There
is something in the water beyond the pull
of tides, something released into the air.

Lake

And the little brown frogs plop into the lake
as if keeping time to footsteps. How still it is.
Acorns lie on the ground, the leaves are falling
so silently, so lightly. There is nothing to shake
the trees, only the nearby sea, the invisible cities
hidden under it, full of darkness and loss.
In the submarine city traffic is crawling
past paper-thin apartment blocks, across
wide boulevards, but here there is only the moment
before time begins. The water is smooth and tight
in the lake. The sea nearby is almost silent.
Water and water. And then the frog springs
and leaps with its tiny splash and time sings
for an instant as it might do this or any other night.

Speech

The noise of fear remains long after the cause;
becomes itself a cause, and habits die hard.
You hear it in the speeches, watch fraught slips
of paper circulate, or see a questioner pause

and remain silent. The Black Sea purses its lips
at the facing villas and draws us in to her
like a dull secret. Shall we walk in and stir
the waves a little? Pick a few cowries? Reward
ourselves for our exhaustion? Feed the dogs
that scamper about our feet? There are lists
to cover the darkest recesses of your heart
but the wind sweeps them away. What is it clogs
the arteries and blows the official files apart
reminding us the outside world exists?

Delta

Hour after hour, cruising through high reeds
in the Delta. Phalaropes, egrets, delicate
yellowish necks. Fishermen, cabins, then nothing.
More nothing. More reeds. The odd pocket
of humanity, then floating. Each channel breeds
an identical silence in regulation clothing.
Good to die here perhaps, or simply to dream
in the continuous sun that blisters our skin,
to move into an entropic state, to survive in
our own decay. Idyllic too: the stream
lapping at the boat with its tonnage of words,
the endless black coffee. We are part of the river,
drifting among spirits of pale waterbirds.
One should stay here, if possible, for ever.

Beach

Two figures on the beach in the dark.
A car cruises by. Two more figures approach.
Slurp, say the waves, licking at their feet.
Night shimmers and crackles with stars. Dogs bark
in the distance, sniffing the air with its sweet
tang of sufficiency. The moment is stable.
The sea frozen. Never again will it encroach
on the cities on its fringes. But underground
the faults widen and slide to a predictable
if imprecise rhythm, to a low rumbling sound
beneath the metro that precedes panic. One man
is making deals, another is counting names,
and the sea begins to move more subtly than
either can know, in tongues, with cold black flames.

439

Hospital

You press the button but the lift won't start
however you keep slamming at the door.
You must get out. The hospital needs treatment
more than its patients. There is a secret art
to finding the right staircase. Every floor
could be another. Your appointment
is with M.C. Escher, dying in a ward
suspended in a wing elsewhere. The lost
are fading into kindness or are restored
to a fading kind of health. We have crossed
some great divide into this. There is sea
in the walls, sea in the blood, in the head
of the man on the ventilator. The dead
sing down the lift shaft. The lift itself stands empty.

Sweet

There are places to get drunk in. The wedding night
at the hotel. The presidential villa with its terrace
overlooking the water. The bedroom with its freight
of sharp mosquitos. In the company of Cerberus,
the dog in the driveway, and his friends. We are alight
with dowsed bulbs and the television flickering
in the corner. It is inexpressibly sweet
all this, among the lost fireflies of a state
in its dotage or birth pangs, whichever it is,
waiting for hands or lips or languages to meet
in the lottery of improbabilities.
The sea is murmuring under its black wing.
The frogs by the lake hesitate, then fly
away, dropping like light rain from a clear sky.

Body

The spirit is compact with the body. This one
is seen by night, by a flickering television
that plays on the inside of the skull and in
the fingers, amplified through the heart.
A long way past twelve, new programmes begin
but none can keep spirit and body apart.
Pictures stutter, fizz into music, then slip

440

between the eyes. Voices, more voices. A curved
shadow turns to tears down a fingertip.
Regular news bulletins continue their well-preserved
list of disasters. The sea continues lapping
at the shore. Outside the window the dark
presses its face to the glass and starts tapping
out reminders, its eyes brilliant and stark.

Song

Inside every other is a you, and this you
is what I would sing, if I had a voice to sing it,
because the song would be poignant, pointed,
unmistakeable, rejoicing, eternal and blue,
the way a horn tails off into silence or an unlit
room. And I'd hear the Black Sea as it shunted
slowly to an fro, its joy made of desire,
of loss, and sheer astonishment. Perhaps
at its core, in its dying deep bed, it moans
and hums in a voice we can't hear, that laps
at the place where our hands were, where a silver wire
of foam creeps beneath the skin into the bones
and goes on living there, I don't know how,
but it's as if I heard that singing now.

The Matrix

Also, in the ambience and the ethos of my birth and upbringing
there was an unconscious directing and moulding of my future life
A Prevailing Wind: Memoirs of the Life of the Rev William Upchurch

Darling, out of what mould have we emerged
from our birth that we should speak as we do
in the moments we have? Can the story be true?
Has someone set us up? Could our paths have diverged
and gone separate ways once the course we have run
was determined? Is there a shape that is ours
and had to be once we had spent the first hours
in the cold matrix of the genes? What's done is done,
say the truisms, who rarely are wrong. Just yesterday
I was sitting with once-lovely Helen. I couldn't take
my eyes off the face in the skin and the trick
she must have mastered early of a delicate flick
of the eye that was for ever not sixty-five, and the grey
hair swinging across it as if she were half-awake,

like the unconscious directing perhaps of gravity
which was also directing the skin and the slow beat
of the heart in the fingers and the gradual loss of heat
in the flesh, with wonderful impassivity;
which is to say I wondered at it, as I do at my own
and at yours and the whole matrix thing, that scene
where Keanu Reeves floats in the air, guns blazing between
wide pillars and the brief moment of being is blown
open with special effects like a myth about winning
possession of space, time and death, and I trace
the path of the bullets in the air, seeking the holes
in our lives, in our curiously combined souls
which must somewhere have had a beginning
and come to this point in your hands and my eyes, in one space.

Cities

Good God, he says, looking at his watch.
Is that the time? The century ticks
inside their hearts. They feel the sun's light touch
on their foreheads. Raw vermilion bricks
blur and soften opposite. Now, where
were we? Was it this moment or the last
the sentence spoken was hung out to air?
And was it finished? A whole life flutters past
like a shadow, but do we know whose it is?

Everywhere broken voices, small talk of leaves
and flies. A piano treads and spins in
circles. He is stroking his unshaven chin.
She feels her back ache. Something deceives
the clock and expands in them like cities.

                    *

Sun in the city: high heat in the streets,
blinding exits from doorways, exhaust fumes
suddenly statuesque, walls in flat sheets
of uncanny thinness. The map assumes
an inward dimension, spreads into the lungs.
We eat the world and, over the years, become
like it, ascending the haunted concrete rungs
of ancient stairwells, passing our own children, dumb
on the landing in the shadows. In discreet squares,

on park benches, isolated moments
wait to be introduced to each other. They ache
for tenderness. And look, from under the pediments
we ourselves emerge, the pavements bake
in heat, and people are going about their affairs.

Three Separations

David and Ellen

Don't talk about it, do it, she said and turned
her face to the wall. David stared at the ceiling.
The space behind his eyes burned.

He was trying to locate an elusive natural feeling
somewhere in the halo of the lamp.
Her shoulder strap had slipped revealing

a patch of skin he wanted to touch with his damp
hot fingers. But the moment had passed. Hers, his,
both. They were stuck there in some kind of cramp.

Impossible to move without pain beyond the crisis,
impossible to imagine beyond it. As once before
a long time ago, in a shower of roses and lilies,

he had met her walking across a sunlit floor
having slept late. And it had been like rain,
or a gust of wind in a draught under the door

but brilliant and accompanied by pain.
Her body was still now, warm yet frozen.
It's what they'd woken to. How they'd remain.

Robert and Emily

When she reached for him under the covers
he seized her hand and squeezed it till it hurt.
It was a long time since they had become lovers

and now came the turning point, a plain curt
gesture. Enough was enough. No point now
in seductive candlelit evenings, pretending to flirt

in restaurants, no point in having a row
and breaking up in public, and no sense
in scoring points, in tears, not anyhow.

Something was leaking away in the tense
darkness. Robert and Emily. It was blood
of a sort, that deep pressing presence

they'd grown with and had long ago understood.
And so she turned away leaving a clear
space between them as, it now seemed, for good,

and in the darkness the faint noise of fear
began to buzz in their ears with a steep
tonal insistence as if their voices could appear

to haunt them just before they fell asleep.

Zoë and Neil

After the baby died it was as if her heart
had been drawn out on a string through her eyes,
and there was no more rest for them, together or apart.

Whose fault was it? Who should apologise
for the death of one so small? There was a lot
of it about, she read, enough death to surprise

the living. A baby would lie safe, you might think, in a cot
but the bad angel of breath may choose to spread
its suffocating wing over the very spot

the poor child occupies and so the child be dead.
So Zoë's thoughts turned round and round, until
her body rose and hovered and the wind took the head

through which that heart had leapt and made her ill.
The wind took her head, threw it in the air
and a man was there to catch it who was not Neil,

who could not be, as Neil saw to his despair.
They moved through the faint rooms they'd known
and eventually all the rooms were bare,

and Zoë flying ever further and Neil alone
while somewhere the enormous child rested
among others as enormous, once Zoë had flown

like a dirigible, light, and delicately breasted.

Shoulder

Goddess: her shoulder, her back, the round of her rump, I sing.
Though they sing themselves it is not in my language, this language,
But the language of life which is elsewhere, uninterpreted
And therefore incomprehensible and yet singing.

And though it is late, and once, whenever, it was younger,
Like you, Goddess, if you have any age, it is still the same
Shoulder and back and rump, which is hers and the language's
And wholly impersonal, the idea of a back and a shoulder,

And how I shudder to touch it, the shudder of pleasure
And affection, the shudder of itself, which, like a word,
Vibrates in its space, like her breath, which is lovely
And personal, in this room with its clock, with its word.

What is love, Goddess? You whom I address with humble
Generic precision, are you capable of answering
In the language of life? Am I capable of writing
Or thinking or feeling the space of the word?

It is Saturday, Tuesday, Friday, the weather goes on,
I can hear people speaking. There are bombs and bullets,
The usual business of war, which is rarely interrupted.
It is Wednesday and Thursday and Monday.

In a Sunday of the mind our bodies roll closer
And each part feels like a morning, an afternoon, an evening.
I want to sing the body on terrible Sunday,
On disastrous Monday and Tuesday, the days of my life.

ACCOUNTS

Retro-futuristic

It is cruel to feel the climax of depression on approaching
your own land, and to see it as a grim retro-futuristic mirage.
ANTONIA APOSTOLOVA

Everywhere in the city, gangs of labourers
are digging up brown fields where banks and shops
once stood in a lost quarter of mirages
full of phantom metro stations, bus stops,
news-stands and fast-food outlets. Great white
concrete towers shimmer and vanish at once
in constantly flashing beams of sunlight.
A neon sign hangs in a cloud. Empty carriages
on the railway bridge are almost transparent
as they speed past, still accelerating
into the outskirts through inner-city slums
where invisible workers gather, patiently waiting.

It is cruel to feel the depression rising, and harder still
to maintain belief in what's gone and never was,
a notional history of the soul, like some urban infill
between a more concrete emptiness one daren't
demolish for fear of losing everything.
It is cruel to wake without visible neighbours
in disappearing apartments to the faint buzz
of houseflies feeding on mountains of damp stinking
refuse. How can one live here? How to define
a space among illusions? An aeroplane curves
between buildings. The calendar says 1989.
There is nowhere to go except the future,

or down to the cinema where they are playing
Blade Runner again. There is Harrison Ford
hanging on for dear life while Rutger Hauer
turns to stone. There is something dismaying
about the scenario, like listening to a cracked record.
And then the beautiful white dove of the soul
rises into perpetual rain above the tower
with its half-recognised high-tech furniture.
The buildings throng with stucco cherubim.
It is Sofia, Tirana, Bucharest, New York. The rain
washes away the rubbish. There is a tight scroll
of froth in the street. Certainly it is grim.

Climate

The sky is broken. There is the usual scud
of dense cloud: showers, lightning, a shower
and then the cycle begins again. Each hour
is a new foray into a thin skim of mud
beside the river. Ducks huddle under leaves
then waddle out into brief sunshine. Nowhere
will you find any fixed point that might bear
your weight or even your spirits. Nothing receives
the imprint of your shoe. It is England of course,
not one of the dependable climates. Things fly
in muscular gusts: flags, bunting, news-sheets.
It is as if there were some irresistible force
blowing us over into a strange new century
that billows beyond us, between our thin heart-beats.

Decades

First Decade: To Be Recited at Times of Trouble

The best lack all conviction while
  The worst have gone the extra mile,
  And must, therefore, arrive there first
  Where worst is best and best is worst.

Justice lays a clutch of eggs
  Out of which climb
  Creatures with a thousand legs
  Given the time.

Chickens roasting on their spits
  Are genuinely thrilled to bits.
  It's good to hear the customer speak
  So warmly of their curve of beak.

Revenge is a dish best eaten cold.
　　You sit so long at the table waiting to be served,
　　But someone eventually brings you
　　The meal you have deserved.

You could fuel an airforce with that hatred.
　　Watch how a single aircraft taxis
　　Across a crooked runway
　　On its mischievous axis.

Open the box and out fly all the names
　　Of despair loudly caterwauling,
　　Immediately to engage in their favourite games
　　Of hyperbole and name-calling.

Pity wears too many faces. She complains
　　Of exhaustion and fever,
　　It seems her destiny is to suffer shooting pains
　　Every morning, forever.

Genocide
　　Has no funny side,
　　Nor can survival
　　Brook a rival.

The peculiar carpentry of the coffin
　　Constructed by a gun
　　Ensures that it falls apart the moment it's laid in the ground,
　　And yet fits everyone.

When God at first made man
　　Having a glass of blessings standing by
　　It seemed a good idea and, after all,
　　It does behove a deity to try.

Second Decade: The People of the Book

The People of the Book
    React with bookish fury,
    Adding another chapter to
    The troubled tale of Jewry.

It doesn't take much,
    It never takes more
    Than a delicate touch
    And some blood on the floor.

It's not a matter
    Of life or death,
    The old man assures us
    With his last breath.

They were too meek.
    They were compliant.
    Says the Holocaust Dwarf
    To his grandson, the Giant.

Between Chagall and Chaim Soutine
    There's room left for debate:
    And on such grounds of argument
    We may well found a state.

In creating a state as a refuge
    They might have foreseen
    That they'd carry with them the dust
    Of the places they'd been.

Once the displaced had settled down
    And their pulses had stopped racing
    They spread their belongings out on the lawn
    And set about others' displacing.

When God is under the weather
    He looks upon his chosen,
    Shrugs with disgust and leaves them
    In the desert, frozen.

Under the magnifying glass
    Toothpicks become stakes,
    And people in their hundreds die
    Because a man's tooth aches.

Life is nasty, brutish and short
    So what harm in making it shorter?
    All it takes is a bit of paste
    Or the distant sound of a mortar.

Third Decade: On Trespasses

When they scored they bent
    And kissed the eighteen-yard-line
    As if the pitch were sacred
    And scoring a sign.

Mahmoud, Jamal and Hicham,
    The girls arrive and press
    Your lips; sleek Ruth, bright Hannah
    and Judith in her Sabbath dress.

Europa has a party and invites
    All ranks of city-dwellers
    Into her penthouse bedrooms
    And filthy cellars.

There is a long music
    That moves in a slow stream
    Within our blood. To wake from it
    Is like breaking a dream.

God does not forget,
    So how can you ask of a man
    To repeat the same mistake
    Time and again?

We do not inhabit land,
    Land inhabits us:
    On that point our scribes
    Are quite unanimous.

Great leaders with beautiful manners
    Have mastered the trick
    Of command. Speaking softly is hopeless
    Without a very big stick.

They hurt our pride and broke
>The neck of our god under their yoke.
>Into the void his head falls
>For ever, and his voice calls.

Believe unto death! they cry
>As they strap on the belt
>Of death. Believe! they cry
>As their bones melt.

The defeated have ceased to exist.
>One cannot stop existing.
>Once the living have been killed
>The dead can start enlisting.

Fourth Decade: Editorials

The wind blew hard. There was
>The usual rain of blood.
>The *Apocalyptic Herald* landed
>On the mat with a dull thud.

Major world figures made speeches,
>The press bit its nails,
>As the flawed engine of Good Will
>Ran off the rails.

World is stranger and suddener
>Than leader writers think.
>You can't tie it down in its trolley
>With a dose of printer's ink.

One after another they frowned
>And spoke as if their hearts
>Were laden down by what they had
>To say in their various parts.

Something corrosive was eating away
>At the fabric of the tongue.
>The breath froze in the mouth of the word.
>Alarm bells rung.

So much righteousness
> Concentrated on a page:
> One item tagged onto another,
> Rage on rage.

There are things that happen,
> And there is the news,
> A whole electric industry
> On a single fuse.

Listen to the incidental music
> Of what happens as it dies
> In the ear, and beyond it the sound
> Of faint, barely audible cries.

The camera's brief intimacies.
> One glass eye must serve all those
> Who crowd in to touch death
> At the point the lids close.

Death's production values
> Are low-tech and demeaning.
> You need to frame things properly
> To give them meaning.

Fifth Decade: The Palace of Art

In a classical porch two angels
> Are steadily beating their God.
> You must train your deities properly.
> No point sparing the rod.

St Veronica lends her hankie
> To the fallen. Next day
> she opens it up: Oh my god!
> I have taken his face away.

A wheel on a pole. A raven.
> The crowd has formed a ring.
> In the centre: death.
> And still they keep coming.

Always this bare hillside and the crowd
        huddling and thinking aloud,
        thoughts that collect in the valley beneath
        with folded spectacles, shoes, gold teeth.

It is awfully black down there,
        And their limbs are terribly bent:
        How lifelike the darkness is
        We seemed to be doomed to invent.

Hell is muscular and crowded
        Like a gym where the demons work out
        Their frustrations on apparatus
        Unhindered by rust or by doubt.

God slides down the chute of his robe:
        His body seems almost to float.
        The late romantic chorus of love
        Belts on in full throat.

We watch the universe collapsing
        About the victim's head.
        The living are turned away from us.
        Not so the dead.

Soldiers asleep, he stands
        Stiff backed: his eyes burn.
        Resurrection begins.
        Now it is our turn.

You put your fingers in the wound
        Gingerly, since you doubt.
        The problem is not so much poking it in
        As getting the damn thing out.

Three Poems for Sebastião Salgado

Preface to an Exhibition

How beautiful suffering is, and how sad:
As the waste flies the wind catches.
The wasted drift among dispatches,
Above the debris, the dirt and the spent matches,
Well-lit but ill-clad.

How beautiful suffering is, and how wild
When the dead scream as loud as the dying
And the cracked glass of the terrifying
Intruder shows the dead child flying
Past the living child.

How statuesque the lost are, how well defined
Each graceful gesture of grief,
Each moment as perfect and brief
As the burning curl of a napalmed leaf
Or a motion of the mind.

The pity, the beauty, the horror and the calm,
The flight of birds in a swirl of smoke,
The deafening noise, the brilliant stroke,
The click of a button like a tender joke
With its offer of balm.

How beautiful suffering is and how soon:
The sense of home as a distant speck,
And mud and night and an endless trek,
The beauty of the rifle's slender neck
In the light of the moon.

How beautiful suffering is as a theme
Where the eye shuts like a shutter
On blood in a gutter
Or moves like a knife through melted butter
Or the dark through a dream.

How beautiful suffering is, and how numb,
Where the moving are stilled
Where no one is killed
And the sound is your breathing forever distilled
And the loud are the dumb.

The wicked boy by the pylons

I am the wicked boy, I walk by pylons, my scowl
Is a terminus, my eyes are beyond you,
I am Rimbaud and the dead, and the black faced owl
In the ruined shed, I am the whoo

In your *who is it*, I am lost for ever in sand,
In the industrial wasteland of the desert, grey
As the sky, as this, my very own wicked hand.
Will you take it and dance with me today

In the sand by the pylons where the shadows cross?
Will your smile heal me and swallow me whole?
Will your pity negate my eyes with its pathos?
Will you erase entirely my wholly wicked soul?

I am the lost boy, the sick boy, the deaf dumb
Malevolence I once met in the street
And became. Let me teach you therefore. Come
With me. Feel my hot head, feel my body heat.

Water

The hard beautiful rules of water are these:
That it shall rise with displacement as a man
does not, nor his family. That it shall have no plan
or subterfuge. That in the cold, it shall freeze;
in the heat, turn to steam. That it shall carry disease
and bright brilliant fish in river and ocean.
That it shall roar or meander through metropolitan
districts whilst reflecting skies, buildings and trees.

And it shall clean and refresh us even as we slave
over stone tubs or cower in a shelter or run
into the arms of a loved one in some desperate quarter
where the rats too are running. That it shall have
dominion. That it shall arch its back in the sun
only according to the hard rules of water.

Account

When the sacred being had said what he had to say
They set off as ordered into the autumn sunlight.
It was neutrally brilliant, a perfectly calm day
And business was brisk at the appointed site.
The mind struggled, as it usually did, to write
Letters of dismissal, memos of loss or delay,
When all it wanted to note was how it was all right
With the account healthy and time enough to pay.

But it wasn't and wouldn't be when phones were ringing
With all the lost messages, most of them much too brief,
Full of exploded phrases and broken sentences.
But the sacred being had written off their absences.
His accounts were already balanced out with grief
And he bade the heavenly choir continue singing.

Arrival

Finally we arrived at the city of silence,
enormous, high-walled, its furious traffic lights
signalling in panic. The streets were covered over
in thick rugs. It was a place without doors, a series
of moving mouths.
              Their eyes, of course, spoke volumes,
vast encyclopaedias. There was little light reading.
Their white gloves fluttered before them
with grotesquely dancing fingers.

It was written that all this should be as it was.
Their thought-crimes, hand-crimes, and heart-crimes
were listed in long numbered chapters.
Policemen pulled faces or pointed at notices.
The civic authorities were sleeping in the park.
DO NOT DISTURB, said the signs.
ASK NO AWKWARD QUESTIONS.

The rest went on feeding and breeding.
They were planting tongues in the cemetery,
thick flowering shrubs of silence.

Tent

The cool blue tent is a jag on the red sand
among nineteen types of palm
in an early phase of night.
The tick of insects at the palm tree's root
is the sole music: a beetle glooms through the leaves.
You wave away a fly in the iron dark of the tent.

Tent is a beacon, tent is a harbinger.
It peaks on the ribbed sand like a sign.
It is your clown's hat, your little scoop of night.
Beyond the trees the skyscrapers huddle,
their lifts tingling with muzak
as they zip up the sides of the buildings
and seal them off from moon and stars.

Where is she, your love? It is lonely on the planet,
though the tent is cool and blue and means you well.

The Morpheus Annotations

(for Katharina Hacker)

Morpheus

The calls of Morpheus, once irregular, grow
still more irregular. You sense him leaving
by the window or the door and follow
his mocassins into the hall, sieving
light from dark, no longer quite believing
in his efficient ministrations in the hollow
parts of night, but he is gone, beyond retrieving,
with his moth-wing lashes. Then you too go,

into the kitchen or lie on the settee to watch
the dying loose flickers of the television,
its alien arctic ice-fields, its comforts such
as they are, lulling you with faint derision,
while Morpheus sweeps up the black snow of sleep
which once was lent to you, but not to keep.

*

The whole universe is packed with sleep so tight
you can hardly move an atom through its bulk.
For each short day, there are great fields of night
where a god might take offence, creep off and sulk
or bury his head in acres of black silk
to be consoled by the indeterminate flight
of his own dreams, his blood as thick as milk,
his veins heavy, his heart an ammonite.

Morpheus taps his fingers on the sill
outside the window. The all-night news is lawn
beneath his feet. Dewdrops are beginning to spill
into his eyes. He goes for a piss at dawn
in the bathroom of his consciousness
then, hearing birds sing, slowly begins to dress.

Mnemon

He'd forget his head if it wasn't screwed on. Awake
at last he checks the list by the bed that had kept him awake
for hours last night. This morning a customer calls
with a problem and he spends the day dealing with phone calls.

461

Remember, they tell him, remember the chair she sat in,
something burned on the water, something in satin,
or samite, or something. He dips the hazel wand of his dreamy side
into that unknown something. There are boxes inside
boxes down there and, dreaming them, they come up
drenched and clear. At night he writes it all up
in a ledger, makes lists for the morning. There is something
missing each time. It's his head or something,
it seems to have come unscrewed. Now, where did he leave
the screwdriver? He asks his wife. She tells him: leave
me alone or I'll call the police. I know you, he protests,
we were sharing a bed just now... His protests
fall on deaf ears. She disappears into a barge
on a something river. Into something very like a barge.

Sisyphus

When Sisyphus enters the hotel
he drops his bags. He rings the bell.
This is, he checks, Pensione Hell?

Charon emerges through a door.
It is all that and something more,
What can we do for the signor?

Sisyphus glances at the stairs.
You could relieve me of my cares
by taking my baggage. *Your affairs*

are strictly your own. I assume
you'll want the very topmost room.
Here are the keys. It's like a tomb

up there and Sisyphus sleeps alone,
or would if he could. He's stretched out prone
and wide awake. He hears the stone

muttering in its metal box
sealed in the biggest case. He blocks
his ears. The bed he lies on gently rocks.

Hotel life. Baggage. Minibar.
TV. Remote control. They are
migrating souls who've travelled far

to get to places such as these
as if they cured some vague disease
but were themselves diseased. The keys

are weighing down his pockets. Night
comes on suddenly like a flashlight
or mysterious loss of appetite.

The bedside phone. The trouser press
in the cupboard. Emptiness
in drawers and bins. Last known address.

The stone rolls out along the bed
and comes to rest beside his head.
He thinks, therefore he must be, dead.

The bill arrives some six months later.
The room yawns open as a crater.
The stone comes down the elevator.

Elpenor

Elpenor? We were fond of Elpenor.
Generous, kind, intelligent and brave
    Elpenor, in company, at dinner,
In the bar. There were days he didn't shave,
    When his embrace was abrasive yet gentle,
When he looked at us from beyond the grave
    In a reassuring, faintly parental
Fashion, as if to say, this too is all right,
    As if death itself were somehow sentimental
And lost; when he stumbled through streets at night,
    A familiar arm round a friend's shoulder, blinking
At the world before him under a dull streetlight
    Recalling aloud other nights of such drinking
As is the way with drinkers, and his eyes
    Swam off into themselves, his clothes stinking
Of spilled wine, his hands touching the unzipped flies
    Of his pants, and there would be a marvellous
Story he could tell coherently enough to surprise
    His companions, whose love of him was jealous
And literally supportive, for he too bore
    Them gladly, an inspissated Daedalus
Of rhetorical devices. Ah, Elpenor,

463

They sighed, he was human but could speak
Like an angel, in exemplary manner,
  And they remembered his love of Greek,
His vulnerable mouth, his once-slender
  Body, his moustache (long gone) and his sleek
Aesthetic gait, and felt unutterably tender.
  Nightly he would sup at Circe's in Soho,
Or the Colony Room then go on a bender
  At all the little pubs, and everyone would know
Elpenor and greet him and help him along,
  And women kissed him full-heartedly as though
They recognised their loss in his, their wrong
  In his helplessness, knowing him once adept
At all they loved, at playfulness and song,
  And watched him, heart-in-mouth, as he leapt
Blindly into the underworld, his old body crumpled,
  Their voices soft as he breathed out and slept.

Minotaur in the Metro

I have seen them myself, heard the sound of their hooves
moving down the platform like cattle, driven
down tunnels, weeping, snuffling, bellowing,
their hairy wrists awkwardly stuffed into sleeves,
their lost eyes tiny and furious, rimmed with fur,
framed by spectacles. They clutch briefcases
tightly to their chests, as if they were children
hugging some battered toy for security
and are swept by harsh winds down corridors.
Slim women in pale dresses, faintly Chekhovian
introspective types, demand their attention.
They take a hairy book from the depths
of their cases and cover themselves for fear
their expressions might betray them. The whole train
is thick with the smell of them, the sound of their breathing.

Sometimes I hear their otherness breathing
gently down my windpipe, travelling on the ghost train
of whatever passes through the blood like a fear
without an object, seeking the unknown depths
of itself, and then my body is all attention,
a terrible bull in an orderly Chekhovian
orchard, watching for movement in the corridors
of the house at the end of the garden, wired for security,
with its freight of grown-up familiar children.

I personally have owned and known briefcases
that demanded obedience, have felt the lice on my fur
gather and revolt, have carefully studied my sleeves
with their attached appendages, heard myself bellowing
silently in fields only dreamt of, where cattle are driven
to slaughter in underground mazes on delicate hooves.

Ariadne observed by the Eumenides

A

Whose heart would not be moved by the plight of this woman,
Cheated and abandoned on Naxos, poor soul, having given
Her heart like the others before her, whole femme-loads deserted.
Who'd not be driven to fury by evil- or faint-hearted
Wooers and louses? Who after all are the masters?
The sailors? Bull-slayers? I tell you: all men are bastards.

B

One winter night by the bus stop I saw a girl crying,
Her make-up quite smudged with her tears. I was dying
To seek out the arsehole and hex him. Her heart was a broken
Axle, her chassis was holed, there was about her a terrible shaking.
She hovered before me like a wisp of fog in the fury
Of the downpour and how I longed to do him an injury.

A

I saw her too. I could look clean through her trembling body,
Cities were alight there, her organs were screaming. Had he
Appeared that moment, I would have torn him asunder.
Can anyone explain why men are happy to slander
The tenderest feelings and leave behind them such agony?
Let's fuck him up now and haunt him to buggery.

B

Disaster will come to him too in due season,
Any day now, on that hardly distant horizon.
Let him arrive there. Let her mourning be beautiful.
I hear drums and leopards. Some gods at least can be useful.
Bacchus will look after her, from now on, for ever.
The rat's almost home. I can just see the face of his father.

Charon

Dans le vieux parc, solitaire et glacé
I saw a couple pass and move away.

There was the pond, the little boats were moored
Along the edge, bobbing and faintly bored.

The boatman sat by his hut, reading a fat
Slab of a book with an embossed title. That

Was all. The couple were lost to view. The moon
Silvered and sharpened as if all misfortune

Were concentrated in it, somewhere over
And above the hut. The book with its cover

Closed. Charon got up. My love stood out clear
On the far side, calling but I couldn't hear

Her. The trees too closed. The water grew
Rapidly colder, the sky a deeper blue.

Three Pieces for Puppetry

1 *The Garden of Earthly Delights*

In the garden of earthly delights a maid sings
in the moonlight and hands escape from their
supporting roles
to act out erotic fantasies as lovers or wings,
or fish in sensually drifting shoals
of light and coloured air.

A frogman appears in the deep like a drowned
monster pulling faces through his goggles.
A plump red heart
floats above a manequin to the sound
of drums. Two old grotesques start
a fight. One struggles

with the other, they knock their heads together,
rolling over and over. It's all about money
and lust – what else is there?
Scraps of cloth, bits of old shoe leather,
stuff from the junkshop, all things spare
and cheap and funny.

All this in a tiny theatre the size of a man's head,
a man with a big head, a completely outrageous
capacious and outsize
head who is telling a story composed of fraying thread
held together by conventions, tricks and lies,
the discarded pages

of ancient directories to the business of living.
The grown ups are being graceful to amuse
their notional child.
They are trying to impose order on the unforgiving
minute. Like poetry, it is the formal dance of the wild,
news which stays news.

2 *The Glove Puppet's Inquisition*

Fancy having a hand up your backside
all your life! To be so filled with Hand
that hand is all in all.
This is a religious proposition. You're tied
by the puppeteer's laws. By them you stand
or (more probably) fall.

It may be only convention but I'm filled
with hand as with holy spirit, am wholly possessed
by another's will.
Perhaps I am merely a helpless child
born without legs, helplesly overdressed
and terminally ill.

The hand that rocks the cradle rocks me
to kingdom come. Do I have an identity
I may call mine?
Is there a centre? My author shocks me
with his terrible lack of pity.
Is it by design

or by some Darwinian joke I have survived
so far? Do I believe in that moody
God with cold stumpy digits?
What makes me cruel? What makes me hide
within myself and beat poor Judy?
Why do I get the fidgets

and make ridiculous noises some mistake
for wit? Is the world like me? Excuse
the rhetoric – I know
we are different but which is real, which is fake?
The world or my self? If it's me, then whose
words are these? whose thoughts flow

through my papier-mâché head? whose lust
blows me out, expands me inch by inch?
What is it to play glove
to a God whose own essence is dust?
Does God at all care for Mister Punch?
Could this be love?

3 *My Love Is of a Birth as Rare*

It is an ordinary dream and a mundane urge
the dream contains. It is romance
in the pleasure dome,
a sense of falling off the undefined verge
of the world, or taking part in a dance
in an aerodrome

while bombers approach down the runway
droning and darkening the sky.
It is the ridiculous
limb movements, the twitches, the mad gay
leaps in the air, the lips going dry,
the painful rictus

in mid-scream, the unsayable words
that are left behind after the flight
has landed or
is taking off in a shower of birds
when the sky goes black as night
or a closed door.

It is the terrible hunger unsatisfied
by the nature goddess, the weird
acrobatic judder
in the spine, it is the voiceless bride
in the cathedral waiting for Bluebeard,
the mad cow's udder.

It's the magic of moonlight and rain
and the weightless heart bursting
in the wooden breast.
It is the moth's wings beating in vain
at the window, the desire, the thirsting
and flying. And all the rest.

Elephant

Imagine this: somewhere, in a far-off land,
you are reincarnated in the form of an elephant,
ponderous, grey, inscrutable, all your old silkiness
hosed off you abruptly. Now you aspire
to wisdom and gravity: frivolity you abhor,
all social graces you dismiss as farce.

It is as if you were watching an old Whitehall Farce
with Brian Rix blundering about in an England
of seaside postcards. The things you used to abhor
as vulgarity, though beneath your dignity as an elephant
seem oddly apt now. The little men who aspire
to vast women in one-piece stripy swimsuits are lost in the silkiness

of the sea where other leviathans sport. It is the only silkiness
allowed you. That and soft rain. Meanwhile the farce
you're engaged in lumbers on. The little men aspire:
the fat ladies in spotty knickers conspire and billow. The land
is all ruts and scrub, which is small beer to an elephant
but not likeable either. And there are creatures to abhor:

scrofulous monkeys, bloated crocodiles, foul-breathed bears. To abhor
is to avoid, to laugh is to snort, to loathe is to sneer. O silkiness!
O crêpe-de-chine! Sweet flim-flam! O delicate elephant
of the imagination! Dream on, big boy. Consider the farce
of the universe with its bumbling planets. See meteors land
with an almight cosmic thump. What is it to aspire

to sky-dust, moonshine, deodorant, hairspray? Aspire
to be an atom drifting in desolate glory. Do not abhor
a vacuum. Be not like nature. Be spirit not body, air not land.
Inhabit a galaxy of conceptual silkiness
where Venus is disembodied desire, where farce
turns to wit or light irony, as befits an elephant

with memories of lightness. For what is an elephant
but condensation of cloud? Is it not made to aspire
to lightning and cloudburst somewhere beyond the farce
of sheer tonnage? What is there, after all, to abhor?
Is the elephant's hide not a hornier silkiness?
Is his bulk not a balloon lilting above the land

like a brilliant thought to whose silkiness anyone might aspire?
Don't we love and abhor death? Is not the elephant
the image of corporeality in a land of fury and farce?

Wasp

Their truly horrible softness seems not to bother them,
nor their lack of mobility. They really are very slow
and fearful of perfectly ordinary things such as me.
What harm do I do them as I blow
on a whim through the window, lighter than a bee
or mayfly with my superior aerodynamic system?

My small sharp voice is as nothing to theirs,
their slow, billowing, mountaineous exhalations,
their spitting, the low dull explosions of their lips.
They are insensible to my more eloquent orations.
I slip between them like a speedboat among ships,
my tiny motor whirring with fine expensive hairs.

And think of the food they put down! Fair enough,
they are large, their requirements such as they are,
but the copiousness of their appetite would appal
the most generous of gods with a taste for the bizarre.
It is, I can tell you, illuminating to crawl
across their tables at mealtimes and gawp at the stuff.

Conspicuous consumption? Whoever invented
the phrase deserves a medal. Spot on, I'd say.
I like to get them ruffled, to raise their hackles
and send the slimebags on their graceless way
with a flea (or wasp) in the ear. Of all God's miracles
they are possibly the least. Their heavily scented

carcasses are an offence to the senses. Were I lord
of the universe I'd boil them down for glue,
use them for something or stop their mouths with wax.
The beautiful would inherit the earth along with the true
and our lot would be kicking their heels down the barracks
with a couple of them to amuse us, should we get bored.

Endragoblins
(for Olivia Cole)

You little green friend, read my father
from Dan Dare. No, *fiend*, I told him
The endragoblins were at it again,
monkeying with the language.
The Mekon sat in his saucer,
his green eyes bulging with venom.
The Eagle had landed. My father
was busy with the endragoblins
who populated every available nook of the universe,
calling to my father on his dying planet.

Winter Wings
(Wymondham Abbey)

How brilliantly the sun
for a moment strides
through the glass
then hides
in deep
recesses
in the very aisles
it so briefly caresses,

so the heart stops and restarts
without noticing
it has stopped:
a swing
lurching,
an eye lost
in mid-blink, dark birds
in full-flight, swimming through dust.

NEW POEMS

(2008)

America

Homage to Robert Frank

When I fell out of the car I tried to blow
through the waves to test the power of my lungs. I tried
to take deep breaths of the inky air but it was no go,

something had already sunk. There was darkness inside.
I could see the road up ahead beyond the bank and thought
it might be reached by a person if only I cried

loud and long enough and could stop feeling so overwrought,
but I had no trust in my temperament, nor in the circumstances.
It was America I was seeking, that I had long sought

and had failed to find and now I was losing her. The chances
were she was gone already beyond the lake
with her comforts, her liquid provinces.

The Child as Metaphor

The child pushed out the boat of his small voice
To see how far it would go. It floated free
Of him, drifting between blocks of ice.

Endangered voice on an indifferent sea
Turning its vast grey back: how would he sound
At the pole where so many had died already?

Under the ice fish screamed at newly drowned
Babies. Whales clicked their tongues and boomed
Disapproval. Creatures with teeth unbound

Their powers and terrifying voices loomed
Like buildings. It seemed the world was against him,
That any child's voice as small as his was doomed

Because there at the arctic all chances are slim
And everything, even love, freezes and disappears
Or snaps in two as the long night draws in.

So she listened to the deep voiced-child. Her ears
Were muffed against the cold but there, and there!
She heard him and she leaned down with her spears

Poised over the water. Mothers, the air
Is dangerous at the north pole. The metaphor
That is your son is crying out. Beware.

Plunge

You can hear them screaming from here. In the dark
      their voices are fins suddenly plunging upwards
from the walled garden. These are the rewards
      of childhood and first darkness. Here is the bark
of the tree that scratches you. Here is the dead
      lane with its berries and the cloud's mussed head.

Here is the steep, the boiling and the loss
      of memory. Most noises are lost in the pitch
of the moment, the yawl of light an ordinary switch
      plunges to oblivion. Far off, voices cross
like beams. Someone shudders on the lawn,
      retching and rising. They'll sober up at dawn.

Fire

1

I saw a distant fire across a field
as I was driving past. It touched a spring
of longing as fires often do and I was running
through an old playground, an eight year old child
without desires that he would call desires.
Then someone struck a match. It flared. I turned
to follow his quick hand as the match burned
until it died.
          You know too much of fires,
their terror, rage, impatience, agony.
Sometimes you might be made of fire, a shape
leaping and dancing, shrunk over or blowing
through dry grass. It is like anything in memory:
nowhere, yet fixed, an image of escape,
the windows wide, the whole room glowing.

2

The windows open wide, the room is glowing
as if possessed by light. So we wake
to pre-traffic silence, hardly daring to make
a noise ourselves. Time, it seems, is slowing
to a bare passage of moments. Meanwhile, far off,
small fires are igniting and dying at the tip
of someone's finger. Lives burn and slip
between time-zones, between the rough
edges of mornings and nights. No solid grief
rolls past us here, no parades, no bands,
no cannonade. We wait. The faintest scratch
of wind at the pane: a branch in full leaf
is playing its imitation game of hands
in rapid movement that sounds like a struck match.

Horse Painter

1

Oh but they are inordinately proud
and calm, my people, these distant grooms
performing like machines in an elegiac
landscape where nothing irregular is allowed.
My horses are braced in their cool rooms,
framed and gazed at, hearing the crack
of dawn like whips, dreaming of courses
where thunder builds. I build myself into
their hooves and fetlocks. I rearrange
their manes, comb out their tails, brush through
each tight coat until they come up strange
and glowing, more furniture than horses,
polite yet beautiful. It is my privilege
to lay them bare with a scalpel's edge.

2

Earth is nature but landscape is property.
Against such backdrop this magnificent
remnant of earth: a horse rising. One rears
under a lady. It is a minor event
in England, a function of anxiety,
of order maintained by stewards with guns.
Nothing is as calm as it appears.
Under the skin, between our nerves, blood runs.
Everywhere men think and gather. The fields
make chomping noises in the mud. Harvesters and reapers
with stoical expressions remark on weather that yields
a good crop. Elsewhere other croppings. Our keepers
keep us as we keep our horses, on a tight rein.
Our horses have mad eyes, but we are sane.

Geneva

(for Gerald Dawe)

where the good people
walk their dogs

1

There will always be good people walking their dogs,
usually at the side of a lake of unremitting glassiness
under snow-capped mountains and clouds like rags
of memory, who will politely address

each other in the detached, faintly guarded sort of way
that underwrites a proper civilisation. There,
by that lake, both reason and passion watch the sky
calmly, and move through cold air

at even pace without fear. In the country of dreams
there can be no nightmares. In the slim
volume of hope death is the blank spaces of poems.
Light is ice in the street. The terraces are trim.

2

Meanwhile stray dogs make their own wars in faint
yards, in deserted car parks, in vacant plots,
between ruined buildings without constraint
of tether or master. Those are not gunshots

far off in the distance but barking, not cries
but yelps. Even here you register the sound
of things collapsing somewhere. Those are flies
not aircraft zipping drastically to ground.

These are our terraces and gardens. This is our lake.
These are our gestures. These unheard screams
are our glassiness. We are not asleep but awake.
We are good people. We live here. These are our dreams.

Clear

...It is not your system or clear sight that mills
Down to the consequence a life requires
WILLIAM EMPSON

To be clear about all this, to be clear at all,
is a disgrace not a virtue, I tell
myself, here where I hear no bombs fall,
where all is – relatively speaking – well.

So says the child to the hole in the ceiling
if it could but say it, to the tongue
that bursts into light, to the lost feeling
in its limbs, to the debris in the lung.

The only clear thing in history is pain.
The only clear thing in history is silence.
In suffering there is no equality. In the hot rain
of silence there is no balance.

Checkout
(for Colette Bryce)

Life is first boredom then fear, I once heard,
and thought it fair enough then, but now I don't know.
Were I myself to look for the right word
it would be neither boredom nor fear, but vertigo –
the dizziness, the height of the world as it drifts
past you. The exhaustion. The crevices. The rifts.

How Long Are Your Hours? asks Penelope Shuttle

My hours vary. See the sign on the door.
Some days I'm out twenty-four hours or more,
stacking my hours neatly across the floor.

The hours line up. They tend to speak in chorus.
Their eyes are sharp, their skin porous.
Are you against us? they demand. *Or for us?*

My hours are easily broken down. They break
into ever smaller pieces. They shimmer and shake
their dazzling heads. They give me a headache.

My hours are constantly sloping off. *We belong
to other schemes of time*, they say. *Our song
is there if you listen close.* My hours aren't long.

Look, even now they have wedged themselves between
two thoughts in the tiniest space. They dream
of history. My parents dream them. Hard they are, and lean.

Cards in the Garden

They're playing cards in the garden, or it might
Be a country chalet, a *dacha* of some sort.
The table folds, you think. It serves to support
Their elbows as they lean forward in a tight
Group. Time is the unborn child about
To be born in the mechanical eye that you know
Must be present. You watch them now in slow
Motion, the pack on the point of being dealt out.

Not so much slow motion as stillness, and not
The authorial *you*, but *I*. The man in the dark
Shirt is my father, horrifyingly slim,
As if time reversed had eaten him or cut
Half of his substance, leaving just this mark,
This light kiss, as if it could not help but love him.

Flight

Consider the mayfly, petals of clematis,
The broken sunlight's shrapnel on flint walls,
The way wind shifts through thrust leaf, all that is
Trapped in the smallest hour, or hangs then falls
As if for ever, because it is never the same,
One moment never quite equal to the next,
Each of them engaged in the long game
Of no discernible message or set text.
    So it seems we have fallen right through death
Having begun in one brief frame of time,
Negotiating as if by great luck or high art,
Still and framed, still framed, the short breath
Of the long game stopped, the terrible crime
Missing its target while blowing leaves apart.

The terrible moment, for all moments are
Potential terrors, is stuff through which we swim
Beating our arms, afloat, swimming as far
As the long game allows. Who knows what slim
Chance thins down to? Who can count the hairs
On your precious head? Who can see
The girl at her wedding, the bride who prepares
Herself in the mirror as if for eternity?
    We are swimmers in deep waters. The light
On the wall breaks up, the long game lasts
As long as it cares to, crimes are committed, leaves fly
In the wind as is their tendency and right,
And the hours gather futures, presents, pasts
As they choose. The eyes of the stars are dry.

Our eyes are different. They absorb and shine
In the same sunlight that breaks on glass or flint
Year round, in every season. They define
The world in terms of hue and shade and tint,
And enrich it with their own hazel, gray or blue.
I have studied yours so often, reading sky
And sea in them, as if eyes were to look through,
As if mind were an element they could supply.
    I think we are here just once, that here is where
All hereness lies. Perhaps tomorrow the sea

Will be mere water, the sky nothing but light,
But light is good enough when it lives in air
That is forever bridal and understands eternity
In its own terms, as moments in full flight.

Snowfield

1

Snow takes form: the shapes it makes mount up
and vanish against sky, a paler more transcendent
cloud, a broader emptiness, briefly dependent
on whatever it clings to, fit for the hands to cup
and pack solid. The quiet solidifies
into a firmer block of silence that shuts
off streets and gardens. Stillness. No wind cuts
our faces. We listen out for whispers and sighs
in the furniture but it is little enough
this light layer: it doesn't change the state
of the world or even Norfolk very much,
only appearances and the curious stuff
of illusion we require to operate
things that we thought were clear and ours to touch.

2

The *One Stop Shop* stays open. The stationer
and gift shop, the butcher, the winebar, the pub:
commerce happens. Money, white goods and grub,
hygiene products, light fittings, the pensioner
at the Post Office window. Cold fingers at tills,
on the counter, in the pocket. We are a scene
from a Dutch painting moving against a screen
of well-worn properties: frozen ponds, windmills,
spires and barns. Our rural sports are gazing
and passing water. We are our own TV.
Children are born, we listen to their bones
growing, watch hair sprout. They move at amazing
speed through slow-motion air. Our brevity
is startling. We're outlived by trees and stones.

3

Brief snow. It sits on the roof as though it had
always been there and always will be. It seems
permanent in its grave weirdness. There are reams
of it to be read in invisible ink. It makes sad
comical entertainment discovering its history
of anecdotes, like an elaborate joke that is told
over and over again. The dead and the old
know it by heart as does the snow-covered tree
in the flat field. As do I myself, or I think
I am starting to learn it: that snow is beautiful,
that it settles on us like a hand that is raised
sooner rather than later, that we can sink
into it as into a frozen bath, that each petal
of its crystal flower is lethal and perfectly phrased.

Beckmann's Carnival

Some prefer rough music, a blast of brass
In the ear, the judder of the resined bow
Or the boom of the tuba. Some like to pass
Wind aloud, long for raspberries to blow
At silence or to lie flat on the floor
Apelike with a horn between their feet
Squeezed into a corner behind a door
That leads nowhere but the irregular beat
Of the heart that is shell-shocked forever.

And how is it now that the apartment fills
With strangers, clutter, and the peculiar noise
Of half recognised women, apes and boys?

Rough music is terror. It is terror that shrills
In the corner, the same phrase blown over and over.

Say

Try to imagine death as a phone call. Say
you have just called your mother or the friend
you met last week before you went away,

and say they answer just at the perfect end
of a perfect life, as the moon rises full
of a benign pearly joy that should portend

more joy, just as the tide begins to pull
away from you and that is the very spot
on which you die, in that calm, most beautiful

of places; and say you die, because it's your lot
to perish by the sea, though it catches you unaware
at the time like a possibility you forgot,

because why after all should you have gone there
but for the possibility of a moon full of joy
and not a death you could meet just anywhere;

say that you know it takes a moment to destroy
a life, to snuff out the moon and the sea and the sand,
to become a distant speck like the dark buoy

bobbing on the tide, to be far from firm land,
a kind of human flotsam, or a space
between constellations, an invisible band

of sky, the weeping memory of a lost face
in another's grief, the friend, the mother, the pet
left puzzled by your absence; say the trace

you leave behind fades in time as people forget
your precise dimensions and the exact
pitch of your voice, that the vast internet

of the imagination registers you as a fact
without context, swimming in the immense
indivisible particularity of a compact

universe beyond summoning, say that a sense
of loss can be anticipated and is so,
or has been, as a whispered confidence

from one part of your brain to another and you go
round knowing all this for ever, my darling,
as do I, as does the voice saying yes, *I know*

in the poem, would that be at all consoling?
Say it were so: say it to the moon and to the ear
listening on the phone, to the waves rolling

towards your feet in the darkness, to the fear
of falling and let it go, my dear, let the rain
fall, let waves lap, let the invisible appear.

Esprit d'Escalier

Suddenly there we all were, talking together
but not to each other. It might have been I
who had started it, muttering as I do
to myself, or rather to a figure to whom
I have something to say in the manner known
as *l'esprit de l'escalier*, that ghostly meeting

on the staircase with a person already past meeting
for whom we now have an altogether
brilliant answer, one we have always known
but had failed to produce when required. And now, I
and the others were talking, all of us, to whom
it would finally concern us to talk to, as we do

each day on the bus, knowing just what to do
and to say at this and every other such meeting.
There were friends, fears, ghosts, and past selves whom
each of us had to answer, all of us speaking together
every which one a distinct and separate *I*
in a world where everything has always been known.

The air was packed solid with voices we had once known
or were ours, it was hard to tell which, for how do
you tell the inner from the outer, or distinguish the I
from the *not-quite-I?* And soon each intimate meeting
had spilled onto the street, all voices singing together
to make one thundering chorus, each *who* with its *whom*,

in doorways, on staircases, singing to whom-
soever could hear and respond to the known-or-unknown
harmonies we were producing as if we were together.
We were ghosts. We were dead. There was little to do
but to listen and sing and be dead and be meeting
each ghost on its staircase. And so it was I

myself spoke to the dead ones within me since I
was their only voice, the lost hum of their *whom*.
It was crazy this sound, the music of meeting
all of them now, there on the bus, having known
only the steps to the top deck, knowing what to do
only in emergencies when we're all thrown together

and have to make do as we are, no matter with whom
we travel or have known, these voices with their *I*,
their you, their singing together at each and every meeting.

Song
(for Linda Grant)

The floor just goes, and the floor just went:
No standing room in your own dumb head
And though the room's well lit, the rent
Is deeper than you can see to tread,
The rent is deeper, the hole too wide
To make it over the other side.

So floors just go and down you come
And fall is further than you thought,
Some depths there are you cannot plumb
Dread heights from which you won't be caught.
You won't be caught in the silky light
That might have tempted you to flight.

The heart gives out and all it gives
Is vacant air up an empty sleeve;
The darling one, the one who lives,
Is darling fit enough to grieve.
You're fit to grieve if your heart is strong,
But who can tell where such hearts belong?

Life's not for me, whatever else
Remains on offer we shall see.
Once there is neither voice nor pulse
The heart floats off like hearts set free.
The life looks on as the life is spent.
The floor just goes and the floor just went.

Happiness

He watched her skip across the street and take
a moment to look back at him. His heart
stopped in its tracks, as though it had fallen apart
for a moment then reassembled. It was the ache
remained, as though life had suddenly shrunk
to one thin cord that was being sounded deep
beneath the flesh, like being half-asleep
then awake, like being doped or drunk
yet clear, as if life had been this dizziness
of atoms and molecules and chance events
out of which the towering moments rose
on stilts, on points, balancing on less
than atoms and was a transforming of moments
if only because the floor vanishes, the moment goes.

The Street in Movement

A shout in the street, Stephen answered, shrugging his shoulders.

The street in movement. The cars at such speed the eye
Can't follow them. Houses turn on invisible spindles
Like old fashioned records,
Their music the orchestrated, chance cry
Of centuries of childhood and forgotten scandals,
More sound effects than words.

Cities, the business of streets, the tenderness
Of districts, the small patient words of houses
Where lives write themselves out.
Early mornings they feel the wind caress
Their faces as they mutter in their sleep. Light rouses
Them and they rise with a faint shout

Into clarity, hope and routine. Soon feet
Shift over pavements or you hear an engine turn,
A door slams in the memory
Then suddenly it is as if time were a sheet
Of hard rain. Water in sewers begin to churn
A subterranean sea.

Storms in a teacup, nursing of tiny precisions.
The long drowned voices of the vanished call
Down delicate whorls of the ear.
Where do such voices come from? Whose visions
Trawl these washed-away streets? Whose fingers crawl
Over the glass? How utterly queer

To be alive, to feel rain soften, to stand in the street
Or enter a square that appears to be still but is spinning
On its axle, terrible and sweet.
Come here, my darling, let me touch you. Stroke
My face the way rain does, tell me what's happening,
How long is it since we woke

To this chance noise? Where are we? Is God
still shouting in the rain? God is the rain,
The noise rain makes that seems
A voice, not quite a language but a flood
Of inchoate music in which we recognise the refrain
Of something that gathers and streams.

Exhortation

Go you then, drive faster than greased lighting
down major trunk roads skirting the storm
following long vehicles of fortune
through to the blue horizon where it's warm
and days are dressed in sun-bleached uniform.

Follow the arrows of the good consignment.
Be magus and potentate eating up the road
towards the miraculous birth of distant thunder
and blowhard rain, cheerfully bearing your load
to those on whom it is to be bestowed.

Believe in miracles, confident of convergence,
in coincident signs, in the sheer shock of light
as it strikes into the distance like a favourable doom,
in the meeting point of slim day and huge night
where dim stars flicker waiting to ignite.

Lilac in the rain

The lilac spreads as if the weight of air
  were something it had to accommodate.
    Its frailest branches are laden with bloom
      so the flowers point downward in the rain.

    Last night there was thunder and the skylight pane
   snapped and popped echoing through the room
  along with the thunder in crisp, separate
hammer taps and all the flowers were bare

to the elements, beaten down but still rich
  in their range of pinks, dowsed in shades
    of fragility, in the dark, under flashes of light
      while we slept and woke and slept again till now

    it is difficult to understand just how
   the rules of sleep work or how the lilac might
  survive such beatings or how dreams fade
into objects so we can't tell which is which.

One Summer Night

Inside the house it was like gold, a pool
Of precious metal, and the windows spilled
Warmth, as if unable to contain it. It was cool
Outside, a summer evening fading into gilt.

First dusk, and then the gradual rubbing down
Into darkness. In the road a musky breeze
Was raising boughs until the whole gown
Of night settled over town and the trees'

Dense heads grew thicker still with starless air.
Then owls and bats: the hoot, swoop and flutter
Of seconds and minutes. A radio somewhere

In the drive made a faint noise in its throat
While the tiniest lives scuttled in the gutter
Each with its own peculiar sweet note.

                              *

Whose was that house? And who had left the light
Burning and billowing like that? Perhaps
A figure in the dark house opposite might
Be able to say, or account for the odd lapse

In housekeeping. It was a sensible
Neighbourhood, almost puritan
In its habits, used to the dull scribble
Of diaries, bills and memos. No policeman

Patrolled its thoroughfares, and the moon
Visited there most times unobserved.
But now that light. Something would happen soon

To alter things and turn the music up,
And it would be no more than they deserved,
As brittle and full of night as an old cup.

Heat

When the heat kicks in, its face pushed right up to yours,
Its breath of summer menace stifling and dense
And nothing moves on the washing line but light pours
Into the dark room and settles there
Holding the air quite still so it's not quite air
But a foretaste of permanence,

You hold yourself and your block of flesh compact
And close, like an accordion that won't open out,
Unable to gasp or sing, lungs impossible to contract
Any further, and so the soul stands bare
Before you in that room emptied of air
Its mouth gaping as if caught in mid-shout.

And the thunder begins to roll somewhere to the west
Of here, grinding its way forward to relieve
The heat and the stillness, its lips compressed
Preparing to blow through the soul
In its room and the dark scroll
Of cloud whose promises you believe.

Clouds

The clouds are drawing out of the station
at infinite leisure.
Two men on scaffolding make miniature
architecture.

The sunlight places its hands
on my face
like a small child. Its hands are all
tenderness, grace,

as if wanting to discover
the true form
of the figure it holds and explores
while it is still warm.

Chairs

It was the empty chairs he feared,
not those with a proper behind rammed into them,
not those littered with stray bits of food or waste paper.

It was the voices that did not speak,
the wheezes and creaks the chairs didn't make.
The kicking over, the collapse,
the broken legs of chairs, the everyday business.

To see them ranged about a table
turned in on themselves as for a ritual,
that was the unsettling thing, and that one there,
yes, that one with its open arms
and its invitation to sit,
its somnolence, its stab at dignity,
its emptiness, was the very devil.

Rochdale 1990

They were acting from the best of motives,
Professionals making the best of what they knew,
When in walked the devil with a glint in his eye,
Took a look at them and said, *'Screw you.'*

And he screwed them all by setting them loose
On the inarticulate estate of the poor,
Devotees, every one, of the cult of bare existence,
With the devil to pay pounding at the door.

Running man blues

(for John Mole)

when the money ran out, they all ran away
they hit the road running with runs on the board
but the bills they'd run up meant no prospect of play

they ran to breakfast in a seedy café
run on a shoestring they could barely afford
where the money ran out and they all ran away

they were running on empty with the devil to pay
the meter still running on the rusty old Ford
with the bills they'd run up still up on display

they'd run into trouble and ran through the day
with running repairs they would once have ignored
but the cash had run out, they were running away

there were runs on the Bourse and the Bank on the way
one ran himself through with a samurai sword
the bills he'd run up left him no room to play

running scared, running low, running down, it was they
who had once run the world or had run in and scored
with the bills they'd run up in the games they would play
till the money ran out and they all ran away.

Dust skin glove bowl

(after Helio Oiticica)

You plunge your hands in wearing gloves,
You plunge your skin in the dirt in the bowl,
In earth the colour of mouse or mole
Or the burnt edge of the planet where droves
Of creatures sift through living rust.

And this is the colour, your own dust,
The dust of the self in which you lurk,
To which you and your eyes belong,

Where your parched mouth sings a raw song
Of dunes and gardens, where you work
Your eyes and hands and where all art
Is lexicon or colour chart.

Here dust becomes you. Gloves become your skin.
You wear your body as you might a gown:
Dust skin glove bowl, median brown,

Like washing clothes, like a good scrubbing down
With the colours you live and die in.

Silk

It was around your neck, or I was, with my ideal hands
loose about your ideal shoulders lost in a storm
of ruffs and frills in the middle of a night's sleep.

The sleep was silk, or I was, slithery with silence
in the rain that was an articulation of something
I did not understand but would continue to trouble

the sleep remaining to me. A wardrobe left open
always brings good luck, and maybe this was luck
folding out of the mud of the shower, in the earth

beneath the trees, where I, or it, or that sheer bolt
of silk lay unrolled, unfolded, my ideal body
curling its lip in disgust and, I must admit,

pleasure, at your neck and shoulders and your trees
and all the invited adulation of the rain
in that dead sleep where I was around your neck,

where your head emerged out of its shimmer,
or my shimmer, or that nothing that was sleep
or simply took the tree's or sleep's or my own form

and you lay there, pure silk, pure storm.

Questions for Stan Laurel

How could the body not be comical
when the music it plays is the fiddling of bones,
the deep fart of flesh in the stalls,
the high whine of bagpipes in the ear,
a fusillade of drumming automatics,
a small rattling of hollow balls,
the faint harmonics of the queer?

How could the body not be comical when one
is fat, the other thin and the belly droops
to the crotch, and the sliding trombone
is the ripping of pants in the sunshine,
when comedy is being unhurt in the shadow
of the great cliff having fallen from air
and proving the hard ground harmless?

How could the body not be comical when grace
is the other name of loss, along with *scapegrace, disgrace,*
the un-grace entailed in clumsiness?
How could your body not be mine and mine yours
in the constant exchange of bodies, from the svelte
athlete, the ploughman with his lunch, the groan
of the almost defeated Bulgarian weightlifter,

when it is the child's body that holds
no surprises. When the song and dance
you break into begins as something twangs
in the doorway and the barbershop boys sing
you into the eternal bar kept open for such as you,
and the terrible force of the mallet on your head
makes you break into your one true falsetto.

Apology for a Broken Glass

(for Katharina Hacker and Christian Strub)

And suddenly objects were falling from the table.
Precariously perched and impossibly unstable.
On sideboards and shelves they trembled as if already
Lost in a world condemned to be unsteady.
Otherwise balanced in the hostile air,
Glass and ceramic items everywhere
Yielded to touch and were soon beyond repair.

Fierce winds seemed to be blowing the child
Over the war-torn landscape he had made,
Rough shapes sang to him out of the wild,

All of them awkward, embarrassed and afraid.

Bigger bodies than his moved without disaster,
Reasonable, graceful entities that could somehow
Orchestrate their limbs in ways he could not master,
Keep order between objects and allow
Each thing clear passage or hold the world still,
Never themselves subject to its independent will.

Grave and serious was the world and that was right.
Life could be negotiated with proper foresight.
Apologies were required. His mother was calling
Softly in the next room. It was late at night,
Sleep too was broken and everything was falling.

Six Airs for William Diaper

Here is a young fellow has writ some Sea Eclogues, poems of Mermen resembling pastorals of shepherds, and they are very pretty, and the thought is new. Mermen are he-mermaids; Tritons, natives of the sea. Do you understand me? I think to recommend him to our Society to-morrow. His name is Diaper.

JONATHAN SWIFT, Journal to Stella

1

My child, listen. When you and I arrived
fresh from our mothers' wombs we floundered
in red air and bawled our guts out, shocked
by everything: the fearsome slap of hands
we could not see, the barbarity of cold
we needed wrapping against; the light that pressed
hard fingers against our firmly shut eyes
though we did not know it. Air was dangerous,
the terrible air we needed for survival
yet needed first to survive. And you and I
we were together in this as was the one
who nurtured you in darkness, eely, frothed
and struggling like Blake's babe ready to sulk,
the alien familiar as we are still, my child,
you with your closed heart and I with mine.

2

He came to visit Swift who said: 'It is a poor
little short wretch but will do best in a gown,'
though later he called at Diaper's door
and found him 'in a nasty garret, very sick'
in an admittedly poor part of town,
so gave him 'twenty guineas from Lord Bolingbroke'
for his considerable gifts and knowledge,
as appropriate for a fellow of Balliol College.

3

A deep-sea fishiness is half of sex,
all wriggle, squirm, thrust, muscle, ooze and flex,
plus otherness and drowning as if this
were necessary to perfect our bliss.
Now fish, now slime, spermatozoa swim
from rampant pecker into depths of quim,
and so our eelets swell and drowse in heat
their limbs more fin than human hands or feet.

Too long in genial beds, we rise for air
as fish might rise for bait that soon must tear
the delicate mouth. Then watery substance parts:
light shoots barbed arrows through our fishy hearts.

4

To silver poets scaled in silver, gaining
the silver medal of the moon
like a delicate staining,
the small fry
who die
unremarked and soon,
whose skin is pale and silvery as a pond,
whose hair is frond,
who dance
according to the slim chance
of names like Diaper, Edward Chicken, Stephen Duck
with a year or two of luck,
then greeted by no Gotterdämmerung,
but by the greater silver
of John Crowe Ransom, Norman Cameron.

5

Wrote couplets enough to furnish a whole choir
of scales and fins. His objects of desire
were human beings coupling, pair by pair,
each doubled vision swimming through the air.
now twisting, now cording like rope:
warmest flesh, the perishable face
packed with hope.

6

My child I sometimes despair of the loss
of that which is not clear to the naked eye.
When I myself was a child the table rose
like a giant, its sharp edges sky-high.
I did not know sky from ceiling, my mother
from God. The words would open and close
their fishy gills by my microscopic ear
until I learned to distinguish one from the other.
And so I watched the wordlings shuffling across
the deep spaces of my attention like specks
cavorting within the dimensions of their sex,
smaller than I was but more sweet and clear.

Fish

1

Whatever it is that has eyes and stares
Through the edges of the world as though
Water were bounded, rectangular, frozen
Into slabs of motion and counterflow
Is enough to strike fear into the heart
Since whatever exists beyond prepares
The end of the world. Business continues –
The sly glug, the terrified dart, the amorous
Lazy hover with every scale alert, ineffably part
Of the world so threatened. No denizen
Of our deep stares like that. Our affairs
Are open eyed, unblinking and indifferent.
But the eyes out there are at the core of an event
That awaits us and remembers us forever.

2

Whatever lives there is lithe and looking to pass
Itself off as something utterly other.
Within the tank delight drifts like glass
In pale green weather.

My eyes are full of light, little swimming dots
Of crystalline wonder.
How beautiful life is as it moves and rots
Or explodes into thunder.

Smoke

I have been examining
the souls of animals,
the way they chuff and poo,
and gaze with melancholy eyes
at saucer and lightbulb

as if something inside them were burning;
from which I conclude
that animals have souls
they emit and cannot see
but leave behind like vapour trails

that mingle with the one that trails behind me
like a useful tail and helps
me keep my balance,
climb trees and things like that
maintaining my essentially vaporous nature.

Known Them

Known a fair number of them. Heard the first
squeak of them from inside a box or cage.
Watched them dart, look puzzled, scamper, wage
war on shoe-laces, yowling fit to burst,
mumbling of hunger, restlessness and thirst.

Known them draw blood from a fingertip. Known
them attack a flick of hair. Known them leap
off unpredictable ledges and fall asleep
on a doorstep as if it were a throne.
Known them like company but walk alone.

Known those eyes that search yours then grow bored
and turn into themselves, the world gone flat
as sadness. Known them fixed on the faint pat-
ter of rain or the spinning of an old record,
or shirt-sleeves dangling from the ironing board.

Known them asleep for hours. Known the grace
of their long backs arching. Known their mad
devil-possessed scramblings, their jihad
on anything that moves from place to place.
Known set expressions flit across one's face

as if they were ghosts of thoughts or faint beams
of perception. Known them stretch out and purr
at the slightest touch of brush on tangled fur.
Known them hunched, lost in enormous daydreams
of killing and sexual capers. Watched their schemes

of world domination come a cropper when
distracted by a paper clip on the floor.
Watched them in two minds at an open door
unable to commit. Saw them expect ten
lives, not nine. Saw them hiss and sharpen

their claws on furniture so far pristine.
Saw right into their souls, or what I thought
were souls. Saw the dead things they brought
into the house. Saw them fat and thin,
and saw them end soon after they begin.

Have shared rooms with them. Fed them. Played a while
with the young ones. Have yet to see one cry
though sickening to death. Have seen them die
in old age. Have seen them crocked, immobile,
wounded, run down, left in a bloody pile.

Have known the names to which they gave no heed,
the names of spaces in the human mind.
Have known them hanker after their own kind.
Have known their stomachs blown out from pure greed.
Have known the loss of them. Their mirrored need.

Geometry

To be divided out of the morning
into the falling sun where no one was
around on the empty grass that glowed
in the heat of itself, was to be a shape
as close to a self as possible.
I was watching her hands, the tiny degrees
of her fingers as they sat in the air
then moved to divide it into perfect forms.

A pair of shoes by the table. The forms
of the body occupying weightless air.
The perfect circles proceeding by degrees
to describe as closely as possible
what it meant to be a shape. This shape.
Which was the loved shape that glowed
wherever anything and everything was
in the falling sun, in the dangerous morning.

In the Pizza Parlour

She sat in the pizza parlour with the river
Rushing behind her. The trees were involved
With the wind. There was something fearsome and resolved
About the way water was running for cover
Into the dark edgewise of time, as rivers do,
Being emblems of time, and our two faces
Dropped with it into their own dark spaces
As if we could watch our mortality falling through
The air. Just so had queens died young and fair,
And there was dust in the food, in the light, in our eyes,
Caught in our lashes, and this was love, its thin
Fingers moving through our dust-laden hair,
Its heart in its mouth, its mouth stopped with sighs,
Calling for us to enter, and we stepped in.

Secret

And so she remained young forever.
All the best words gradually fell
Into perfect order and sang. Over

And over again her breasts would fill
With milk, her face smooth out, her eyes
Sharpen, her heart revive to baffle

The doctors. She'd rise at sunrise
With supple limbs, breakfast on air
And float about the house on sighs

Of wind, then out through the front door
Where she was lovely as the birds
That sang as she passed. She was more

Of everything. She was words
And air in appropriate patterns, as time
Continued, in its usual way, to move forwards,

As if time itself were simply a game
You could play then drop like a ball
In a playground, turn around and come home.

The Old

The old, as always, are right. These days the days
seem to be collapsing: week blurs into week,
spring and summer vanish in a heat-haze

followed by thunder and sea-mists and sleek
autumnal showers. It is early morning. You lie
beside me as I trace the contours of your cheek

with my finger. The first week of July.
The frail light on your skin opens and spreads
its hands across the pillow. The windows sigh

with light, dissolving in faint blues and reds
and creams, one moment among millions
that fly past us trailing luminous shreds

through the room, which is ours and no one's.
Slowly the radio wakes to the world. Words start
on wrecked sentences. All the well-known patterns

fall into place. We know our place and part
in this. We know time's way with the alarm clock's
pale green regular pulse and bursting heart.

Mirrors

1

When I am ninety-eight I shall listen to music
For a very long time and I will think
Of your shoulder as you stand in the doorway.

Whether I will be man or woman then
Will not matter much because at ninety-eight
A person's gender is of little importance

Growing, as we do, into nothing or permanence,
While not knowing either. Because then I can wait
As now I can not, because never again

Will things be the same. That's why I play
A little music now and why I want to drink
time slowly, tick by tick by tick.

2

When I am ninety-eight I shall be an old woman
Remembering what it was to be a woman. My ears
Will be vast as an elephant's because I shall want

To hear every drop of music as it passes
Into nothing or permanence. Each passing noise
Will mean all it can mean and I will be quiet

When trouble breaks out and there is riot
In the streets and gangs of small boys
Rampage through derelict premises,

Because music is neither pleasant or unpleasant
Merely an earnest of everything that disappears
Into that past where I was still a man.

Sestina: Hullaballoo

Always at this beginning of the year
towards the end of the Christmas hullaballoo,
taking the tree down, unplugging the light
fantastic, watching the long icy rain
in free fall through the window, the wind brisk
and loutishly loud throughout the short dark day

time winds itself back. It was the day
she was born in the bedroom, in the year
of the hot summer to come. There was the brisk
French midwife, the blunt hullaballoo
of birth in a huddle of women, and time like rain
falling precipitous in the electric light

as she too was falling out of dark into light
on a dark and typical January day,
the sense of incipient snow gentling to rain
in the distance. It was seven o'clock. The year
was thirteen days old. What hullabaloo
in the house. Outside it was cold and the brisk

traffic kept moving homeward to equally brisk
households, but without this source of light
coming into our own world's hullabaloo,
the making a living, the paying for one day
with more days, days that ran though the year
full of noise and demands, steady as rain,

fierce as the wind. But here was life in the rain
of the body, bawling and waving its brisk
little limbs. The year before had been a year
of death and it was ironic and joyful to light
up the new one with cries and see the day
open on a child that knew nothing but the hullabaloo

of light and air, which is perhaps the only hullabaloo
worth all that bawling, and lightly to wipe the rain
of birth from its small body on its very first day
in the world, because life is generally brisk
and gets on, with just enough leisure to light
the odd candle to its possessors once a year

so that love focuses on a day full of hullabaloo
when the whole year seems to shimmer in rain
and a kind of brisk joy, the turning on of light.

506

New Year Canticles

1

The new government is the old government,
The new year is the old year in new shoes,
The new testament is the old one reversed,
The new man is the old man newly cursed.

The new poor are the old poor plus a few.
The new itinerant is the old bum.
The new lie is the old lie, and then some.
The new *Titanic* steams on through old scum.

2

When they blew away the dust they found
a brand new darkness underneath.
It surprised them. They prodded it with sticks.
It didn't move for ages, then it stirred.
It wanted naming but they couldn't find the word

3

You think of your children in the early light
of the new era. You think of birds in flight.
You think of a cup in the kitchen in the broad
sunlight of mid November, of the faint noise of the road.

You think of the rhetoric of time
as a faintly bombastic ticking. You think of buds
ticking away in the branch under the rime.
The emblematic delicacy of soap suds.

4

And the notion of an uninterrupted passage
towards happiness, the joy of the unkissed moment
waiting to fly past you, reassuringly off-message,
like a ludicrous, airborne, angelic monument,

Cupid on a bender, a sweet urgent gust
of well-being. Love among the just.

A Poster of Marlene, 1937: After Brassaï

Marlene is monstrous. Her great blonde mane
Is the wind in the walls. She laughs and beams
At the sky. *Marlene!* young men exclaim
As they cycle to work. Everyone dreams

Of laughing Marlene, her high-arched brows'
Absolute precision, of her white teeth
Glinting through the lush Parisian boughs
Of the *Boulevard des Capucines* while, beneath,

Life moves forward, as it must, into the great
Unknown future and a boy in plus-fours
Stops his delivery bike to contemplate
The beatitude of Marlene who adores

Paris as it adores her, and the glance
She casts across the whole of *La Belle France.*

Wedding Photographer with Wedding, Budapest

These are the courtyards of the ordinary.
These are the floors of the tenement;
the floor of the woman who trails them, of the plain
wings of windows, the silent courtesy
of iron railings, of the intensely white event
of a wedding dress that will never be worn again.

Below them the vortex of the yard in which tears
gather like rain in buckets along with other encumbrances.
The woman dreams a city. The bride makes the bed.
The groom strokes the bride's hair. Nothing appears
to be missing. Nothing vanishes. Light dances
all by itself as if the building were untenanted.

INDEX

Index of titles and first lines

(Titles and sub-titles are shown in italics, first lines in roman type.)

516